Why Our Culture and Our Country Have Stopped Making Sense—and What We Can Do About It

Telling
the Truth

Lynne V. Cheney

Simon & Schuster

New York   London   Toronto   Sydney   Tokyo   Singapore

Simon & Schuster
Rockefeller Center
1230 Avenue of the Americas
New York, NY 10020

SIMON & SCHUSTER and colophon are registered trademarks
of Simon & Schuster Inc.

Designed by Karolina Harris

Manufactured in the United States of America

10 9 8 7 6 5 4 3 2 1

Library of Congress Cataloging-in-Publication Data

Cheney, Lynne V.
    Telling the truth : why our culture and our country
have stopped making sense—and what we can do about it /
Lynne V. Cheney.
        p.   cm.
    Includes bibliographical references and index.
    1. Postmodernism—Social aspects—United States.   2. Learning and
scholarship—United States—History—20th century.   I. Title.
HM73.C489   1995   95-23625
303.4—dc20   CIP
    ISBN 0-684-81101-4

?~ Acknowledgments

DURING the two years that I was writing this book, I held the
W. H. Brady, Jr., Distinguished Fellowship at the American Enterprise Institute; and so my first thanks are to the Brady Foundation
(in particular, Elizabeth Lurie) and the AEI (in particular, Christopher DeMuth) for their generous support.

Many people provided research aid and assistance. I am particularly indebted to Michael Boskin, James Cicconi, Robert Costrell,
Katherine Kersten, Erich Martel, and Thadd Prisco. I would also like
to thank the Center for Media and Public Affairs for supplying copies
of their newsletters and the Media Research Center for making vid-
eotapes available. Kathy Ruff was particularly helpful in providing
tapes of news programs from the Media Research Center's splendid
archives.

Many of those who directed me to the sources I needed—and
often even provided them—were colleagues at AEI. I would like
especially to thank Marvin Kosters and Karlyn Bowman. To Evelyn
Caldwell, the resourceful librarian at AEI, I owe a special debt of
gratitude. Sean Littlefield and Amy Rash, efficient as they are, made

sure that I never missed a deadline (or, at least, that I felt guilty when I did). A number of AEI interns and assistants spent time working on this project: Michelle Van Gilder, Rob Witwer, Todd Johnson, Simon Yee, Megan Fernstrom, Julie Nicholas, Christina Cannon, John Giarrusso, Amy Wallace, Allison Schoenthal, and Scott Wastak. With their resourcefulness and wit, these young people should give us much hope about the future.

Celeste Colgan, John Ellis, John Fonte, Victor Gold, Andrew Goldman, Leon Kass, Thomas S. Kingston, Michael Malbin, Jerry Martin, Anne D. Neal, Ricki Silberman, and James Q. Wilson read parts or all of the manuscript at various stages and provided sage advice that I have tried to follow. These readers and I know well that there is no way to insulate a book like this fully from the attacks that are—given the times in which we live—inevitable, but their insights helped me to strengthen it against reasoned criticism. As for the unreasoned kind, one reader suggested a strategy. Challenge your opponents, he suggested, by pointing out that name-calling and labeling help prove your thesis that reason and the search for truth are not sufficiently honored. The challenge is hereby issued: Try to show I am mistaken if you wish, but do so with sound evidence and sound reasoning. Invective and accusation will merely serve as evidence of the low status into which truth has fallen in our time.

I would like to thank my agent, Bob Barnett, for his continued assistance. I am also grateful to my editor at Simon & Schuster, Bob Asahina. He has a remarkable gift for seeing how a chapter or organizational scheme might be made stronger and for pointing it out in such an intelligent way that a fifth or sixth rewrite begins to seem like a perfectly wonderful idea.

To my research assistant, Lynne Munson, I would like to express special gratitude. No challenge was too big or too small for her as we worked our way through this book. I have been particularly blessed during this project to have had the help of someone whose judgment is so sound, whose organizational skills are so impressive—and whose future is so bright.

To my granddaughter, Kate

❧ Contents

"Any attack on intellectual liberty, and on the concept of objective truth, threatens in the long run every department of thought."

—*George Orwell, "The Prevention of Literature"*

&~ Introduction

"Not merely the validity of experience but the very existence of external reality was tacitly denied by their philosophy. The heresy of heresies was common sense."

—*George Orwell, 1984*

As one witness reported it, "the scene . . . recalled the daily 'minute of hatred' in George Orwell's '1984,' when citizens are required to rise and hurl invective at pictures of a man known only as Goldstein, the Great Enemy of the state."[1] And I was Goldstein, one of the enemies whose very name evoked jeers and hoots from the assembly—which, somewhat surprisingly considering their behavior, happened to be composed of academics from Duke University and the University of North Carolina. And what had I done to deserve demonization by this distinguished group? As chairman of the National Endowment for the Humanities (NEH), I had written a pamphlet entitled, innocuously enough, *Humanities in America: A Report to the President, the Congress, and the American People.* In it, I had observed:

Viewing humanities texts as though they were primarily political documents is the most noticeable trend in academic study of the humanities today. Truth and beauty and excellence are regarded as irrelevant; questions of intellectual and aesthetic quality dismissed. . . . The key questions are thought to be about gender, race, and class. What groups did the authors of these works represent? How did their books enhance the social power of those groups over others?

I went on to describe what I saw happening as a diminishment. "The humanities are about more than politics," I wrote, "about more than social power. What gives them their abiding worth are truths that pass beyond time and circumstance; truths that, transcending accidents of class, race, and gender, speak to us all."[2]

Stanley Fish of Duke University, a superstar of the academic world, was one of those at the North Carolina conference whom these mild words seemed to drive crazy. A report came back to me of his waving my pamphlet around, while—to shouts and jeers and other noises of encouragement from the audience—he derided my suggestion that the humanities have transcendent value. "Once you take away gender, race, and class, what else is left?" he demanded. I imagined all of the distinguished professors rising as one and chanting, "Nothing, nothing, nothing."

This conference, which took place in 1988, was not exactly the picture of the humanities that I had in mind when I was nominated to serve as chairman of the National Endowment for the Humanities. At my 1986 confirmation hearings before the United States Senate, I talked about the models of excellence that can be found in history. I talked about the enduring truths that emerge from the study of great authors: Homer and Euripides, Milton and Shakespeare, Locke and Montesquieu. I talked about Matthew Arnold, the nineteenth-century poet and essayist about whom I had written my doctoral dissertation. As Arnold saw it, humanistic study was "a disinterested endeavor to learn and propagate the best that is known and thought in the world."[3]

I had not been chairman for long, however, when I began to see a vast discrepancy between what I was saying and the direction the humanities were taking. I had been away from the academic world for a decade or so working as a writer and editor, and in those years there had been a sea change. Although there were still many faculty members who thought of the humanities as I did, a new group of academics was coming into power who viewed the humanities as a political tool, a weapon to be wielded in a variety of causes, but most especially multiculturalism and feminism. To them, Homer, Shakespeare, Milton, and their ilk were icons of the corrupt civilization of the West. Matthew Arnold was among those they most disdained since he had spent so much time propagating oppressive notions like objectivity and excellence.

Thinking a little frank talk to be in order, I began to speak out about what I saw happening, enraging the leadership of the humanities community whenever I did. The name-calling and invective that my forays brought down on my head struck me as curious. Why didn't my opponents offer counterarguments to what I had to say? Why didn't they try to show where weak evidence had led me to false conclusions or where a lack of knowledge had kept me from seeing the truth?

A second curiosity had to do with the way those on the other side defined politics. Every statement in every text (or not in a text, for that matter) was said to be political, said to be aimed at advancing the interest of the speaker or writer. This often came up in connection with teaching. I or someone who thought as I did would object to the classroom's being used to advance a political agenda, which would inevitably lead to the response that all teaching is political and that today's activists are simply being honest about what they are doing. What was clearly happening is that something that was trivially true (we can never get totally outside ourselves and divorce ourselves of all our interests) was being inflated. Politics writ small had become politics written so large that it drove out the possibility of human beings doing anything nonpolitical—such as encouraging the search for truth. Sometimes this view was advanced in a self-serving way—as an excuse for politics in the classroom—but what intellectual climate, I had to ask, would allow anyone to think that such a defense would be effective?

What I gradually came to understand was that in the view of a growing number of academics, the truth was not merely irrelevant, it no longer existed. They had moved far beyond the ideas that have shaped modern scholarship—that we should think of the truth we hold today as tentative and partial, recognizing that it may require rethinking tomorrow in light of new information and insight—to the view that there is no truth. They had leaped beyond the common-sense observation that people's descriptions of reality differ to the conclusion that there is no independent reality and thus no basis for making judgments about truth—or falsity. As these academics saw it, all those things that we think are true are really the constructs of dominant groups, the creations of the powerful. Might makes right, in other words; and so intimidation was a perfectly natural way to try to gain assent. Politics was writ large because, in their view, there was no countervailing force. When I had conjured up a picture of the professors in North Carolina chanting "nothing, nothing, nothing," I had imagined better than I knew.

The fact that an increasing number of academics viewed the world in this way—this "postmodern" way, as many call it—created great difficulties for the functioning of the National Endowment for the Humanities. Founded on the principles of traditional scholarship, it had been authorized for public funding on the basis that scholars would search for truth, seek objectivity, and strive for excellence—none of which were goals that the postmodern generation had in mind. These scholars were not only seeking financial support for projects that advanced their agendas, but sitting on NEH panels recommending that taxpayer dollars go to politicized projects. This meant that I sometimes had to override panel recommendations, as, for example, in the case of a proposal for a television program that charged Columbus with genocide, but portrayed the Aztecs—who practiced human sacrifice on a massive scale—as a gentle, peace-loving people. My refusing to fund such projects inevitably brought cries of outrage and, ironically, charges that I was politicizing the Endowment.

Even more important was the postmodern generation's impact on colleges and universities across the country; and in my last year as NEH chairman, I wrote a pamphlet, *Telling the Truth: A Report on the*

State of the Humanities in Higher Education, that focused on some of the consequences of radical relativism for our campuses.[4] After returning to private life, I increasingly saw the importance of another dimension: the impact of these ideas on the larger culture. The idea that truth is something to be invented rather than pursued has passed beyond narrow academic circles to influence many fields of endeavor. As I shall show in this book, it has affected schools, where, in the name of group politics, students are taught fantasy rather than fact: that the ancient Egyptians flew in gliders and that the Greeks "stole" their culture from Egypt. It has changed cultural institutions such as museums, where curators now see politics as an important part of their mission. It has affected private lives, as psychotherapists, believing objective truth to be an outdated concept, urge patients to lodge accusations of sexual abuse even when there is no evidence to support such a charge. It has changed public life, as journalists have come to disdain objectivity and as public figures have felt less and less constrained by reality. Consider the case of Mr. Joshua Steiner, lately of Yale and Oxford Universities, testifying before the Senate Banking Committee in the summer of 1994. He had written in his diary that his boss, Roger Altman, had "gracefully ducked" a senatorial inquiry, but what had really happened, claimed Steiner before the Senate, was that Altman was "truthful and forthright." Pressed about the contradiction, Steiner sounded as if there were no objective reality to control descriptions but only various purposes that descriptions might serve: in the case of his diary, the purpose was "to reflect upon personal and professional experiences"; in the case of the hearing, "to be as precise and accurate as I can."[5]

On a wide range of subjects, cultural and political leaders tell us that we are foolish to be too concerned about truth. New York University professor Thomas Bender labels scholars who insist on accuracy "fact fetishists."[6] White House aide George Stephanopoulos, pressed about presidential inconsistencies, accuses his questioners of "an excess of literalism."[7] A writer for the *Nation*, considering Tawana Brawley's charges that she was abducted and sexually assaulted by a

gang of white men, argues: "In cultural perspective, if not in fact, it doesn't matter whether the crime occurred or not," since it represents "what actually happens to too many black women."[8] A commentator on the Anita Hill–Clarence Thomas hearings advises, "Anita Hill must be believed not because she was personally speaking the truth, but because her affective language is symptomatic of the collective 'sexual condition' of working women."[9]

In fields ranging from education to art to law, the attack on truth has been accompanied by an assault on standards. The connection is seldom made clear. Indeed, one of the characteristics of postmodern thought is that it is usually asserted rather than argued, reasoned argument having been rejected as one of the tools of the white male elite. But the thinking seems roughly to be that absent external reality, distinctions of any kind are meaningless. No accomplishment can be judged superior to any other—except as it promotes the interests of desired groups. Without the objective measures that an external reality would provide, who can really say, for example, that the work of some students is better than that of others? And so the usual grades are A's and B's, with feminists arguing that even that much hierarchical ordering is patriarchal and oppressive. In the art world, the idea that aesthetic standards are nothing more than white male constructs is so influential that artists who seek originality or formal coherence in their work are often marginalized, while those who mock the concept of quality and strive through their subjects— puddles of vomit, piles of excrement, photographs of corpses—to be as disgusting as possible become the center of attention.

Feminists and critical race theorists claim that legal principles represent white male thinking and particularly attack the notion that the law ought to hold everyone to the same standard. They argue that overcoming inequities demands different standards for different groups—a claim that has been institutionalized in affirmative action practices, spectacularly so in recent years. Consider a 1994 directive at the Department of Defense that requires any official who wants to promote a nondisabled white male to a senior management position to obtain special permission to do so.[10] Or a decision by a school

board in New Jersey: Faced with having to lay someone off, they fired a white teacher solely on the basis of her race, arguing that her absence from the rolls would improve the school's diversity. The U.S. Justice Department, after first defending the teacher, switched to defending her firing.[11]

As George Orwell showed in *1984,* in a world where objective truth is denied, definitions become exceedingly slippery; and anything can mean almost anything else. Two of Big Brother's favorite mottoes are "war is peace" and "freedom is slavery." In our own time, *fairness* and *merit,* words often used to explain why accomplishment rather than group membership ought to be the basis for judging people, are said to be "code words continually in the mouths of up-to-date bigots."[12] *Quality* is said to enable "white, male, Western culture . . . to exclude or marginalize all other cultural practices."[13] Even the word *individual* has come under attack on the grounds that its use "privileges the 'individuals' belonging to the largest or dominant group."[14]

Sexual harassment, which once meant activities on the order of unwanted fondling or sexual blackmail (e.g., "sleep with me or lose your job"), now might mean being insufficiently appreciative of feminist approaches to literature or disagreeing with a feminist professor.[15] On the basis that sexism and racism require power to practice, these concepts have been narrowed so that they are sins exclusive to men and white people. As a Washington, D.C., diversity trainer puts it, "Racism is a white problem."[16] But at the same time these ideas have been dramatically expanded to include not only deliberate acts of discrimination, but also any situation that produces unequal results. If a college or university faculty does not represent racial groups in proportion to their presence in the population, the reason is said to be racism; and no matter that there is a disproportionately small number of minorities in the hiring pool. (While 12 percent of the population is African-American, for example, only 3 percent of those who earned Ph.D.'s in 1991 are.)[17]

So much that follows from denying the idea of truth is deeply unsettling. We have to worry not only about whether our educational

19

and cultural institutions will pass along an accurate and balanced history to our children, but also about whether they will communicate to them the importance of reason, of trying to overcome bias, of using evidence to arrive at conclusions—understandings that they will have to have if they are ever to be able to judge what they are told. And how are we to teach the next generation to work hard and strive for excellence when ideas like merit and quality are impugned? Indeed, what does it mean for our own lives when we are told that it is wrong to demand fair treatment and wrong to expect to be considered as individuals? Meanwhile, we live, each of us, with a tiny dread in our hearts. What if, amidst the rules and definitions that mutate in ways that seem beyond the power of reason to comprehend, what if we should be found guilty of a violation?

While writing this book, I came across a particularly haunting story. It was about Michael Bullock, a math teacher in Fairfax County, Virginia, known for passing out soft drinks in class, calling his students by nicknames, and enlivening his instruction with a sarcastic humor that his many admirers appreciated, although other students were sometimes offended. One day in the spring of 1993, a female student, joking around with Bullock (and, according to one account, repeatedly poking him in the chest), remarked how large his chest was. Bullock, who was greatly overweight, was irritated and responded with a comment about the small size of the student's chest. She filed a sexual harassment complaint, causing school authorities to put Bullock on administrative leave and launch an investigation. When their efforts turned up other students who said Bullock had made inappropriate remarks to them, authorities held a meeting with Bullock that left him with the impression that he was about to be found guilty of sexual harassment for having created a "hostile environment." On the following weekend, Bullock, who had been teaching for more than twenty years, committed suicide.[18]

A few days after the *Washington Post* reported the Bullock story, a reader wrote in to ask, "What on Earth is happening to our society?"[19]

That is the question I intend to take up in this book. I want to show how we have come to live in a world where offenses are constantly being redefined. I want to consider the distortions and divisions being wrought by a kind of thinking that denies there is truth and to examine how it is that this postmodern approach has become entrenched and powerful. I want to look at the origins of the radical skepticism of our time; examine its claims to legitimacy; and, finally, suggest what we can do to blunt its force and restore truth and reason to a central place in our lives.

Politics in the Schoolroom

"Ignorance is strength."

—*One of the mottoes of the Party in George Orwell,* 1984

• A Massachusetts educator warns teachers about using *The Story of Babar* because it "extols the virtues of a European, middle-class lifestyle and disparages the animals and people who have remained in the jungle."[1]

• A teacher of "radical math literacy" warns against bombarding students with "oppressive procapitalist ideology." Among the practical applications of mathematics that she says should be avoided is totaling a grocery bill since such an exercise "carries the nonneutral message that paying for food is natural."[2]

• The author of a textbook for future teachers urges skepticism for the idea that the people now known as American Indians came to this hemisphere across the Bering land bridge. Indian myths do not tell this story, she writes. Moreover, she observes, the scientific account has nothing "except logic" to recommend it. A committee of parents and teachers in Berkeley, California,

subsequently offers this argument as reason for rejecting a
fourth-grade history text.[3]

Disparate as these examples seem, the people in them have a common goal. They want to be sure that American schools show no
favor to—and, indeed, positively downgrade—ideas and practices
associated with the United States and its Western heritage, including, in the last instance, the Enlightenment legacy of scientific
thought. While such efforts can seem foolish and extreme (someone
really wants to ban *Babar*?), it would be a mistake to overlook the
trend they represent: the growing tendency for politics to drive the
education of the young in this country, very often at the expense of
truth.

A teacher in New Jersey describes at length her way of teaching
fourth-graders that Columbus wasn't a hero who "discovered" America, but a "greedy" man and a "murderer" who "stole" it. In order to
help them understand why they have been taught lies about 1492,
she has the children in her class imagine that every year the principal
of their school speaks of Columbus as a man to be respected. Meanwhile, the fourth-graders are further to imagine, the principal regularly leads an army of the school's strongest students on raids of
neighboring schools where they confiscate valuable materials and
round up prisoners to be the principal's servants. By asking the
fourth-graders "to explain the connection between the principal's
spirited promotion of the Columbus myth and the invasions of
neighboring schools," the teacher claims to help her students understand how the positive Columbus myth is used by their government "to forestall any critical questioning of U.S. imperialistic foreign
policy today." As the teacher explains it:

> Widespread belief in the myth makes it easy for U.S. officials to
> get away with invading Vietnam, Grenada, Panama, and so on.
> Those books [containing the myth] teach children that any nation
> with sufficient military power has the right to invade other lands.
> In particular, they reinforce blind patriotism and the belief that

the United States has a moral imperative to control the "New World Order."[4]

Although this teacher is particularly expansive about the views she presents in the classroom, she is hardly unique in conveying to those she teaches that the events leading up to their country's founding should be regarded with loathing. At a multicultural conference in California, a teacher offers her colleagues an example of how to deal with students who want to be positive instead of negative about Columbus and study him as an exemplar of the Age of Exploration. When faced with this in her own classroom, says the teacher, she simply told the student, "That would be like a Jew celebrating Hitler because he had a dream."[5]

Fourth-graders in Chapel Hill, North Carolina, have had to use the following words in a fill-in-the-blank test about Columbus: *conquer, genocide, holocaust, subjugate, annihilate,* and *propaganda.*[6] A seventh-grader in Minnesota recounted for me her difficulties with a writing assignment about Columbus:

> The history teacher wanted us to write a story for first-graders, wanted us to tell the story over the way it was supposed to be. We were supposed to write a negative story on the bad things Columbus did.

The seventh-grader went on to explain that she didn't follow instructions: "I didn't think we should go out and tell first-graders he was so awful." As a result, she got what she called "a really bad grade." She wrote the story again, "half and half" this time, and thus managed to get by.[7]

We should not, of course, retreat into the old myths, should not hide from students that Columbus and other European explorers were often brutal. But there was also brutality in indigenous cultures—as well as much to be admired. And much to praise about Europeans as well, who did, after all, bring with them the foundations for our legal, educational, and political institutions. But instead of being encouraged to search for a complicated truth, students are increasingly presented with oversimple versions of the American past that focus on the negative.

Sandra Stotsky, a researcher at Harvard University, reviewed teaching materials being used in the Brookline, Massachusetts, high school and concluded in 1991 that there was "one major theme" running through the course outlines and examinations for social studies: "the systematic denigration of America's Western heritage." A ninth-grade exam on ancient history, for example, asked students to identify the "Hellenic epic which established egotistical individualism as heroic." Almost all the questions on Greece and Rome, according to Stotsky, emphasized negative aspects, while "all items about ancient China . . . were worded positively or drew attention only to China's positive features, such as 'Chinese belief in pacifism and relativism.' Not a word, for example, about the existence of slavery in ancient China and the thousands of slaves who built, and died building, the Great Wall." Similarly, Stotsky observed:

> Students . . . learn about racism as an American and European phenomenon only. Even though Islamic and African history are extensively covered in the curriculum . . . students learn only about the trans-Atlantic slave trade and nothing about the slave trade conducted by African kings or Arab traders for centuries preceding and following the trans-Atlantic slave trade.[8]

The National History Standards developed at the University of California at Los Angeles and released in the fall of 1994 are the most egregious example to date of encouraging students to take a benign view of—or totally overlook—the failings of other cultures while being hypercritical of the one in which they live. Published in two volumes—one for U.S. history and one for world history—and intended for schools across the nation, the standards suggest that students consider the architecture, labor systems, and agriculture of the Aztecs—but not their practice of human sacrifice. The gathering of wealth, presented as an admirable activity when an African king,

Mansa Musa, undertakes it, is presented as cause for outrage when it occurs in the American context. One suggested student activity is to "conduct a trial of John D. Rockefeller on the following charge: 'The plaintiff [sic] had knowingly and willfully participated in unethical and amoral business practices designed to undermine traditions of fair and open competition for personal and private aggrandizement in direct violation of the common welfare.' "[9]

Although the standards for U.S. history neglect to mention that George Washington was our first president or that James Madison was the father of the Constitution, they do manage to include a great deal about the Ku Klux Klan (which appears seventeen times in the document), Senator Joe McCarthy and McCarthyism (cited nineteen times), and the Great Depression (cited twenty-five times). The U.S. standards also pay little attention to scientific and technological achievement. Among the figures *not* discussed are Alexander Graham Bell, the Wright Brothers, Thomas Edison, Albert Einstein, Jonas Salk, and Neil Armstrong (or any astronaut). The exquisite consciousness of race and gender that characterizes the standards may have contributed to the omission of this group (its members are all white males), but it is also the case that science and technology are now held in extremely low regard in certain parts of the academy. Feminists argue that science represents destructive male thinking. Why not call Newton's *Principia* Newton's "rape manual"? asks one.[10] Both feminists and environmentalists argue that because of the high value that science places on objectivity and rationality, it is now in deep and deserved crisis—information that tends to come as a surprise to practicing scientists.[11] Did the authors of the U.S. standards decide that in the case of a field so disdained by so many of their colleagues, the less said the better? Whatever the motive, to overlook American accomplishment in science and technology is to omit some of our most dazzling achievements.

The World History Standards do mention Edison and Einstein; and while there is heavy emphasis on the role that technological advancement has had in increasing the brutality of war, there is also some recognition that science has played a role in improving quality

27

of life—though it is usually coupled with a reminder that not everyone has benefited equally. Students are asked, for example, to assess "why scientific, technological, and medical advances have improved living standards for many but have failed to eradicate hunger, poverty, and epidemic disease."[12]

In the World History Standards, the fact that women generally had different roles from men in the ancient world is seen simply as a matter of gender "differentiation"—until it happens in Athens, the birthplace of Western civilization. Then it becomes a matter of "restrictions on the rights and freedoms of women." Just as sexism is first introduced in the context of Greek civilization, so, too, is ethnocentrism—as though in previous cultures in Asia and Africa, people had never considered their ethnic group superior.[13] Nowhere is it mentioned that it was, in fact, in Western civilization that the unjust treatment of women and minorities was first condemned and curiosity about other cultures first encouraged.

In one of the sillier sections of the World History Standards—and one of the most quintessentially politically correct—students are asked to read a book about Michelangelo, not in order to discuss art, but so that they can "discuss social oppression and conflict in Europe during the Renaissance." In what may be the most irresponsible section of the World History Standards, fifth- and sixth-graders are asked to read a book about a Japanese girl of their age who died a painful death as a result of radiation from the atomic weapon dropped on Hiroshima in 1945.[14] No mention is made of why American leaders decided to use atomic weapons, about the casualties they believed an invasion of Japan would have entailed, for example. No mention is made of death and suffering caused by the Japanese. The rape of Nanking is not discussed, nor is Pearl Harbor, nor the Bataan death march. What fifth- and sixth-graders would be likely to conclude is that their country was guilty of a horrible—and completely unjustified—act of cruelty against innocents.

In the World History Standards, as in those for the United States, the Cold War is presented as a deadly competition between two equally culpable superpowers, each bent on world domination. Ignored is the most salient fact: that the struggle was between the communist totalitarianism of the Soviet Union, on the one hand, and the freedom offered by the United States, on the other. One might almost conclude from reading the standards that it would have made very little difference in terms of human freedom how the Cold War ended.[15]

It is sometimes said that the negative slant to what we are teaching now is overreaction to a too positive slant in the past, and it is true that in the past we sometimes presented celebratory history in our schools. But this explanation is of no help to students who were not around when prideful, positive stories were told, and who, day after day, are presented a drearily distorted picture of the society in which they live. Nor is this explanation complete. For those intent on political and social transformation, a bleak version of history is better than a balanced one. The grimmer the picture, the more heavily underscored is the need for the reforms they have in mind.

In recent years, some activists have been remarkably frank about the political goals they have for education. Betty Jean Craige of the University of Georgia argues that "multiculturalism" has the happy "potential for ideologically disuniting the nation." As American students learn more about the faults of this country and about the virtues of other nations, she writes, they will be less and less likely to think this country deserves their special support. They will not respond to calls to use American force, and thus we will be delivered from the dark days of the early 1990s, when President George Bush was able to unify the nation in support of war against Iraq, and be able to return to the golden days of the late 1960s and early 1970s, when no president was able to build support for Vietnam. Writes Craige:

> Multicultural education may well be incompatible with patriotism, if patriotism means belief in the nation's superiority over other nations. . . . The advantage to the nation of multicultural education thus may be increased reluctance to wage all-out war.[16]

Classicist Martha Nussbaum has also made a case against patriotism, calling education that encourages it "morally dangerous."
Writes Nussbaum, "To give support to nationalist sentiments sub-
verts, ultimately, even the values that hold a nation together, because it substitutes a colorful idol for the substantive universal values
of justice and right."[17] A central confusion in Nussbaum's argument,
and in Craige's, is that neither considers the ways in which the
American system has uniquely nurtured justice and right. The idea
enunciated in the Declaration of Independence that all men are
created equal has, for example, been a driving force behind the
changes we have made to achieve a greater degree of equality than
exists anywhere in the world for women—and for racial, ethnic, and
religious minorities. The principles of freedom and liberty that have
inspired our political system have also informed our economic arrangements and made the United States a beacon of opportunity to
people everywhere. If we do not teach our children these things,
they may well conclude, as Craige wishes, that this nation deserves
no special support. They might well become "cosmopolitan," as
Nussbaum prefers. But we will have accomplished these ends at the
cost of truth—a truth, moreover, that calls into question the wisdom
of the political goals that Craige and Nussbaum advance. Why deny
special support to a nation that has become a political and economic
lodestar to people around the world?

One of Nussbaum's concerns seems to be that our schools will
foster arrogance and self-righteousness, that they will encourage the
view that "Americans as such are worthy of special respect." And,
adds Nussbaum, "that, I think, is a story that Americans have told
for far too long."[18] But no one is suggesting that we hide our flaws
or neglect the achievements of others. The point is to give students
as accurate an accounting of the past as we can; and when we neglect
our accomplishments and emphasize our failings, while doing exactly the opposite for other cultures, it is not the cause of truth that
is being advanced.

The fact that the history of the United States and Western civilization is so often presented in a negative light has spawned an

occasional backlash. In 1994, the school board in Lake County, Florida, complied with state directives to teach multiculturalism with the following caveat:

> This instruction shall also include and instill in our students an appreciation of our American heritage and culture such as: our republican form of government, capitalism, a free enterprise system, patriotism, strong family values, freedom of religion and other basic values that are superior to other foreign or historic cultures.[19]

The school board was denounced and derided for its action, largely by people and groups focusing on the phrase "superior to other foreign or historic cultures." A University of Central Florida professor called the policy "close to racism." The Lake County Education Association maintained that the board's action violated the state's multicultural education law.[20] In the face of this criticism, one of the members who had voted for the statement resigned; and when a subsequent election further changed the composition of the board, the statement was repealed. But the original board action made an important point. There are, to be sure, many ways in which we are not superior to other cultures. We have produced "no Mozart, Beethoven, Brahms, or Bach," as columnist Richard Cohen noted in connection with the Lake County decision. Nonetheless, there are also many ways in which we are the light of the world; and one of them is that we have created a single nation out of people from every part of the world. We have created one from many and should celebrate the spirit that has enabled us to do so. Richard Cohen's description is apt:

> The true glory of American culture is its eclectic nature—its plasticity, the wonderful adaptability that not only has produced ham and Swiss on croissants but, more important, the throat-catching letters of immigrants to their relatives back home. So many of these people were simply stunned by the hearty openness of

American society, its willingness to accept them as individuals, not as tribal representatives. This emphasis on the individual is very American. It can be overdone, but overall it's wonderful.[21]

American students should learn where we as a nation have fallen short. But if they are to have a true understanding of past and present, it is crucial that they also know about what we have done well—very well, indeed.

ɜ∾

One of the ways in which schools have changed—and for the better—is in recognizing the contributions that women have made and will continue to make to our society. But a 1992 study sponsored by the American Association of University Women (AAUW) claimed that education reformers have ignored girls, left them on the sidelines. Entitled *How Schools Shortchange Girls*, the report concluded that schools were biased in favor of boys, though, in fact, research in this area—including research cited in the AAUW report itself—is hardly clear on this point.[22] As education historian Diane Ravitch has pointed out, when one compares the educational record of females to males, it is very hard to find evidence that girls are victims of gender bias:

> While boys get higher scores in mathematics and science, girls get higher scores in reading and writing. Boys in eighth grade are 50 percent likelier than girls to be held back a grade, and boys in high school constitute 68 percent of the "special education" population.[23]

Research done shortly after the release of the AAUW report was especially devastating to its conclusions. A 1993 survey showed that female college freshmen—recent products, most of them, of American elementary and secondary schools—have higher aspirations than male college freshmen: 27.3 percent of the women declared their intention to pursue medical, law, or doctoral degrees; 25.8

percent of male freshmen had the same ambitions. Numbers for 1994 showed an even higher percentage for women—28.1—and a slightly lower one for men—25.6. These numbers represent an enormous turnaround from a quarter century ago when three times as many male as female freshmen said they intended to pursue advanced degrees.[24]

The AAUW report found textbooks to be discriminatory, a claim that was repeated uncritically in many news stories about the report. But as anyone who has looked at textbooks recently is aware, they have undergone enormous change. In order to make this point, I frequently cite for audiences a study showing that 83.8 percent of seventeen-year-olds know who Harriet Tubman is—more than know that George Washington was the commander of the American army during the Revolutionary War.[25] When I use this example, the over-thirty-five-year-olds in the audience almost always look disconcerted because they haven't the least idea of who Tubman—so familiar to seventeen-year-olds—was. Their puzzlement is testimony to how much textbooks—and, as a result, school curricula—have changed.

A group of researchers at Smith College in Massachusetts analyzed three leading high school American history textbooks and found that they not only include women, but show a pro-female bias. Wrote Robert Lerner, Althea K. Nagai, and Stanley Rothman:

> Of [the figures] they do evaluate, textbooks portray 99 percent of the women positively. Only one female character is portrayed both positively and negatively; no woman is depicted in a negative light. When textbooks rate men, they also portray them positively, but only 71 percent of the time. By contrast 14 percent of the men rated mixed portrayals, while 14 percent are portrayed negatively.

The researchers also noted a pro-feminist bias. The National Organization for Women (NOW) and the Equal Rights Amendment (ERA), for example, both received uncritical, favorable coverage. Opposition to groups like NOW and legal measures like ERA was uniformly ignored.[26]

33

A study of elementary school textbooks published in 1986 found:

> Not one of the many families described in these books features a homemaker—that is, referred to a woman principally dedicated to acting as a wife and mother—as a model. . . . There are countless references to mothers and other women working outside of the home in occupations such as medicine, transportation, and politics. There is not one citation indicating that the occupation of a mother or housewife represents an important job, one with integrity, one that provides real satisfactions.[27]

In light of the results of this research—indeed, in light of what any parent who opens up a recently published textbook will see for him- or herself—it is astonishing that the president of the AAUW, Jackie DeFazio, in defending her organization's report, would write, "Textbooks rarely include references to the achievements of women, and when women are included, they are generally in sex-stereotyped roles."[28] Not even the report she was defending made that claim. Its primary concern, in fact, was almost the opposite: that the women in textbooks tended to be famous; that is, they had succeeded by supposedly male standards, rather than being representative of "women's perspectives and cultures."[29]

In 1993, the AAUW issued a second report, this one on sexual harassment. According to *Hostile Hallways,* 81 percent of students had experienced sexual harassment in school. Some of the instances of harassment cited were quite serious: 11 percent said they had been "forced to do something sexual at school other than kissing." But others were much less so. Two-thirds said they had been harassed by "sexual comments, jokes, gestures, or looks."[30] One of the commentators to point out how expansive is the AAUW definition of sexual harassment was Albert Shanker, president of the American Federation of Teachers, who wrote:

> *Hostile Hallways* defines sexual harassment so broadly that it can be anything from being raped on the stairs to "unwelcome" words

or gestures from someone you don't find attractive. . . . And the glance/gesture/remark kind of harassment is by far the most frequently reported.

Observing that an all-inclusive definition of sexual harassment trivializes the harm done to students who suffer serious abuse, Shanker asked, "What possible benefit is it to anyone to define sexual harassment so broadly that it includes most of the kids in a school—a girl who doesn't like the way a guy looked at her as well as one who suffered several broken bones when she was attacked?"[31]

The political point of the AAUW's research became clear when a "gender equity" bill was introduced in the Congress in 1993. In 1994, many provisions of this bill were enacted into law as part of the Elementary and Secondary Education Act. Millions of dollars of federal funds were thus dedicated to the purpose of making schools more congenial places for girls—despite statistics showing that males, in fact, have at least as much if not more difficulty than females at succeeding in school.

The research efforts of the AAUW illustrate well a point made by Cynthia Crossen in her book *Tainted Truth* about how postmodern thinking has affected the research enterprise. "Researchers have almost given up on the quaint notion that there is any such thing as 'fact' or 'objectivity,' " Crossen writes.[32] Instead, the point has become to amass data in order to support an agenda, in the case of the AAUW, an agenda that is moving sharply left, aligning it with organizations like the National Women's Studies Association. Vivien Ng, who as president of the NWSA expounded at that group's 1993 convention on her love for "political work, both inside the classroom and outside it,"[33] is a member of the AAUW foundation that funded *Hostile Hallways*. The other AAUW study, *How Schools Shortchange Girls*, was written in part by Peggy McIntosh, associate director of Wellesley College's Center for Research on Women, who has gained a certain measure of fame lecturing to parents and teachers across the country about how schools must stress the "lateral" thinking typical of women and minorities and deemphasize the "vertical" thinking that white males exhibit. Lateral thinking, as McIntosh defines it, aims "not to win, but to be in a decent relationship with the universe." Vertical thinking, on the other hand, is what makes "our young white males dangerous to themselves and the rest of us—especially in a nuclear age."[34]

One of the worst ideas that vertical thinking produces, according to McIntosh, is the notion of excellence. It holds "in thrall," she explains, those who think of life in terms of advancement upward.[35] Many feminists—and other political activists as well—maintain that we should do away with the idea of excellence not only on the grounds that it is oppressive but because it is an illusion. Although they usually assert this point rather than explain it, their view seems to be that since complete objectivity is impossible, any judgment about excellence is completely subjective and meaningless. That this line of thought sets up a false dichotomy (complete objectivity and complete subjectivity are not the only choices; varying degrees of each are possible) and makes all valuations thoroughly arbitrary (including those that feminists would substitute) does nothing to slow down the attack. In her book *Ed School Follies*, educator Rita Kramer tells about listening to one of the most popular professors at Columbia University's Teachers College, one of the most prestigious institutions of teacher education in the country, condemn "norms of success, effectiveness, [and] efficiency"; assert that "we have to do something about our preoccupation with rewards and competition in this country"; and declare "relativism" to be "a *good* thing." "There are no 'objective standards,' " the professor tells her students, "there is no such thing as 'objective norms.' "[36]

Inspired particularly by Harvard psychologist Carol Gilligan's *In a Different Voice*, as well as by *Women's Ways of Knowing*, a collaboratively written book, many feminists have declared excellence and objectivity to be male constructs, part of a male sphere where abstract principles, intellect, rationality, and logical thinking are valued.[37] The research on which these books depend is idiosyncratic and limited. *In a Different Voice* is based on three small studies, including one of twenty-nine women considering having an abortion; *Women's Ways of Knowing* reaches its conclusions on the basis of 135 open-ended interviews. The authors of these books do not claim to offer conclusive evidence (indeed, attempting to amass the data needed to do so would, by their lights, be a decidedly masculine undertaking). But despite this and despite the fact that the theories they offer portray women in stereotypical ways that previous generations of feminists would have found highly offensive, *In a Different Voice* and *Women's Ways of Knowing* have become widely influential. Among many professional educators, the conventional wisdom is that for female students, caring, sharing, and connectedness are what matter; that for them, feelings, emotions, and intuition provide natural ways of proceeding. Schools, which have traditionally undervalued these ways of knowing, must—so the thinking goes—now bring them to the fore.

One of the first steps in achieving this transformation is to do away with situations that create hierarchies, thus elevating some at the expense of others. Grades do this, of course, and one of the trends of our time at all levels of education has been to do away with meaningful grading:

- According to research reported by Randy Moore, editor of the *American Biology Teacher*, high school teachers gave twice as many C's as A's in 1966. By 1978, the ratio had changed dramatically, with the number of A's given exceeding the number of C's. By 1990, 20 percent of entering college students reported an A average for their entire high school career.[38]

- According to a survey conducted by the Higher Education Research Institute at the University of California at Los Angeles, in the fall of 1994, 28.1 percent of college freshmen reported average high school grades of A- or higher.[39]

The same phenomenon has occurred in higher education. At Stanford, over 70 percent of undergraduates get A's and B's; at Princeton, the number is 80 percent.[40] According to Harvard instructor William

Cole, the "gentleman's C" has been replaced at his school by the " 'gentleperson's B,' and A- is gaining ground fast, especially in the humanities."[41]

Grade inflation is certainly not the accomplishment of feminists alone, but they have contributed mightily to the notion that the world in general and schools in particular have for too long been run according to standards that have no justification except to advance the interests of white males. "Relativism is the key word today," explains Harvard's Cole. "There's a general conception in the literary-academic world that holding things to high standards—like logic, argument, having an interesting thesis—is patriarchal, Eurocentric and conservative."[42] So out of fashion has meaningful grading become that the *New York Times* declared Stanford University's 1994 decision to reinstitute the grade of F "an event of seismic proportions."[43]

One also senses the radical egalitarianism espoused by many feminists in the movement to do away with other kinds of competition in the schools. In a section of *How Schools Shortchange Girls* that Peggy McIntosh helped write, current events and civics curricula are condemned for their tendency to focus on "controversy and conflict." Debate clubs are said to be harmful since they take for granted an "adversarial, win/lose orientation."[44] Other examples of this kind of thinking abound:

- According to an article in the *New York Times*, physical education is no longer what it used to be: "[In] the new P.E. . . . competition is out and cooperation is in." In every part of the country, schoolchildren are dancing and jumping rope, activities that do not involve competition, instead of playing games like dodgeball, from which a winner emerges.[45]

- A mother in Michigan reports to Ann Landers that her child's school no longer has spelling bees because they are regarded as unfair to children who are not good spellers.[46]

- The president of the Independent Schools Association of the Central States reports that the Illinois Junior Academy of Science prohibited a small independent school in Downers Grove, Illinois, from competing in the 1995 State Science Fair. The Downers Grove school, which makes a point of encouraging excellence, puts other schools at too much of a disadvantage, an Academy of Science official said: "We want to spread the wealth around."[47]

• Meanwhile, the executive director of the Maryland Coalition for Inclusive Education argues that honor rolls should be abolished. They rely on "objective" cutoff points, he complains, and reinforce "some of the least attractive aspects of our culture."[48]

Meritocracy in general has come under assault in the schools. A few years ago in the *Harvard Educational Review*, there appeared an article that has become something of a classic in the annals of educational egalitarianism. Entitled "Tootle: A Parable of Schooling and Destiny," the article warned about the lesson implicit in the Little Golden Book story *Tootle*. The story is about a talented young train who, after going through a period in which he breaks the first rule of trainhood and repeatedly jumps the tracks in order to wander through the meadows, learns that success, in the words of the *Harvard Educational Review* article, comes from "deferred gratification, hard work, and an achievement orientation." While one might think these good lessons to teach children, they are, according to the *Harvard Educational Review* article, part of the repressive "masculine world of technology [and] competition" to which Tootle's "sensitive, emotional, and relational qualities . . . must give way."[49]

Although this heavyhanded analysis of a simple story reads like a parody, it has been taken quite seriously. In her book *Ed School Follies*, Rita Kramer reports on a class for future teachers at Eastern Michigan University in which the professor assigns the *Harvard Educational Review* article. An older woman in the class is skeptical about the analysis it offers. "What would a six-year-old get out of [the story of Tootle]?" she asks. "I read it to my kid. 'Work hard in school'—isn't that what we all want?"

The teacher pounces on her question. "What does that sound like? Anyone?"

A young woman named Amy—the star of the class, according to Kramer—knows exactly what mistaken notion the older student is advancing: "Meritocracy! And if it doesn't work, if you don't succeed, you think, What's wrong with me?"[50]

The idea of a nurturing female sphere distinct from the competitive male world has led to a feminist interest in witches and witchcraft, as readers of the New York Times discovered on Mother's Day a few years ago. A Times editorial described nature rites being conducted by a priestess/witch: a bowl of water being passed around, prayers being put into it, the water poured onto a tree whose leaves would pass the prayers into the wind. "Such is the practice of goddess worship," the Times editorialized, "a new development in America's spiritual life, and one worth acknowledging on Mother's Day." The editorial went on to describe the reasons for this new movement in terms that Peggy McIntosh and Carol Gilligan would no doubt appreciate: Societies that worship goddesses are "peaceful, cooperative and egalitarian," explained the Times, while societies that focus on male deities are "violent, authoritarian and stratified."[51]

Not surprisingly witches and witchcraft are now making an appearance in school curricula. A teacher in an extended day program at Seeds University Elementary School at the University of California at Los Angeles tries to relieve her students of negative stereotypes they have of witches and to get them to think of them in positive ways. She begins by telling the children, "What I know is that the real women we call witches weren't bad. They really helped people." In the following days she sets up a number of activities, such as a "witch-healer" table where children can concoct their own potions. The children are taught chants:

Stirring, stirring, stirring the pot;
Bubbly, bubbly, bubbly hot;
Look to the moon, laugh like a loon,
Throw something into the pot.[52]

The state of Arkansas has a Governor's School, a special summer session for outstanding high school juniors. At the 1992 Governor's

School, some of the readings assigned were by well-known authors such as Ursula K. Le Guin, Annie Dillard, and Albert Camus. But the single longest assignment was an autobiographical meditation by Emily Culpepper, a self-described "semi-anarchist witch." Culpepper described how her Christianity had become "compost," how it had "decayed and died, becoming a mix of animate and inanimate, stinking rot and released nutrients," and how she had turned to witchcraft:

> Feminist witchcraft has become one important vehicle for spiritual/political liberation. . . . Many women are inspired by its spontaneous creativity in rituals [and] refusal to solidify into fixed book or creed or hierarchy. . . . Being a witch has always meant to me, not joining a faith, but developing an identity that channels anger and ecstasy into creativity. Being a witch means believing in magic as part of politics; it's part of dancing in the revolution, as Emma Goldman would put it. Being a witch means understanding ourselves to be on the boundaries and beyond of patriarchal realities.

As an example of how magic might be made part of politics, Culpepper recalled participating in a 1967 antiwar march on Washington that concluded with an attempt by Allen Ginsberg and the Fugs to levitate the Pentagon.[53]

To some parents, teaching about witches and witchcraft is not merely a bizarre aspect of contemporary feminism, it constitutes religious instruction; and they have tried to stop it. One target has been a book series for elementary school students entitled *Impressions*.[54] While the series contains many poems and stories to which no one would object, about two dozen selections (out of more than eight hundred) are about goblins and witches. In one, a monster chases a child and tears off his head while other children cry, "MORE, MORE, MORE." In another a witch denies her true nature—and in doing so manages to turn children into frogs and their parents into pigs. Horrified at what she has done, the witch corrects her mistake, earns the gratitude of those she has made human again, and regains her self-esteem. She learns to accept herself as she really is—a witch.

Parents complaining about the series have particularly objected to exercises in accompanying teacher's guides that call for students to pretend to be sorcerers and witches and to cast spells and chant incantations. In one exercise, students sit in a circle, pass a candle, and try to transport themselves to distant lands by chanting to "candles bright" and "cats black." In another, they attend a wizard's meeting in order to exchange spells and stories of magic they have performed.

As a result of parental pressure, a few school districts have stopped using the series, but more have not; and the disgruntled parents have been unsuccessful in court. One judge ruled that the inclusion in the classroom of "isolated instances of . . . activities [that] may happen to coincide or harmonize with the tenets of two relatively obscure religions," that is, witchcraft and neopaganism, did not constitute the promotion of a religion. While acknowledging that some of the classroom exercises resembled witchcraft practices, the judge wrote that "38 exercises out of over 9,000 exercises and activities does not amount to a government message of endorsement."[55]

The concerned parents have lost not only the legal battle, but also the public relations fight, thanks in large part to People for the American Way, a liberal organization that consistently portrays them as zealots who not only want to censor what children read, but bring down the public school system. As law professor Stephen Carter of Yale University has noted, it has become common in our culture to perceive parents who complain about school curricula on religious grounds as "backward, irrational, illiberal fanatics."[56] But it is important to place complaints such as those made about the *Impressions* series in a larger context and ask, for example, why it is permissible to have "isolated instances" of witchcraft practiced in the school when not a single instance of organized prayer is permitted. If the former does not violate the establishment clause of the First Amendment, why does the latter?

Some Christian parents object not only to what is being taught in schools, but also to what is not: namely, creationism, or the idea that life developed under the direction of God, as described in Genesis, rather than as a result of natural selection. This battle has also been lost, mainly because there is such a powerful argument on the other side: that creationism is a matter of faith rather than science and that it should not be the purpose of the public schools to teach matters of faith. As Nobel Prize winner Murray Gell-Mann puts it, "Fundamentalists have a perfect right to their beliefs but no right to control the teaching of science in the public schools."[57]

One can only wish that figures like Gell-Mann would look at instances in which belief rather than fact has actually entered the curricula of schools—at what is being taught (and not taught) in the name of feminism, for example. If the principle that ideology should not dominate what children learn in public schools is a sound one—and generations have held it to be—then surely it deserves the widest possible application.

౭౿

In a 1989 New York State education report, *A Curriculum of Inclusion*, Leonard Jeffries, Jr., chairman of the Department of Black Studies at the City College of New York, demanded that elementary and secondary school students be taught that "the Crusades and the corruption of the Roman Catholic Church" had led to the "negative values" of Europeans, to the "greed, racism and national egoism" evident in their desire to "discover, invade and conquer." He insisted that teachers present the idea of Columbus's "discovery" of America as "an essential part of the ideology of 'White nationalism' designed to justify the exploitation and eventual genocide of indigenous Americans."[58]

One might have expected the task force assembling the report to shy away from such inflammatory notions, but instead it embraced them. This kind of teaching would raise the "self esteem and self respect" of students from minority cultures, the report asserted, "while children from European cultures will have a less arrogant perspective."[59]

A Curriculum of Inclusion was thus explicit in making something besides truth the goal of history teaching; and within two years, a second New York State report, *One Nation, Many Peoples*, would expand on this idea. In a particularly instructive section of *One Nation, Many Peoples*, Edmund W. Gordon, then of Yale University, and Francis Roberts, the superintendent of schools in the Cold Spring Harbor school district of New York, explained and embraced many of the postmodern notions that now enter into thinking about what should be taught in schools. They presented truth as a more or less dated concept, an idea that people still worry about from time to time, but one that has been called into question by newer understandings. One of these is that knowledge is "situated": What we believe we know and think is true reflects our circumstances and interests. Different groups, being situated in different circumstances, will have different truths; and while in an earlier time, we might have tried to gather information to decide which views were accurate, we now understand, as Gordon and Roberts explain it, that such efforts do not take us very far because information is itself "situated": "Facts . . . are insufficient and often so situation bound as to limit their utility."[60]

Thus, *One Nation, Many Peoples* recommends that we not burden students with too many names and dates and places: "The information-dominant approach to the social studies curriculum fails as a vehicle for multicultural education." Instead, we should emphasize that history is "socially constructed," that it reflects the circumstances in which it is written rather than the reality of the past. We should teach students to appreciate different interpretations and work to open their minds to "multiple perspectives." We should give credit to "noncanonical knowledge and techniques"— including, presumably, the kind offered by Leonard Jeffries.[61]

These arguments have many weaknesses, chief among them a problem that exists whenever relativism is espoused. If there is no truth, then there is no basis for making statements about truth—or anything else. One of the best illustrations I know of this point was provided by a young man who once worked for me as a summer intern. He recounted how a professor of his at Amherst College had proclaimed in class one day that there is no truth—which led the very sensible summer intern to raise his hand and ask, "Is that statement true?" Similarly, Gordon and Roberts, once they have declared all knowledge to be "situated," have no authority for making broad declarations about what schools should teach.

But the weaknesses of postmodern thought have not done much to slow its advance, and the fact that the epistemology of postmodernism has made its way from campuses to schools helps explain the presence of a great deal of nonsense in elementary and secondary curricula. It is surely worth noting that one of the groups wholeheartedly endorsing *One Nation, Many Peoples* was the American Association of University Women.[62] The philosophy that the report sets forth justifies the noncanonical knowledge and techniques of feminism—notions about teaching horizontally rather than vertically, for example—as well as providing a rationale for Afrocentric teaching. Should Leonard Jeffries advance one of the axioms of Afrocentrism—the idea that the skin pigment melanin determines character and intelligence, for example—on what grounds can the relativist object? The melanin theory has no basis in fact, but what does that count for in a world where the best that can be said for facts is that they are "situation bound" and "insufficient"?

Early on in any discussion of Afrocentrism, it is important to note the responsible and enlightening work that has been done on Africa and the African-American experience. An important academic tradition that aims to get at truth traces back to scholars like W. E. B. Du Bois; has been carried on by John Hope Franklin, Kenneth B. Clark, and others; and in recent years has been invigorated by the kind of work being done by Henry Louis Gates, Jr., of Harvard University. There are also scholars such as classicist Frank M. Snowden, Jr., professor emeritus at Howard University, whose books and articles have advanced understanding of the black experience in antiquity. White historians have also explored the African-American past, and their work, like the work of black scholars, has helped enlarge and enrich what is taught in schools. A generation ago, students learned little about the non-European world and gained only the vaguest notion of the African-American experience in the United States. Now they read about ancient African kingdoms, encounter frank discussions of slavery and racism in the United States, and learn in detail about the struggle for equality. Careful research and sound scholarship make it possible for today's students to have a much fuller, richer, and more accurate understanding of the past than their parents had.

But also having impact are the ideas of the Afrocentrists. School districts across the nation have introduced Afrocentric curricula, and a primary source for them is the *African-American Baseline Essays* developed for Portland, Oregon, schools under the direction of Asa Hilliard III, a professor from Georgia State University who served on the *One Nation, Many Peoples* committee. The *Baseline Essays* purport to detail African contributions to history and knowledge; but in all too many instances what they actually do is make ill-founded claims about ancient Egypt: that its inhabitants, for example, were not only masters of the natural world, having discovered everything from the particle/wave nature of light to the theories behind quantum mechanics, but they also commanded the supernatural world with their powers of "precognition, psychokinesis, remote viewing and other underdeveloped human capabilities."[63]

Hunter Havelin Adams III, the author of the *Baseline* essay on science, writes that "this process of investigation, called science, is not value neutral; nor is it culturally independent; furthermore, there can be no ultimate objectivity."[64] What this seems to mean in practice is that one can base the most extravagant claims on the slenderest reeds. Wayne State University anthropology professor Bernard Ortiz de Montellano, who has reviewed the *Baseline* essay on science, describes Adams's method of reaching conclusions this way:

On the basis of a creation myth in which the word *evolved* is used, the *Baseline Essay* claims that Egyptians had a theory of species evolution "at least 2,000 years before Charles Darwin developed his theory. . . ." On the basis of a 6″ x 7″ tailless, bird-shaped object found in the Cairo Museum, supposedly a scale model of a glider, Adams says that Egyptians had full-size gliders 4,000 years ago and "used their early planes for travel, expeditions, and recreation."

The science *Baseline* essay, de Montellano concludes, is "a farrago of extraordinary claims with little or no evidence." He also points out that its author, though described as a research scientist at Argonne National Laboratory, is actually an industrial hygiene technician there whose highest degree is a high school diploma.[65]

Egyptologist Frank Yurco of the Field Museum of Natural History in Chicago concurs, calling the *Baseline* essay on science "a mixed bag of misinformation, misinterpreted data and documentation, some outright gaffes, and distorted information."[66] The *Baseline* essay on the social studies, Yurco says, is even worse. Written by John Henrik Clarke, professor emeritus of Black and Puerto Rican Studies at Hunter College in New York, the social studies essay is so full of inconsistent and conflicting data, Yurco writes, that it amounts to "sham scholarship." By way of example, Yurco notes that the social science essay promotes "the undocumented, unproven, and unscientific argument that Cleopatra was a black person."[67] The main evidence cited by Clarke is a reference to her as "tawny" in Shakespeare's *Antony and Cleopatra*. Frank Snowden, Jr., also a critic of the *Baseline* essays, has noted:

> There is no evidence that Shakespeare, who lived more than sixteen hundred years after Cleopatra, had reliable evidence that Cleopatra was black. Nor can it be demonstrated that Shakespeare intended to suggest by his use of "tawny" that he regarded Cleopatra as "black."

Snowden also points out the ways in which the Afrocentrists ignore evidence that runs contrary to their ideas—such as "the ancient portraits of Cleopatra, including those on coins commemorating her marriage to Mark Antony, [which] depict her with features as Caucasoid as those of the other Ptolemies," who were of Macedonian, or Greek, descent.[68]

Debunked though they have been, Afrocentric myths dominate many classrooms. When journalist Fred Barnes visited the Robert E. Coleman Elementary School in Baltimore, Maryland, he encountered schoolchildren who had been taught that melanin, supposedly responsible for everything from creativity to paranormal powers, is the source of black racial superiority. When Barnes tried to initiate a discussion about what people of different races have in common, a young student's first observation was, "You don't have enough melanin."[69] A *Washington Post* report on Afrocentrism in schools in Atlanta, Georgia, begins with an account of a sixth-grade student who "drew on her Afrocentric instruction for her prize-winning exhibit in the city social studies fair. Her thesis: Cleopatra and the pharaohs of ancient Egypt did not descend from Greeks but were black Africans." In a paper that was part of her project, the sixth-grader explained that such information was not widely known because "the rise of capitalism called for 'degrading and discrediting the Negroid peoples.' "[70]

Afrocentric teaching commonly implies not only that Egypt was a black nation, but that it provided the Greeks with their culture and that scholars of European descent, driven by racist impulse, try to cover this up. All the evidence indicates, however, that Egypt was a multicultural nation, populated by different races, including black people. While Egypt influenced Greece, most obviously in art and architecture, there was influence from other cultures as well, including those of Semitic peoples.[71] For this and many other reasons— including the creativity and inventiveness of the Greeks themselves—it is gross exaggeration to suggest that Greek culture was borrowed *in toto* from Egypt.[72]

One of the sources for a curriculum intended to bring Afrocentric teachings into public schools in Prince George's County, Maryland, is George G. M. James's *Stolen Legacy*. The thesis of James's book is that "the Greeks were not the authors of Greek philosophy, but the Black people of North Africa, the Egyptians."[73] According to James, the Greeks began purloining Egypt's legacy when that country was occupied by the Persians, but the major theft occurred after Alexander the Great conquered Egypt. Aristotle and other Greek philosophers then descended upon Egypt, taking books of Egyptian learning from the library at Alexandria and otherwise turning that storehouse of Egyptian knowledge to Greek uses.

Classicist Mary Lefkowitz of Wellesley College in Massachusetts has pointed out the flaws in James's book, including the author's casual attitude toward chronology:

> For example, in the initial chapter, James never mentions that the city of Alexandria (as its name suggests) was founded only after Alexander's conquest of Egypt, and even then remained a Greek city and was never fully integrated into the rest of the country. Neither does he mention that the library of Alexandria was built only after Aristotle's death in 322 B.C., so that he could not have sacked it, even if he had been in Egypt.[74]

Nonetheless, in the Prince George's County world history curriculum, one finds George G. M. James's book relied upon and quoted. After Alexander's invasion, according to a passage of *Stolen Legacy* cited in the curriculum, Egyptian culture continued to thrive, but the Greeks relabeled it, putting their own name upon it: "Egyptian culture survived and flourished, under the name and control of the Greeks."[75]

Mary Lefkowitz also reports hearing the story of Aristotle sacking the library at Alexandria in a lecture at Wellesley by Yosef A. A. ben-Jochannan (whose work is cited as a source for the Portland *Baseline Essays*). When she and a colleague pointed out the problems with chronology in this account and the fact that there is no evidence that Aristotle ever went to Egypt, ben-Jochannan accused them of arrogance and insolence. Further, Lefkowitz reports, "One student apologized to the speaker for our rudeness, and walked out. After the lecture other students surrounded us, saying: 'You think you know the truth, but HE is telling the truth. What you learned is wrong.' "[76]

Some Afrocentrists use the idea that the Greeks plagiarized Egyptian philosophy to argue that Western culture is essentially corrupt and therefore should be excised from the schools. At the Second National Conference on the Infusion of African and African-American Content in the High School Curriculum—a gathering chaired by Asa Hilliard III, and sponsored by a number of major American corporations and textbook publishers—Wade Nobles, a prominent Afrocentrist from California, used the following metaphor to describe the process of learning about Egyptian philosophy through the Greeks:

> It's like someone drinking some good stuff, vomiting it, and then we have to catch the vomit and drink it ourselves. . . . The Greeks gave back the vomit of the African way. . . . Don't become the vomit-drinkers!

John Henrik Clarke, author of the social studies *Baseline* essay, also spoke at the conference. His target was religion in general and Christianity in particular:

> At what point do we stop this mental prostitution to a religion invented by foreigners? All religion is artificial. All the major religions of the world are male chauvinist murder cults.[77]

How weak the intellectual underpinnings of Afrocentric education can be was made particularly clear in the fall of 1993 when details of an Afrocentric project to be undertaken at Webb Elementary School in Washington, D.C., became public. The project, developed by Abena Walker, trained teachers at an unlicensed, unaccredited university founded by Walker and from which she claimed her master's degree. Paid $248,000 for her work, Mrs. Walker presented vague plans characterized by predictable misinformation ("The ancient Africans left to the world a legacy of achievements so brilliant that non-African people took it and called it their own") and suspicious pedagogy. "African educational ideology spawns . . . particular methods," Walker wrote, among them "the use of Nommo, the African concept of the magic power of the word in all subjects, including character building." Mrs. Walker went on to explain:

> The concept of Nommo is not cloaked in any hocus pocus, fairy tale notion of magic. . . . Given its African roots, it has a pronounced sociopolitical thrust which symbolically interprets and advocates change in a multicultural milieu. Thus, its transformation of information becomes an act of acquiring power in a social setting that many times is perceived as hostile. Nommo is word magic; to control Nommo is to control the generation and transformation of sound energy, thoughts and action.[78]

The *Washington Post* asked Russell L. Adams, the chairman of Howard University's Afro-American Studies Department, to review Mrs. Walker's materials. He in turn passed them on to his senior seminar. "They were speechless," Adams reported. "And then they said, 'Please, they cannot be serious.' "[79]

The response of the District of Columbia school system to the controversy was to let Mrs. Walker's plans go forward. Franklin Smith, superintendent of schools, defended Mrs. Walker's qualifications:

> She has worked with one of the top Afrocentric scholars, Dr. Asa G. Hilliard of Georgia State University. He praised her work in a letter to me earlier this year. He wrote: "She is among a small group of well-prepared educators who understand an African-centered approach to education."

Moreover, said Smith, "During its three-year life, not one parent or teacher has complained about the project. Instead, they have emphasized the positive changes they have witnessed in their children since the project began in 1990."[80] According to 1994 articles in the *Washington Post*, however, some parents did have strong misgivings.

They called the *Post* to complain that children in the Afrocentric classes weren't allowed to play or eat with other children at the school. They said their children were taught "anti-white" lessons. Reported one parent:

> They taught my daughter that [President] Clinton wasn't their President, that [South Africa President Nelson] Mandela was. I didn't like that. My daughter lives in the United States. Clinton is her president.[81]

Attacks on the intellectual quality of Afrocentric education failed to have effect here, as they often do, because the goal of this teaching is not intellectual. In an interview in which it was pointed out to Portland, Oregon, school superintendent Matthew Prophet that the *Baseline Essays* compiled and published by his school system are deeply flawed, he responded:

> We think that the content of the essays themselves is of less importance than the overriding principle of respecting all geo-cultural groups. . . . I think too many of us in our country have become too involved with trying to refute or to prove certain factual content rather than to really know the purpose. The purpose is to gain recognition that all people have made contributions.[82]

But correct "factual content" is not incompatible with recognizing the contributions of different groups; to the contrary, it is the basis for an accurate understanding. Looking at the evidence of the American past leads one to conclude, as columnist Alan Keyes has described it, that "the survival of black people in America, through slavery, racist assaults and economic deprivation, is one of the greatest sagas of the human spirit the world has ever seen."[83] No distortions of history are necessary to arrive at this lesson. It is simply true—a fact that makes all the more dispiriting Prophet's muddled allegiance to something besides the truth.

It is often argued that Afrocentric education is important because it increases the self-esteem of African-American students; but as Gerald Early, professor of English and Afro-American Studies at Washington University in St. Louis, points out, there is scant evidence to support this claim.[84] Even if it were to be shown that Afrocentric education enhances self-esteem, one should ask whether education should be used therapeutically: Doing so hardly encourages truth-seeking and may even discourage achievement. An international comparison of skill in mathematics, for example, showed American youngsters doing worse in mathematics than almost any other group tested. On one measure, however, they were superior. Asked how good they were at mathematics, they revealed themselves to be more confident in their abilities than any other group.[85] Equally telling, students from the District of Columbia ranked next to last when their mathematical skills were matched with other U.S. students (only U.S. Virgin Island students ranked lower). Students from the District ranked first, however, in their own estimation of how good they were at math.[86] The inverse relationship between real and perceived ability suggests that if self-esteem is to have a role in education, it should be a secondary one, something that students earn by working hard in the primary quest—acquiring useful skills and accurate knowledge.

What African-American children—what all children—require are models like the ones now appearing in some textbooks of figures who earned their place in history through struggle and accomplishment. In her new series for grade-schoolers, *A History of US*, Joy Hakim tells of Frederick Douglass growing up a slave in a time when it was illegal for anyone to teach him to read. Understanding from this that slaveholders wanted to keep slaves ignorant, Douglass devoted himself to learning. "I understood the pathway from slavery to freedom," he wrote; and working enormously hard and fighting against incredible odds, he taught himself not only to read, but also to write and speak in a way that could touch hearts and change minds.[87] Hakim also tells about John Manjiro, a nineteenth-century Japanese boy whom an accident of fate brought to the United States, but whose hard work and determination got him a Western education and a way back to Japan. There, as Commodore Perry was trying to open trade with Japan, the emperor called upon Manjiro; and some historians think he was able to provide mediation between two extremely different cultures.[88]

As Hakim shows, history is full of stories of people whose confidence in themselves is confidence they have earned. Students also need to be encouraged to look to today's achievers and to appreciate the hard work that lies behind the accomplishments of the general or the mayor or the cabinet member. And they need to be encouraged directly as well as indirectly to work hard themselves. "Just as athletic gifts are relatively useless without good coaching and long hours of practice," columnist William Raspberry reminds us, "native academic potential remains untapped without good teaching and long hours of study."[89]

But these ideas assume norms of success, objective standards, competition—all the things that many students are now being taught to view with disdain, taught to regard as artificial constructs put in place to oppress them. The idea that one might be able to distinguish oneself, to stand above the crowd, is powerful motivation to hard work—and we take it away from female students when we tell them that trying to make it to the top of a hierarchy is a quintessentially male activity. The excitement of debate is a spur to learning—an impetus to finding out more and perfecting techniques of analysis and refutation so that one can do even better in the contest next time. And it is an incentive that we take away from girls when we lead them to think that debate, analysis, refutation, and contests are somehow unnatural for females.

But the saddest consequence of the idea that different groups should have different standards is found in the inner city, in Oakland, California, for example, where a young woman, Za'kettha Blaylock, who wants to work hard and go to college and become a doctor is ridiculed by her peers for "acting white."[90] Or in Washington, D.C., where a hardworking young man like Cedric Jennings of Frank W. Ballou Senior High School finds himself virtually without friends because his classmates see his ambition as a betrayal of race. One of them, a gang leader, explains his contempt for Cedric and other students who try to get ahead this way: "Everyone knows they're trying to be white, get ahead in the white man's world. In a way, that's a little bit of disrespect to the rest of us."[91]

It is hard to imagine anything more damaging than taking away from young African-Americans the idea that hard work and high aspirations lead to better lives. That this is the way things work may not be a truth on the order of the sun's being 93 million miles from earth, but it is, nevertheless, one for which evidence abounds. This is the way our society usually functions, and to encourage black students to think that for them it is otherwise—to think that their group has a separate truth—is to rob them of possibilities that young people who are being taught to work hard and aim high have.

Postmodern thinkers have helped accomplish this theft, no doubt unintentionally. But the result is no less tragic.

Chapter Two

PC: Alive and Entrenched

"Only the Thought Police mattered."

—*George Orwell, 1984*

LIKE most sophomores, Shawn Brown, a student at the University of Michigan, sometimes did sophomoric things. In October 1992, in an essay he was writing for his political science class, he used the following example to illustrate why people sometimes give pollsters the brush-off:

> Let's say Dave Stud is entertaining three beautiful ladies in his penthouse when the phone rings. A pollster on the other end wants to know if we should eliminate the capital gains tax. Now Dave is a knowledgeable businessperson who cares a lot about this issue. But since Dave is "tied up" at the moment, he tells the pollster to "bother" someone else.[1]

One might have expected Deborah Meizlish, the teaching assistant grading Brown's essay, to suggest that he use more elevated examples, but she and the course instructor, Professor Steven J. Rosenstone, had other things in mind. In the margin of Brown's essay, Meizlish wrote:

This is ludicrous & inappropriate & OFFENSIVE. This is completely inappropriate for a serious political science paper. It completely violates the standard of non-sexist writing. Professor
Rosenstone has encouraged me to interpret this comment as an
example of sexual harassment and to take the appropriate formal
steps. I have chosen not to do so in this instance. However, any
future comments, in a paper, in a class or in any dealings w/ me
will be interpreted as sexual harassment and formal steps will be
taken. Professor Rosenstone is aware of these comments—& is
prepared to intervene. You are forewarned![2]

Soon an account of the incident appeared in a student paper, the
Michigan Review, under the headline "Thought Policed in Poli Sci
111"; and subsequently the *Wall Street Journal* editorialized about
"language censors" at Michigan.[3] The university's administration was
clearly embarrassed, and Edie N. Goldenberg, dean of the College of
Literature, Science and the Arts, wrote to the *Journal*, "I think it is
important for your readers to know that I regard the teaching assistant's response as inappropriate and ineffective."[4]

This pattern of events is familiar to those acquainted with college
and university life today. Campus goings-on are exposed to public
scrutiny, they are quickly found to be outrageous, and sometime
thereafter someone in authority will declare the entire event a misunderstanding that should never have happened. But those who
follow such happenings closely know that any celebration by people
who have found the incident appalling is likely to be premature.
While a particular outrage may have been condemned, the people
who produced the incident remain in place, ready to resume their
work.

An electronic mail conference participated in by some of those
teaching in the University of Michigan's political science department
makes it clear that, whatever Dean Goldenberg might write to the
Wall Street Journal, there was a significant body of opinion that
Shawn Brown got exactly what he deserved. E-mail participants
described Goldenberg's letter as "despicable" and "disgusting" and

claimed that it did not really reflect the administration's position. One participant explained, "When [the administration] found out all the relevant facts, their feeling was that the TA had acted exactly as she was supposed to."

And what were the relevant facts? It turned out that student Shawn Brown had a history of undesirable behavior. A short history, to be sure, involving only one other incident, but one that loomed large in the e-mail exchange: When a handout of the Political Science Department's gender-free language policy had been distributed in Brown's class, he had been observed "slamming it down on his desk."

A few participants in the electronic conference did not think that this incident together with Brown's account of Dave Stud amounted to sexual harassment, but there was a strong current of opinion that it did. And some argued that Brown's decision to drop the course was further evidence of flawed character. "All I see is a very narrow mind," declared one. Another agreed, calling Brown "a close-minded wimp." Still another claimed, without offering evidence, that the *Michigan Review* had taken advantage of the case "so that a bunch of whiny white conservatives can have there [sic] chance to feel oppressed."

Important as it is to bring stories like Shawn Brown's to light, doing so is not necessarily a remedy. Business major Pete Schaub's 1988 experience with a women's studies class at the University of Washington is a case in point. When Schaub could not get into an accounting class he wanted, he signed up for Women's Studies 200, where he soon found himself assigned to memorize a sexually explicit poem. In one lecture session, a dildo was displayed as part of a lecture on masturbation. Schaub objected vigorously to what was going on and argued with the instructors. They had him expelled from the class. When he protested, the administration reinstated him, setting off demonstrations by women's studies partisans and attracting a great deal of attention from the media. It was finally agreed that if Schaub would not return to class, he would nevertheless get full credit, an arrangement that he regarded as a personal victory, but hardly a permanent remedy. "There'll be another Pete," he told a television interviewer.[5]

And sure enough, there was. Six years passed but women's studies partisans were still exerting their power on campuses. Craig
Rogers was enrolled in a Psychology 100 course at California State
University at Sacramento when a visiting lecturer came to class one
day to offer hints about masturbation and show slides of female
genitalia. Offended by the presentation and the disparaging remarks
about men that accompanied it, Rogers asked university authorities
to exempt him from test questions relating to the lecture. When they
refused, insisting he was responsible for the material, he filed a
sexual harassment claim against the university. It was rejected, leaving the guest professor, in her words, "relieved and happy and
pleased to have the support of the university to continue to teach
about female sexuality and the simple joys and pleasures of masturbation." Rogers planned to pursue a lawsuit.[6]

ॐ

In late 1990 and early 1991, there was a period of immense media
interest in political correctness. *Newsweek* magazine ran a cover story
on "thought police" that detailed instance after instance of politically
correct forces on campus trying to enforce an orthodoxy. "It is . . .
the program of a generation of campus radicals who grew up in the
'60s and are now achieving positions of academic influence," the
magazine declared.[7] *New York* magazine also put political correctness on its cover, and writer John Taylor called its proponents "the
new fundamentalists." "They believe that the doctrine of individual
liberties *itself* is inherently oppressive," he wrote.[8] The *New Republic*
followed in a few weeks with an issue that detailed how "the new
orthodoxy speaks power to truth" on campuses across the country.[9]
Soon television shows from *Good Morning America* to *The MacNeil/
Lehrer NewsHour* were giving opponents of political correctness a
chance to state their case.

Like most topics that the media focuses on intensely, interest in
this one waned after a time, leaving behind an impression that not
only had the problem been exposed, it had also been solved. Surely
once it had been brought to light that many faculty members con-

sidered the purpose of higher education to be the advancement of "correct" political viewpoints, colleges and universities, with encouragement from parents and alums, would undertake a reassessment, return to their roots, and emphasize again that the goal was to pursue truth—not to find it necessarily, but to encourage debate in hopes of approaching ever closer.

Reinforcing the idea that political correctness need no longer be cause for concern was a public relations campaign aimed at showing that reports of what had been happening on campus were grossly exaggerated. Among the groups taking up this campaign was the Modern Language Association (MLA), whose policy statements, publications, and conventions had epitomized the politicization of teaching and learning. One of the MLA's contributions to the effort was a survey intended to demonstrate that all the talk about white male authors being excised from syllabi was just that, and to show that literature courses were pretty much what they had always been. Although the survey avoided questions about composition and beginning humanities courses, where there has been the most ferment, and focused instead on upper-division courses, where there has been more stability, the results, nevertheless, indicated remarkable change. Fewer than half of those teaching nineteenth-century American literature, for example, regarded it as "particularly important" to include such a standard work as Henry David Thoreau's *Walden* in their courses. Only a third considered Nathaniel Hawthorne's *The Scarlet Letter* as particularly important to include; only 29 percent, Herman Melville's *Moby-Dick*.[10]

Undaunted, the MLA hired a consultant, longtime Democratic activist Ann Lewis, and then issued a press release giving the survey results the desired spin. "Professors have not abandoned traditional texts,"[11] the headline read; and no matter the artful ignoring of the real significance of the survey results, versions of this headline were repeated by newspapers across the country. Lewis was also hired by the MLA, the *Chronicle of Higher Education* reported, "to make sure that press coverage of its annual meeting runs smoothly";[12] and, perhaps not coincidentally, some remarkably positive coverage resulted. In a major story in the *Washington Post*, the leaders of the Modern Language Association were given an opportunity to present themselves as souls of moderation, misunderstood scholars whose profession had suffered from a conservative disinformation campaign and the media's recycling of a few oversimplified scare stories. "Literature Professors Look Inward and Find Scant Evidence of 'PC,'" read the headline; and the subhead: "But Right-Wing Misinformation, Media Hype Are Problems, Many Agree."[13]

These same charges were repeated by two organizations founded in 1991, Teachers for a Democratic Culture and the Union of Democratic Intellectuals. Conservatives were behind the criticism of the campuses, they maintained; and the purpose of right-wing attacks was not to depoliticize teaching and learning, but to reverse the advances made in recent years by women and minorities.[14] Members of the two new groups fanned out across the land to elaborate on these accusations. Michael Bérubé of the University of Illinois, Urbana-Champaign, wrote in the *Village Voice* of the way in which "the most callow and opportunistic elements of the Right" were playing to the prejudices of bigoted alumni who didn't like seeing women and blacks on their campuses.[15] Cathy N. Davidson of Duke University's English Department suggested that there had been no more than a half-dozen instances of political correctness, and that they were being endlessly recycled by conservatives, whom she lumped together with ex-Klansman David Duke.[16] So little did these assertions have to do with the facts that they seemed an apt illustration of how debased argument can become when one discounts, as so many academic activists do, traditional standards of accuracy and evidence.

The defenders of the newest trends on campuses liked to describe those on the other side of the debate as conservatives, but they were well aware that many of the most eloquent critics of the campuses had been liberal: Benno C. Schmidt, Jr., former president of Yale University; C. Vann Woodward, professor emeritus of Yale; James David Barber of Duke University; and the University of California at Berkeley's John Searle—to name only a few. And when the defenders of academic life came together to confer among themselves, they were rather more honest than they were when addressing the issue of political correctness in public. At a conference at Hunter College in New York organized by Teachers for a Democratic Culture and the Union of Democratic Intellectuals, the same Michael Bérubé who had lately lambasted "callow and opportunistic elements of the right" for creating the political correctness issue now lamented the number of moderates and liberals who had also taken up the battle against PC. Another speaker, Wahneema Lubiano of Princeton University, railed against liberals who objected to radical efforts to politicize universities. She was particularly angry with faculty at the University of Texas at Austin, where she had formerly taught. In 1990–1991, a number of them had prevented the English Department from turning the required freshman composition program into a course more concerned with political reeducation than with writing. In Lubiano's view the "self-described liberals" who "broke ranks during the curriculum dispute" did so because as white males they detected a threat to their power.[17]

The idea that political correctness was a chimera of overheated conservative minds was given some credence in the press. In a front-page article about the founding of Teachers for a Democratic Culture, a reporter for the *New York Times* endorsed the view that criticism of the universities amounted to a "conservative on-slaught."[18] A story in the *New Republic* by Michael Kinsley declared charges of "P.C." to be conservative "B.S."[19] Teachers for a Democratic Culture trumpeted the journalistic turn. A 1992 newsletter celebrated Princeton sociologist Paul Starr's unfavorable review in the *New York Review of Books* of Martin Anderson's *Impostors in the Temple*. Starr's negative assessment of a book that was severely critical of current trends in higher education was, claimed the newsletter, a sign "that the ideological smear campaign against new academic movements . . . may at last be getting exposed."[20]

But it was impossible to sustain this case for long. The ink had hardly dried on a magazine story written by a *Philadelphia Inquirer* reporter claiming that the influence of PC had been "grossly exaggerate[d],"[21] when two incidents occurred a few miles away at the University of Pennsylvania that seemed so out of keeping with the proper spirit of a university that they received massive publicity. A conservative student columnist, Gregory Pavlik, writing on subjects such as affirmative action for the student newspaper, the *Daily Pennsylvanian*, offended a group of black students. In protest, they seized and destroyed thousands of copies of the newspaper, an action for which the university declined to punish them. The policemen who apprehended the black students, however, were ordered to sensitivity training sessions. At about the same time, a student named Eden Jacobowitz gained international fame as a result of yelling at a group of black women students who were socializing loudly underneath his window, "Shut up, you water buffalo." Even when it was explained that Jacobowitz had gone to a yeshiva high school, where the Hebrew term for "water buffalo" was slang for a foolish person, he was threatened with prosecution for racial harassment. His ordeal went on for months, ending only when the women, who claimed they were being persecuted by the press, dropped the charge.

ॐ

One of the reasons political correctness continues is that internal opposition to it is so weak. Those inclined to speak out are many times pressured to convert to the cause—or to leave. Nancy Welch, pursuing her Ph.D. in English and teaching composition classes, as many doctoral students do, offered an example of such pressure on graduate students at "University B":

> When one graduate student said she felt uneasy about the political agenda of the assignments we were giving (a sequence of assignments designed to lead students to an understanding of knowledge and self as social and ideological constructs), one instructor replied, "That's naïve. If you're going to teach, you're going to get your hands dirty. If you don't want to do that, then maybe you don't belong here."[22]

Welch described the students who dropped out of the Ph.D. program: one to backpack in Yellowstone, another to do clerical work, another to teach in a private school, she herself to pursue graduate work at another university. The dropouts, she wrote:

> believed they must either join this congregation or leave it entirely, participate in the program's aims or (especially for those kept in one location by family and financial obligations) abandon their aim of earning a graduate degree. When the voices of other Institutions and Inclinations are banned in a seminar room, it becomes virtually impossible for participants to doubt and debate, question and revise, and find ways of working within a culture without being dominated and enslaved by it.[23]

A Ph.D. is merely the first gate through which a faculty member must pass. He or she must get a job; and here, too, the ideological gatekeepers are at work. Thanks to them, by the late 1980s, according to John Patrick Diggins of the City College of New York, "A white male conservative who admired Madison more than Marx, had about as much chance of getting hired on some faculty as Woody Allen of starting as point guard for the Knicks."[24]

Sometimes the process of insuring ideological conformity in new faculty members is subtle, but not always. A feminist group at the Association of American Colleges developed a questionnaire for search committees. Among the areas of inquiry suggested for potential faculty members:

> How have you demonstrated your commitment to women's issues in your current position?
>
> Have you ever worked actively on behalf of . . . sexual harassment policies? . . . rape crisis programs, including judicial procedures, and so forth?
>
> In your current position, what is your relationship to the affirmative action officer? Have you ever sought his or her help in recruiting?
>
> Of the people you hired in your current position, what percentage are women?[25]

This kind of questioning could be regarded as preparation for what new entries into academia will encounter later in their careers. Candidates for offices in the American Sociological Association (ASA) receive a questionnaire from Sociologists for Women in Society that asks them for short essays on such topics as "the specific actions you would take while serving in your elected position to enhance the position of women in ASA" and "activities . . . in which you have taken part which demonstrate a public commitment to feminism."[26] Economics professor Barbara R. Bergmann of American University recently recommended that candidates for offices in the American Economic Association be sent a similar questionnaire.[27] At the time she made her recommendation, Bergmann was, astonishingly, president of the American Association of University Professors, an organization that would once have waged vigorous battle against such ideological litmus tests.

Sometimes prospective faculty members are asked substantive questions to elicit their political views. An applicant for a tenure track position in American and European history at California's Pasadena City College reports that he was asked whether Columbus was a "genocidal imperialist" and whether the French were more racist than the Spanish in colonizing the New World. "A lot of questions were designed to gauge whether we were PC," observed the applicant, Leon Waszak, who did not get the job. "If we answered one way, we'd be racist. If we answered the other way, we'd be totally undermined as historians."[28]

People who do become faculty members have many opportunities to see the professional disadvantages of failing to conform ideologically. Courses that run counter to prevailing orthodoxies may not be easily approved. Certification of a proposed "Great Books" program at the University of Wisconsin at Milwaukee was delayed for months when nearly two dozen professors signed a petition expressing "serious reservations about the academic and intellectual merit of basing a certificate program on opinions of 'greatness.' "[29]

In order to encourage enrollment, a faculty member might well wish to have a course that he or she is teaching in English or sociology cross-listed in women's studies or African-American studies; but that is unlikely to happen unless the course meets certain requirements that go under the name of "quality control," but are, in fact, ideological conditions. At Pennsylvania State University, courses will be cross-listed in Women's Studies only if they "recognize the existence of patriarchal structures in defining values and social roles" and "empower women students to seek their own paths and define themselves as entities separate and apart from roles that patriarchal societies dictate."[30] At San Francisco State University, the Black Studies Department refused to cross-list a course called Black Politics being taught in the Political Science Department by a distinguished black scholar. Saying "there was no control over the quality," the department chairman claimed the course might have too much of a traditional perspective. Black students in the black politics course subsequently disrupted classes, organized demonstrations against the political science professor, and drove enrollment in the class of forty-five down to five.[31]

An article sent to a journal might very well not be published unless the language is gender neutral. A scholar who submitted an article on seventeenth- and eighteenth-century intellectual history to the *Western Journal of Graduate Research* was told that "the use of sexist language such as 'man,' 'mankind,' 'his' to represent all people" required revision to his text—even though that might be exactly the way the seventeenth- and eighteenth-century thinkers with whom the paper was concerned used those words. Advised the journal's associate editor: "It is imperative that this historical bias be explicitly recognized in your writing or you condone and perpetuate the prejudice of the times."[32]

Success in professional organizations, a junior faculty member will also observe, is today more likely to come to those whose research interests are in certain areas. Jerry Z. Muller, a historian at Catholic University of America, recently analyzed the work of candidates nominated for office in the American Historical Association. "Five of the nominees specialize in class/labor," he wrote, "ten in women/feminism/gender/sex, and seven in race/African-American/minorities." Muller continued:

In calling attention to these statistics, I do not mean that these are subjects unworthy of study, or that scholars who specialize in these areas ought not to be actively represented on the Council of the AHA. But we are now far beyond that point: through a process of self-recruitment, work on the holy trinity of race/gender/class has now become a virtual prerequisite for nomination to the Council of the AHA. The nominees include no historians of the corporation, no economic historians, no historians of international relations, no military historians, no historians of science, and no historians who have written major works for a nonacademic audience. This is what "diversity" means in the Orwellian discourse of the politically correct.[33]

Historian Stephen E. Ambrose of the University of New Orleans has also observed how limited a meaning "diversity" has come to have in academic circles. Looking at the 1993 program for the annual meeting of the Organization of American Historians (OAH), he noted that there were sessions on "black, Indian, Hispanic and other minority history, women's history, labor and radical history, gay and lesbian history, and multicultural history." But despite the fact that the OAH met on the 250th anniversary of Thomas Jefferson's birth and on the 50th anniversary of the invasions of Sicily and Italy, there was not a single session on either our third president or on World War II.[34]

The newly hired professor will observe that there are not only preferred subjects for research, but preferred ways of dealing with them. In articles and books about race and gender, the trend is to move away from objective research and to report on one's own experiences. In *The Alchemy of Race and Rights*, a book that one reviewer calls "feminist jurisprudence" and that the author herself calls a diary, law professor Patricia J. Williams not only takes up subjects such as affirmative action, but also recounts a conversation with her sister, discusses a New York to California train trip, and ends with musings about polar bears. In *Alias Olympia,* art historian Eunice Lipton writes about her efforts to find out about Edouard Manet's model Victorine Meurent. Along the way, she also discusses her own mother's inadequacies, her failed first marriage, and a four-and-one-half-hour meal in a Paris restaurant. English professor Nancy K. Miller concludes her book *Getting Personal*, which is a collection of papers she has presented at various learned conferences, with a chapter titled "My Father's Penis." The attack on objectivity as a white male delusion helps explain why this kind of scholarship is dominated by women, but men also undertake it occasionally. In *The Edge of Night,* Duke English professor Frank Lentricchia gives new meaning to the description "cutting-edge scholarship" by fantasizing about the damage he could wreak if he strapped a Texas chain saw to his penis.[35]

A professor at the University of Pennsylvania asked me if I remembered the scene in the movie *The Graduate* in which Dustin Hoffman's character was advised the future was "plastics." "Today," said the professor, "the future is gender studies."[36] And, he might have added, the more intimate and bizarre, the better.

The junior faculty member who makes it to the point where he or she is being considered for tenure can find the slightest political misstep to be costly. Art historian Stephen Polcari's problem, he believes, was a long footnote in a book he had written and was editing for publication. In it, he attacked critics who judged art ideologically, specifically directing his ire at members of the "political left" who tried to discredit abstract expressionism by associating it with "American Imperialism and the Cold War." Wrote Polcari, "This vein of Late Marxist writing depends on faulty premises; specious associations; perpetuations of original critical misunderstandings; simplistic political recontextualizations and entrapments; quotations out of context; factual errors; dismissal of personal, cultural, and intellectual concerns; sweeping abstractions and generalizations; pernicious political distortions; and willful ignorance of the intentions, subjects, forms, and imagery of the artists."[37]

With its tone—much more combative than the rest of the book— the footnote did call attention to itself. Sharply challenging as it did the idea that aesthetics and politics are one and the same thing, the footnote was also the epitome of political incorrectness. Nevertheless, all the experts who had been asked by the Art Department at the State University of New York at Stony Brook to review Polcari's work gave positive recommendations. One called him the "undisputed authority" in the field of abstract expressionism. Another called him "a voice of clarity, common sense and informed ideas." At least two made enthusiastic reference to his forthcoming book and the impact it would have on the field.[38] Polcari's department unanimously recommended him for tenure; and so did the dean of humanities and fine arts, who, in a letter to the provost, noted the strength of Polcari's recommendations and publishing record, his superior award and grant record, his having taught a large number of the art department's most highly enrolled courses, as well as his having compiled an outstanding service record.[39]

But a faculty committee outside the department, the Personnel Policy Committee, actively opposed Polcari's being tenured. The members of the committee solicited yet more reviews of his work; and though these, like those previously requested by the department, were positive, committee members recommended against tenure; and they were supported by the university's president, who in a letter to Polcari acknowledged, "Your case for promotion is very strong." But, the president continued, "The issue of the state of your manuscript looms so large in the minds of those who advise me on promotions that I am not prepared to overturn their judgment."[40] Particularly since so many reviewers had been so effusive in their praise for his work—some of them specifically for his forthcoming book—Polcari believed that criticism directed at "the state of his manuscript" was really focused on something narrower: the footnote, in which, as he put it, I "shot back at . . . the current attempt by leftist academics to vilify American and particularly Abstract Expressionist art." "This refutation," he wrote, "is what inspired the whole attack."[41]

Polcari was allowed to resubmit his application for promotion and tenure the following year. Although by this time his work had been reviewed—and reviewed positively—by two or three times as many people as are typically asked for their opinions in tenure decisions, the Personnel Policy Committee sought yet more reviews; and this time the reaction was negative. As Polcari saw it, the law of averages finally worked against him. "If you keep soliciting letters," he wrote, "at some point you will find someone to say something negative."[42]

In March 1990, Polcari decided to resign. In 1991, his book, *Abstract Expressionism and the Modern Experience*, was published. One reviewer called it "a challenging, revolutionary reassessment." Another predicted it would become a valued resource for future scholars in the field. Still another wrote, "It combines breadth of outlook with an investigative intensity that presents a plethora of fresh knowledge to which scholars will be indebted for a long time ahead."[43]

Polcari, who is now director of the Archives of American Art in New York, is philosophical about his failure to get tenure. "That is life in today's university," he writes:

> I could never get another decent teaching job because political art history . . . is all that is hired today, so today I am an arts administrator. Pushing papers is much more honest work.[44]

Even a tenured professor is not safe. Early reporting on political correctness set forth story after story of distinguished scholars being unjustly charged with racism and sexism. One at Harvard was accused by students for such sins as using the word *Indian* in class—even though he had explained that it was the word most American Indians use themselves. At the University of Michigan a distinguished scholar was accused of racism not because of anything he said but because of words and phrases that appeared in assigned materials. Although by any objective reading of the situation, these professors were charged unfairly, university administrators did not come to their defense. Both scholars decided to quit teaching the courses out of which controversy had arisen rather than risk further damage to their reputations.

Exposing these situations was healthy, but it did not keep similar situations from occurring. In March 1993, anonymous accusers at the University of Michigan charged statistician David Goldberg with "race and gender-baiting," "inflammatory racial rhetoric," and harassing "entire groups of people based on their particular racial or ethnic identities, gender, or sexual orientation" in Sociology 510, a required statistics course. With their letter demanding that the university no longer allow Goldberg to teach required courses in the Department of Sociology, the anonymous accusers distributed documents intended to substantiate their charges, mainly reading assignments and handouts from Goldberg's class that were supposedly "rampant with racial and gender stereotypes and pejorative assumptions." A typical document presented the case of "the 59¢ button," which is worn by some women to protest their earning 59¢ for every $1.00 earned by men. Goldberg's handout showed the female to male earning ratio actually varied from a low of 53¢ to a high of 93¢ depending upon whether one took into consideration such factors as education and marital status; and the handout asked: "Do you really think 59¢—is a fair representation of sex discrimination in wages?"[45]

Speaking on condition of anonymity, students in Sociology 510 also told a student newspaper about a confrontation with Goldberg following an examination. Some students, who felt that the test had been too difficult, asked Goldberg why it was so hard. He told them that he had been trying to find out how much different students in the class had learned. "Before Goldberg finished," the student newspaper reported, "a student raised his hand with a question. What right, the student wanted to know, did Goldberg feel he had to administer a test that presumed a variance of ability among his students?" As they saw it, his presuming "a variance of ability" was more evidence of his racist and sexist attitudes.[46]

Still another charge against Goldberg had to do with his teaching technique. Everyone, including Goldberg, agreed that it was demanding and confrontational. As he saw it, pushing students was a way of encouraging achievement; but according to one graduate student, such a technique, when applied to all students without regard to race or gender, amounts to racial and sexual harassment of minorities and women, who, operating from a position of powerlessness, easily interpret challenges and demands as "an academic form of social exclusion."[47]

71

Instead of defending Goldberg, the chairman of his department agreed to student demands that he be removed from the teaching of any required course. When other members of the Sociology Department protested, the chairman agreed to let Goldberg continue with 510, but he created a second section of the course to be taught by someone less controversial. A member of the Sociology Department who asked not to be quoted by name commented on what had happened: "There's a sort of 'ethnic cleansing' of inquiry going on at this university, in which the minority is purging the majority."[48]

In the Goldberg incident, students attempted to silence a tenured faculty member. Sometimes members of the professoriate take on this task, as the case of Professor Richard Levin of the State University of New York at Stony Brook shows. In 1988, Levin published a critique of feminist criticism of Shakespeare in the *Publications of the Modern Language Association* (*PMLA*). Some measure of the judiciousness of Levin's article can be gleaned from its opening paragraph:

> Feminist criticism . . . has enlisted a number of intelligent and dedicated critics and has produced a substantial body of publications. Its remarkable growth can be measured, moreover, not only in these statistics but also in the steady enlargement of its range from the first tentative efforts, aimed primarily at rectifying sexist misinterpretations of Shakespeare's female characters, to much more confident and ambitious studies of many other aspects of the canon.

Having praised the achievements of feminist criticism, Levin went on to document the failings of "one major trend of the movement": finding that Shakespeare's tragedies are always about gender, being selective with evidence to support this case, and relying on stereotypes of men that present them all as "unconscious misogynists," people who "grow up sick," while "women grow up healthy." Levin ended his article with an appeal for "study of the complex factors in human development, which would investigate the similarities as

72

well as the differences between women and men, based on evidence that compelled the assent of all rational people, regardless of their gender or ideology."[49]

In response to Levin's article, twenty-four feminist professors wrote a communal letter to *PMLA* condemning him. They declared their irritation with his appeal to rationality—"An Enlightenment dream, long since turned to nightmare," they called it—and indicated that they were "disturbed" that such a person had made "a successful academic career." Moreover, they demanded to know why *PMLA* had printed such an article, since it was clearly "blind . . . to the assumptions of feminist criticism."[50]

"The fact that [*PMLA*] is publishing a steady stream of feminist articles is not enough, in their view," Levin observed; "they also want it to deny publication to any criticism of them that they disapprove of."[51] The episode also led Elizabeth Coleman, president of Bennington College and surely one of the country's bravest administrators, to note: "Even a fairly healthy sense of humor fails one at the suggestion that a colleague should not be allowed to have a successful academic career or to have his thoughts see the light of day if he sees fit to raise questions concerning internal consistencies among certain . . . feminist theorists."[52]

In the late 1980s, philosopher Christina Hoff Sommers, a self-described "liberal feminist," began to critique the extreme ideas that many academic feminists were advancing; and in 1990, the *Atlantic Monthly* commissioned her to write an article on the topic. Subsequently, Sandra Lee Bartky, a faculty member at the University of Illinois at Chicago, wrote to the magazine urging them not to publish Sommers's work on the grounds that Sommers was, in Bartky's words, "known for her implacable hostility to academic feminism" and "as a right-wing ideologue."[53]

When asked about her letter, Bartky denied that she was trying to get the *Atlantic Monthly* to censor Sommers's views: "Editors exercise discretion," she said. "By not asking someone to write a piece, that's not censorship, that's discretion." A senior editor for the *Atlantic Monthly* had a very different view of the episode: "It seemed

73

to confirm some of the darker aspects of Ms. Sommers's article, which pointed out the extraordinary lengths some of these women were prepared to go to shape all discussion in which they had an interest."[54]

When Professor James David Barber and some of his colleagues at Duke University decided to organize a chapter of the National Association of Scholars (NAS), a group advocating traditional curricula and opposing politicized research and teaching, Stanley Fish, chairman of the English Department, wrote to the provost that it was his view that members of the NAS "should not be appointed to positions on key university committees such as APT [Appointments, Promotions, and Tenure], Distinguished Professor, or any other committee dealing with academic priorities and evaluations." The provost rejected the establishment of what he called "an a priori litmus test,"[55] but this incident, like the ones recounted above, shows the intolerance of those who have become powerful in academic life for colleagues who disagree with them. Their lack of tolerance is in some ways the logical outcome of their relativism. Truth does not exist, in their view; rationality is an outdated white, male practice. What is left is power, and one of its more effective uses if one wishes one's own ideas to prevail is to silence all challengers.

Julius Lester of the University of Massachusetts at Amherst, who left the Afro-American Studies Department there under pressure from colleagues who objected to his views, describes one of the methods used to punish those who fail to go along with group orthodoxy as "shunning"; and he describes the experience as "a very profound one":

> I can't describe what it's like . . . to walk down a hallway and people lower their voices or they stop talking or they close the doors as you walk by—just to walk through that atmosphere of hostility, week in, week out. The intent of it, of course, is to make you think twice the next time you sit down to write.[56]

Lester eventually found a home in the Judaic Studies Department at the University of Massachusetts. Alan Gribben of the University of

Texas at Austin was so disheartened by hate mail, anonymous phone calls, and his colleagues' refusal to speak to him that he left the university, where he had taught for seventeen years. By writing letters to a newspaper, he had helped foil an attempt to turn the freshman composition program at the university into a course on racism and sexism, but the price he paid was high. Today he is teaching at the Montgomery, Alabama, branch of Auburn University.[57]

It can be costly for faculty members to speak frankly, which accounts at least in part for an experience that is common for campus visitors like myself who can be honest about what they find. After I lecture at a college or university, I frequently hear from faculty members who want quietly, very quietly, to encourage me in my work. They can't speak out, they say, but they want me to keep on doing so—without ever mentioning their names. I once received a letter from a graduate student at the University of Texas at Austin along exactly these lines. He wanted me to know about something outrageous that had happened, but he also wanted to be sure that I did not contact him through his department. It would ruin his reputation, he explained, if it were known he had corresponded with someone as "disreputable" as I.[58]

ह़्

There are many reasons to be silent rather than speak out on campuses today. Undergraduates have to worry not only about the power of professors to determine grades but also about faculty members' ability to make the classroom a miserable place for the dissenting student. In 1991, Michelle Colitsas, a senior at Mount Holyoke College in Massachusetts, wrote a critique in a student newspaper of a philosophy class in which she was enrolled. As Colitsas described it, students in the course read Plato, Nietzsche, Mill—and Patricia J. Williams's *The Alchemy of Race and Rights.* Although Williams's book presents a very limited (and entirely positive) view of affirmative action, it was one for which the professor "exhibited a strong affinity . . ." Colitsas wrote, "both through her own statements, as well as through her unquestioned support of those student comments similar to Ms. Williams' in sharp contrast with her challenges to those student comments raised in opposition to or in skepticism of Ms. Williams' view." Colitsas maintained that such teaching violated a trust: Students rely on teachers to give them a complete view of controversial issues, not a partial one based on their preferences. "When the teacher professes opinion as fact, subjective concepts and definitions as the truth," Colitsas wrote, "the contract [between teacher and student] is violated."[59]

Although Colitsas did not name the course or the professor, one can well imagine the faculty member's irritation at a student's writing about the problem in the campus press. Still, the professor's response was extraordinary. As a student newspaper described it, the professor "announced that she would be leaving early in order to provide the 20-30 members of the class with the opportunity to share their views." What followed was, in the newspaper's words, a "verbal lynching":

> The "discussion" quickly degenerated into an *ad hominem* denunciation of a single student. As Colitsas put it, "They were no longer attacking my political beliefs, they were attacking my character."[60]

Marc Shachtman, an undergraduate at Ohio's Oberlin College, described a similar incident at that campus:

> In a course I took last year a maverick student said he agreed with a Supreme Court justice's view that a particular affirmative action program would unconstitutionally discriminate on the basis of race. During the next few minutes a couple of students vehemently objected. One raised her voice significantly, the other began to yell at him. In the following fifteen minutes, the professor did not speak; instead, he took other volunteers. Almost all of these students jumped on the bandwagon, berating the one maverick student. The professor gave him one more chance to speak. By this time the student was quite flustered and incoherent.

Noted Shachtman, "The class learned that bringing out such controversial views would carry a high social cost. They would be less likely to repeat the 'error' of their fellow student."[61]

When students do speak their minds, their complaints may have little effect. A feminist professor teaching at the University of Wisconsin listed some of the objections that students had made to feminist teaching in composition and introduction to literature sections. Wrote one student, "I feel this course was dominated and overpowered by feminist doctrines and ideals." Wrote another:

> Feminism is an important issue in society—but a very controversial one. It needs to be confronted on a personal basis, not in the classroom. I didn't appreciate feminist comments on papers or expressed about a work.

Another student complained, "My professor . . . is a feminist and she incorporates her ideas and philosophy into her grading scale."[62]

The professor quoting these complaints did not accord them any legitimacy. She did not ask whether it might be reasonable for a student to object when a course that is supposed to be about how to write is turned into a course on overcoming patriarchy. To her, the complaints were examples of what feminists have to put up with in the classroom. They were simply a starting point for discussing the "resistance" that must be overcome "in order to get our students to identify with the political agenda of feminism."[63]

A professor from the University of Massachusetts at Boston, who used a freshman writing course to teach, as she put it, "leftist politics" and "feminist thought," found herself the subject of a complaint from a young woman named Minnie, whom the professor described as "a young working class woman from Puerto Rico." What Minnie wanted was to learn how to write. She wanted model essays to pattern her work after; she wanted the professor to correct her papers and tell her how to write better; and when these things did not happen, she complained to the writing director. As the professor described Minnie's grievance:

She made it clear that . . . notions of gender politics, notions of student empowerment did not touch her need for the proper style, the proper accent, the Doolittle makeover she had signed up for. It was not that Minnie did or did not wish to embrace her race and her class; it was that she wished to define them otherwise. That is, to define herself as American, middle-class, conservative, genderless: the student, the worker, the citizen.

Even though the professor is trying to disparage Minnie's ideas with this description, it seems quite clear that the young woman knew exactly what she needed—and had every right to expect—from a freshman writing class. And it is equally clear that the professor was determined to see her as a misguided ingrate for wanting to make her way in this society rather than become an expert in its faults. "Minnie's tuition dollar is buying plastic surgery, not literacy," the professor concluded.[64]

Composition courses have become particularly susceptible to ideological teaching. Writing in such periodicals as the *Journal of Advanced Composition* and *College English,* composition teachers offer advice on how to inform such courses with "political consciousness and social action"[65] so that students will become "social and political activists."[66] They discuss how to tailor "liberatory pedagogy" so as to bring students from different social and economic backgrounds to "a critical awareness of the constrictions in their own class position." One would not want, for example, to use the same methods on students from upper-class backgrounds who "have the financial and emotional security to be open to progressive pedagogy and even radical politics" that one would use on middle-class students who "reflect the reflex conservatism of uncritical subordination to established social order and authority."[67]

Maxine Hairston, former chair of the Conference on College Composition and Communication, identifies the new model for freshman writing programs as one "that puts dogma before diversity, politics before craft, ideology before critical thinking, and the social goals of the teacher before the educational needs of the student."[68] Two of the most widely used textbooks for freshman composition, *Racism and Sexism*, edited by Paula S. Rothenberg, and *Rereading America*, edited by Gary Colombo, Robert Cullen, and Bonnie Lisle, support her assessment.[69] Both present essay after essay portraying the United States as mired in racism, sexism, and elitism—not to mention that most hopeless of all states, capitalism. According to the publisher of *Rereading America,* the book was used at almost five hundred colleges and universities the first year it was published.

As politicized as many composition classes are, women's studies classes are typically worse. When Karen Lehrman visited women's studies classes on four different campuses for *Mother Jones* magazine, she was struck by the amount of consciousness-raising she found. Time and again, students were urged to talk about their personal experiences of oppression and their emotions about being oppressed, rather than to consider the status of women in any objective fashion. At the University of California at Berkeley, after the screening of a film, a professor asked her class: "How do you *feel* about the film?" In another class at Berkeley, students took up the topic of faked orgasms. "Many in women's studies consider personal experience the only real source of truth," Lehrman writes.[70]

Professors themselves report on their techniques for consciousness-raising. A professor at the University of North Carolina at Charlotte describes in an article how she encourages students in her women's studies class to tell "life stories," particularly on Mondays, and how she uses anecdotes from her own life to spur them on.[71] A professor at the State University of New York at Brockport informs other members of the Women's Studies List on the Internet of the positive results for her women's studies class of her having confessed her own previously repressed memories of child abuse. An English professor and two psychologists at a small college in Michigan worry about faculty members in a variety of courses urging students to reveal intimate details of their lives. One faculty member, they report, holds special sessions after class for students who reveal they are victims of sexual abuse.[72]

Some students buy into the ideology they find in classrooms. A women's studies major at San Francisco State University proudly tells two visiting researchers that she "got her politics" at State.[73] These students work not only to make sure that their peers conform, but also that faculty members do not stray from the party line. Daphne Patai and Noretta Koertge report on three professors who have decided to abandon women's studies because of their experiences with militant students.[74]

Other students, whether they support the ideology or not, are affected by the thinking that permits the ideology in classrooms: the idea that there is no truth and no reality, that there are only different stories told by different groups in order to advance their interests. One of the clearest examples of this in recent years occurred at Duke University when the student newspaper published a paid advertisement setting forth what has become the standard line among those who deny that the Jewish Holocaust occurred, which is that the gas chambers, the photographs of dead and starving concentration camp prisoners, and the eyewitness accounts of death and suffering were all a fraud.[75] Student newspapers across the country had received the same advertisement, and while many refused to accept it (Harvard, Yale, MIT) on the very sensible grounds that newspapers have no obligation to publish advertisements that are misleading and fail to meet elementary standards of evidence and logic, many had run the ad (Cornell, Northwestern, the University of Michigan). Administrators at these schools typically cited First Amendment reasons, though as Deborah E. Lipstadt, who has written about Holocaust denial, notes, many of these papers had policies in place prohibiting racist and sexist advertising; and some of them had also refused to run cigarette advertising.[76]

But the Duke editor offered a unique defense of her decision: namely, that the deniers are simply revisionists who are "reinterpreting history, a practice that occurs constantly, especially on a college campus."[77] The Duke History Department, to its credit, rose up in protest at the idea that Holocaust denial is simply a new perspective on the past. Revisionism is not about the "actuality" of events; it is about their "interpretation," a department statement said.[78] But the distinction is one that postmodern thinkers, with talk about how facts themselves are "situated," often honor in the breach. The Duke editor's decision may well have revealed less about her misunderstanding of ideas that are now common on campuses than it did about what can happen when truth and reason are dismissed. As Deborah Lipstadt observes, "The deniers are plying their trade at a time when much of history seems to be up for grabs and attacks on the Western rationalist tradition have become commonplace."[79]

Some students—and it may well be the majority—simply try to cope with what they find going on in classrooms. A student at Smith College in Massachusetts told Karen Lehrman that she "quickly discovered that the way to get A's [in a feminist anthropology course] was to write papers full of guilt and angst about how I'd bought into society's definition of womanhood and now I'm enlightened and free."[80] When I visited the University of Pennsylvania, a student told me that she had discovered, "If you write about misogyny, you'll do great."[81] The same idea informs an exchange that made its way into a learned journal not long ago. One male student instructs another on how to succeed in a feminist classroom. "Pretend to be a male chauvinist, then have a conversion. You're bound to get an A."[82]

Upon encountering a teaching assistant "with wild ideas," most undergraduates, a University of Pennsylvania student told me, will "just do whatever is necessary to get a good grade. . . . They'll talk the talk and walk the walk that the TA wants them to." What this produces, the undergraduate went on to explain, is "the conviction that it is not the pursuit of truth [that college is about], it's just getting out."[83]

A student at the University of North Carolina at Chapel Hill told me, "You learn to read professors when you're in college, and you know exactly what they want to hear. . . . You just go ahead and say what they want to hear, which, in my case, was [to] bash Reagan and Bush." When I asked him if he personally had done this, he answered, "Yes. That's totally against my personal beliefs, to bash Reagan and Bush . . . but I'm not here to philosophize my beliefs in Poli Sci 41, I'm here to get a decent grade in the class."[84]

Anyone fortunate enough to have gone to college in years when literature and philosophy and political science classes were indisputably places for expressing views and testing beliefs realizes how much this student and so many of his peers are missing. While it is gratifying that they do not buy into the politics they find in classrooms and heartening that they are usually good-humored about their situation, it is dismaying to think how little they know of the excitement of learning and how well versed they are becoming in dissembling—and in the cynicism that a system that encourages dissembling produces.

ॐ

A student at the University of Pennsylvania observed to me that the classroom is not the only place that students encounter ideology. Describing a university administration that "has its own agenda and is accountable to no one," he noted that while "there are problems in the classroom," there are worse problems "outside the classroom" where administrators' control is more certain.[85] He was specifically pointing to the world of diversity training that has grown up on college and university campuses across the nation. At the University of Pennsylvania, as at scores of institutions, incoming freshmen (or first-year students, in politically correct terminology) get a massive infusion of what University of Pennsylvania history professor Alan C. Kors calls the "ideological analysis" of the "heirs of the sixties."[86] The guiding assumption of this extracurricular training is that the attitudes and beliefs with which students arrive on campus are unsatisfactory and must be changed. "Families have not socialized their children in good values," declared a speaker at a 1995 conference in Washington, D.C., on how to transform not only the classroom but student life outside it as well.[87] Typical lessons in this co-curriculum are that only whites can be racist because only white people have power and that "institutional racism" exists whenever institutions like universities do not produce equal outcomes for all races. Students learn how deeply racist is the college or university they have chosen to attend—even when the facts have to be altered to support that conclusion.

The "Facilitator's Guide" for diversity training distributed at the University of Pennsylvania in 1989 called for facilitators to read to students "incidents of harassment that have taken place at the University over the past few years."[88] One of those to whom the guide was distributed, Michael Cohen, a professor of physics, recognized that in at least three cases, the so-called incidents of harassment had been exaggerated to the point of fabrication. In one instance, facilitators were to describe the following events to students:

> A University professor continually referred to African-American students in his class as "ex-slaves" and said that their comments would be particularly useful when the class discussed the Thirteenth Amendment. It was later discovered that other African-American students who had taken the professor's class had had similar experiences.[89]

Cohen pointed out that the facts in this case were well known. In widely publicized hearings it had been established that the professor had made a one-time reference to African-American students as ex-slaves and had done so in a statement in which he expressed surprise that while he, a Jew, celebrated his liberation from slavery at Passover, African-American students, likewise "ex-slaves," did not celebrate the Thirteenth Amendment. The "Facilitator's Guide" also failed to mention the harsh punishment meted out to the professor: He was suspended and forced to undergo sensitivity training. Concluded Cohen, "I don't know who compiled the list of incidents and who approved the final text, but I do know that they are people with little regard for the truth."[90]

Above all, diversity training emphasizes that students must think of themselves and others in racial terms. Professor Kors observes that when students have their "first contact with the university, before they get into a classroom, they're taught that race and gender are the primary parts of human personality."[91] At diversity training sessions at Penn, freshmen have been asked to label themselves by race and gender so that they can play "human bingo"—before they introduce themselves by name. At Bryn Mawr College in Pennsylvania, freshmen have been asked to construct a "cultural coat of arms" for themselves, filling it in with "their cultural group's greatest accomplishment, a favorite food of their cultural group, a piece of clothing that is symbolic of their cultural group, and an artifact of their cultural group in their home."[92]

At the State University of New York at Binghamton, orientation group leaders have been given definitions of various stages of racial sensitivity, the most unenlightened of which is the stage in which "majority members . . . do not perceive themselves as 'racial beings' and tend to assume that racist and cultural differences are unimportant."[93] To liberate incoming freshmen from this stage, orientation leaders break them up into small groups and have them play "Wheel of Oppression," a game that shows how prejudice combined with social power leads to sexism, ableism, ageism, classism, heterosexism, and racism. One group leader reported on the results of the orientation:

> Most of them didn't know what we were talking about. It was kind of sad. When we first got together they were all friendly, drawn together because they were new. But as we got into the game playing, especially the "Wheel of Oppression" part, they began to split up and draw away into little cliques.[94]

A recent graduate of Skidmore College in New York wrote in the school's alumni paper about how divisive her experience with a student-led diversity effort had been:

> One of my closest friends at that time was from Texas. . . . But then it happened. . . . At the [diversity awareness] meeting a student took the podium and announced her belief that all whites are racist. She then demanded that the audience respond: those in agreement were to raise their hands. I was shocked when I saw my friend raise hers. The instant she raised her hand, a line was drawn. We were no longer simply two friends. Now, she was black and I was white.[95]

Two graduate students at the University of Cincinnati have written about an orientation session required of residence hall staff members. Those attending were separated into groups, given a bag of Tinkertoys, and instructed to "build the tallest free-standing structure." One group had only two white males; and they were the only members of their group to work on the project, "the others showing no interest whatsoever," according to the graduate students. These two white males managed to build a structure taller than any other group's—for which the diversity training instructor berated them. They had "personified all the characteristics of white-male oppression," by being concerned "only with building the tallest structure and of listening only to the other white male in the group."[96]

Many students do not buy into the ideas that have become the staples of diversity training: In a survey done of Stanford University students by political scientist John Bunzel, the overwhelming majority of white students defined *racism* in the traditional way—as either prejudice ("preconceived and unfavorable judgments about people") or discrimination ("selective mistreatment"). A high percentage of black students, on the other hand, defined racism as diversity educators have come to talk about it: in terms of power, so that the phrase "white racism" becomes a redundancy.[97]

From this latter definition flows one of the most disturbing features of college and university life in the 1990s: self-segregation. Minority students demand separate clubs, yearbooks, dorms, and commencement ceremonies, arguing that they provide a zone of comfort and encourage racial and ethnic awareness. Some maintain that group power is the primary goal. Asked why black students choose to separate themselves at Stanford, a black student responded:

> My answer begins with our history of subjugation. Whites have had the power ever since this country got started, and they abused it. The rest of my answer is that they still have the power and they still abuse it. How do you fight against the misuse of power? With your own power.[98]

If one accepts the idea that racism is impossible for minorities, then acts of separatism by minorities cannot be defined as racist. As a black student leader at Stanford declared, "There is no such thing as reverse racism, reverse sexism, because those people don't have the wherewithal to act out their prejudices."[99]

But to white students who do not accept the idea that only they can be racist, black separatism is cause for resentment. Writes Bunzel, "Apart from feeling that they can and deserve to be trusted, [white students] resent the fact that at the same time that blacks are adamant in opposing racism, they continue to segregate themselves from whites. Self-segregation is precisely the kind of action and behavior that whites consider discriminatory."[100] Thus, it should not be surprising that many white students come away from their college years with less sympathy for minority causes than when they started. Almost one-third of the white students in Bunzel's survey reported that their experience at Stanford had made them "more suspicious of the 'anti-racism' of minorities."[101] A student at the University of Pennsylvania described his experience this way, "I have always considered myself an open-minded person, but being inundated with this day after day after day, and seeing how the University is divided, I have much less tolerance than I ever had before."[102]

For students who do not accept the premises on which most diversity training is based, it oftentimes has exactly the opposite result of that intended. For all students, it has the effect of increasing consciousness of race and decreasing consciousness of people as individuals. Instead of bringing us closer to the world that Martin Luther King, Jr., envisioned—a world in which people are judged not by color but by character—diversity training often brings the message that race matters most.

In every part of the university, the range of permitted thought and expression is narrowing. Faculty are constrained in their research and teaching, students in their academic and personal lives. Surely it is one of the sad spectacles of our time to watch great institutions that once encouraged the search for truth seeking now instead to ensure ideological conformity.

From Truth to Transformation

"He tried to remember in what year he had first heard mention of Big Brother. He thought it must have been at some time in the Sixties."

— *George Orwell*, 1984

To understand how we have gotten to where we are, let us begin with a story, a true story of events that began on a June day in 1835, in a house outside the Normandy village of la Faucterie in the commune of Aunay. There, forty-year-old Victoire Brion, seven months pregnant, was preparing a gruel. Two of her six children were in the room with her: seven-year-old Jules Rivière, who had recently arrived home from school, and eighteen-year-old Victoire Rivière, who was by the window making lace. Outside, Victoire Brion's oldest son, Pierre Rivière, was digging in the garden and talking to his grandmother, who was working a bed of peas nearby. Noon arrived, the grandmother went off to milk the cows, and Pierre Rivière picked up a recently sharpened pruning hook and went into the house and murdered his pregnant mother, his sister, and his brother. The doctors who examined the bloody bodies a few hours later reported that Victoire Brion had been nearly decapitated and that the female fetus she had been carrying was dead. The blows that had killed her daughter had cut through the young woman's spine and severed her upper jaw. The boy Jules had been struck in such a way that the top of his skull lifted off easily. The child's brain, the doctors reported, was "completely mangled."[1]

In a memoir explaining his actions, Pierre Rivière wrote that his mother, an assertive woman, had been a great burden to his father, the source of "tribulations he continually endured." In his memoir, Rivière also mentioned—as would the shocked neighbors—his long fascination with violence. He enjoyed crucifying frogs and birds and was said to laugh with delight as the hapless animals he was torturing struggled to free themselves from the nails he drove through their bellies. Rivière also liked to read, and he became particularly interested in warriors who had gained glory in battle by sacrificing themselves for king and country. Wouldn't he, Rivière, gain similar glory by murdering his mother and thus sacrificing himself for his father? "I knew the rules of man and the rules of ordered society, but I deemed myself wiser than they," Rivière wrote. "I wished to defy the laws, it seemed to me that it would be a glory to me, that I should immortalize myself by dying for my father."[2]

After slaughtering his mother, sister, and brother, Rivière hid in the woods. Apprehended after a month, he was tried and condemned to death, a sentence that was commuted to life in prison. In 1840, Rivière hanged himself in jail.

His try for immortality a seeming failure, Rivière passed into obscurity until, more than a century later, in the early 1970s, his story was recovered by Michel Foucault and his seminar students at the prestigious Collège de France. So taken were Foucault and his students with Pierre Rivière's tale that they spent two years compiling and arranging Rivière's memoirs and other documents relating to the June afternoon when he murdered his mother, his sister, and his brother.

The book that resulted, *I, Pierre Rivière*, is not the most famous of Foucault's works, but it does reveal in a very accessible form patterns of thought that have been enormously influential. In the book, Foucault and his students take up in a remarkably detached way a story that is truly horrific. The facts of the pruning hook, the blood, and the mangled brains all move to the background to be replaced by dueling interpretations. The depositions, testimony, and court briefs are important not for what they tell of the murders, but for what they show about the struggle to control the interpretation of the event: doctors battling with other doctors and with judges over whether Rivière was a criminal or a madman; the villagers of Aunay trying to put forward their version emphasizing the singularity of the event—and thus the unlikelihood of its being repeated. "In their totality and their variety," Foucault wrote,

> [the documents] form . . . a strange contest, a confrontation, a power relation, a battle among discourses and through discourses. . . . I think the reason we decided to publish these documents was to draw a map, so to speak, of those combats, to reconstruct these confrontations and battles, to rediscover the interaction of those discourses as weapons of attack and defense in the relations of power and knowledge.[3]

Thus, *I, Pierre Rivière* is a case study showing how different groups construct different realities, different "regimes of truth," in order to legitimize and protect their interests. But the book is about more than competing discourses. In an important way, it deconstructs itself because its authors prefer one of the discourses. Although they assume a pose of neutrality, they are not really neutral. Although they write detachedly about harrowing events, it is, in fact, the horror of those events that fascinates them. They prefer to think of Rivière as he thought of himself: as the murdering hero. Two of Foucault's students elaborated on Rivière as the Nietzschean figure who goes beyond good and evil, daring to transgress the norms that form the warp and woof of his existence and keep him and his like in subjugation. According to Jean-Pierre Peter and Jeanne Favret, the students whose work Foucault chose as the lead essay on the Rivière documents:

> If the peasants had a Plutarch, Pierre Rivière would have his chapter in the *Illustrious Lives*. . . . The enclosed horizon of the

hedgerows was from time immemorial a profusion of lives devoid of all future, deprived of all prospects. Enduring the unlivable, day in and day out. Should one of them perceive it even for a moment, his whole world falls apart and everything around him. Everything falls apart. For the mute horror of the daily round, for the predicament of dumb beast and dupe he has substituted a more flagrant horror, protest by hecatomb. . . . Rivière alone could surmount the barrier and win a bitter victory, only he could simply die, or, in other words, kill. An explosion into a purple ceremony.[4]

It is Rivière's willingness to violate the social order in the ultimate way, through murder of a parent, that makes him so much an object of fascination. Wrote Foucault, "We fell under the spell of the parricide with the reddish-brown eyes."[5]

In much of Foucault's work, one finds the same pattern. In *Madness and Civilization*, first published in 1961, he advances the idea that insanity is a recent invention. There was a time when the foolish and deranged were an accepted, even valued, part of the everyday landscape, according to Foucault. Then the idea of madness was invented, and by the eighteenth century society routinely set such people apart, isolating and institutionalizing them. In describing this shift, Foucault claims to be practicing "a sort of relativism without recourse."[6] But as he lays out the history of madness, Foucault is anything but a complete relativist. Not that he baldly states his preference. It was not his practice ever to state anything baldly. But he loads the case so that the reader is given to understand that the world was a richer, more interesting place before doctors tried to remedy insanity, before the idea of madness was constructed and began to impose its sterile constraints.

By the time of the May 1968 student riots in France, Foucault was one of his country's best known intellectuals; and although he was teaching in Algeria when students erected barricades in the Latin Quarter, people saw his influence at work. University of Paris professor Raymond Aron credited thinkers like Foucault with "the formula 'there are no facts.' " This way of thinking, "much acclaimed in Parisian circles," according to Aron, had led student rioters to overlook "constraints of fact—the need for production, for organization, for a technical hierarchy, the need for a techno-bureaucracy and so on" and encouraged them "to reject one social order without having any notion of the order which might be erected in its place."[7] Foucault's recent biographer, James Miller, sees another connection between the rioters and Foucault in the way that the passionate destruction of the riots mirrors the celebration of violence and irrationality running through much of Foucault's work.[8]

The United States was also fertile ground for Foucault's ideas. According to Betty Jean Craige of the University of Georgia, people involved in the Vietnam anti-war effort had watched those in power give out versions of events tailored to advance their interests; and the activists had drawn a lesson: "that information carried ideology, that there was no 'pure' knowledge."[9] Having this as their driving conviction made 1960s intellectuals the perfect readers for Foucault; and so, too, did their experience on campuses where many people thrilled to the idea of revolution and saw violence as an appropriate response to what were perceived to be repressive institutions. Moreover, Foucault provided a method for continuing revolutionary activity long after American troops had withdrawn from Vietnam. His ideas were nothing less than an assault on Western civilization. In rejecting an independent reality, an externally verifiable truth, and even reason itself, he was rejecting the foundational principles of the West. This was revolution by other means, and in the voice of those who took up the call, one hears the thrill of being part of a subversive movement, the excitement of participating in forbidden acts. Describing the fascination of deconstruction, J. Hillis Miller, then a professor at Yale, sounded much like Foucault explaining the attraction of Pierre Rivière. Wrote Miller, "A deconstructionist is not a parasite but a parricide. He is a bad son demolishing beyond hope of repair the machine of Western metaphysics."[10] Andrew Ross, an academic superstar of the 1990s, calls himself and like-minded colleagues "assassins of objectivity."[11]

Others besides Foucault had an influence on American campuses. Jacques Derrida, for example, rather than Foucault, is most often associated with J. Hillis Miller and others who came to fame as part of the Yale school of deconstruction. Jacques Lacan and other French theorists of the 1960s have also left a mark. Heidegger and Nietzsche, as Allan Bloom explained in his book *The Closing of the American Mind*, had direct and enormous impact in the United States.[12] An American historian of science, Thomas S. Kuhn, author of *The Structure of Scientific Revolutions,* is often cited (and almost always carelessly) by those who want to argue that the days of external reality and truth are at an end.[13] In fact, Kuhn explained scientific revolutions as the result of paradigm shifts that give scientists new angles on reality—quite a different thing from arguing that reality is nothing more than a social construct. Nevertheless, Kuhn's word *paradigm* has become virtually synonymous with what Foucault, much more the relativist, called an *episteme*.

Many thinkers have helped create an intellectual atmosphere marked by claims of extreme skepticism, but no one defined that atmosphere more effectively than Foucault. As Lawrence Stone of Princeton University has described it, by 1983 Foucault enjoyed "an almost unparalleled position of intellectual dominance over the interpretation of many key aspects of the evolution of Western civilization since the seventeenth century."[14] A decade later, it was almost impossible to pick up an academic journal in the humanities or social sciences or to attend an academic conference without encountering Foucault's name and ideas. He had become a staple in undergraduate courses as well as in graduate seminars. Even freshmen could be overheard trying to explain Foucault's theories about knowledge and power to one another. Anyone who wishes to understand the origins of a way of thinking that has turned American campuses upside down and begun to change the larger society can do no better than start with Foucault.

The idea that reality is nothing more than a social construct, a tool that allows dominant groups to exercise power, had, for example, a profound impact on both the civil rights movement and feminism.

Where once the goal had been equal opportunities for achievement, now it became changing the social construct that defined achievement so as to produce the results one desired. If Harvard Law School does not have a tenured female African-American professor, the aim is not to work to ensure that black women have opportunities to meet the standards such a position demands—graduation in the top ranks of a top-rated law school, for example. Nor is the aim to examine the merits of the standards, to ask whether top graduates of Harvard or Yale or Chicago make better professors. Instead, the standards are denounced as tools of the existing white male order and requirements more likely to be met by a minority woman are put forward. Professor Derrick Bell, leading the protest against the composition of the Harvard law faculty (which had at the time six black men and five women in its sixty-four tenure and tenure track positions), told the *Boston Globe*: "By insisting on the same old credentials, Harvard ensures it will only hire more of what it already has: white, well-off, middle-aged men." To transform the Harvard faculty into a properly diverse group, according to Bell, would require new credentials that went "beyond grades—say civil rights experience, or what have you."[15]

Bell argues, as did Foucault, that standards have no objective reality. They are merely ways of perpetuating the preferences of the powerful; and the point, as Bell sees it, is to substitute requirements that perpetuate one's own set of preferences: civil rights experience instead of grade point average, for example, in order to bring greater ethnic diversity to the faculty. (Ideological diversity is another matter entirely. Bell once called black Harvard professors who did not support his stance people who "look black" and "think white.")[16] Bell seems unbothered by the inherent contradiction in his position. If standards have no objective justification, what rationale can there be for the ones he proposes? If standards can be endlessly manipulated until they produce desired results, why bother with them at all?

Bell also seems unperturbed by the way in which his proposal resembles ethnic stereotyping—and what else can one call the suggestion that different races need different standards in order to prosper? Similarly, feminists today often seem to stereotype men and women. When they look at a college curriculum dominated by white males, they are not interested simply in adding notable but heretofore overlooked women. Instead, they want to expose the standards by which all those white males were included in the first place, such as "violence in the service of winning," in the words of Peggy McIntosh of Wellesley College's Center for Research on Women; they want to create new standards that they feel better suit the nature of women. McIntosh suggests, for example, emphasizing "capacities beyond competition and what is called rational analysis."[17] Yolanda T. Moses, president of City College of New York, argues that among the factors that have held women and minorities back is that "institutions of higher education in the United States are products of Western society in which masculine values like an orientation toward achievement and objectivity are valued over cooperation, connectedness, and subjectivity."[18] In Moses' view, it is time for a change, time to transform the university into a place that validates the supposedly different needs of those who are not white and not male.

Group politics in the United States, lacking though it has been in the subtleties and ambiguities of French thought, owes a debt to it; and this nexus has helped perpetuate the ideas of Foucault and other French philosophers long after their influence has waned in France. As philosopher Mark Lilla has observed, a number of events, such as the publication in the 1970s of Aleksandr Solzhenitsyn's books about the gulag, brought home to many French intellectuals the fact that their antipathies had been misplaced. Foucault had made the case in *Discipline and Punish*, one of his most influential books, that dreadful as were the punishments imposed upon criminals in the seventeenth century (drawing and quartering, for example), far more dreadful are the grinding, dreary, and continuous surveillance and discipline to which modern institutions—not just prisons, but also schools and factories—subject all citizens. To French readers learning of the horrors of the gulag such an argument came to have a hollow, even frivolous sound. Writes Lilla, "In the face of [Solzhenitsyn's] compelling account of physical and mental torture directed by a regime many in France still considered the vanguard of social progress, it was difficult to maintain that Western classrooms were prisons and still remain within the bounds of good taste."[19]

To American activists, however, revelations that seemed to undercut Foucault's ideas were less important than the fact that those ideas were such useful tools for advancing group interests; and they not only took up Foucault's thought, they moved relentlessly with it to transform society so that it would correspond to the interests they represented. In a sense, Foucault had prepared the way for this. Although proclaiming himself a relativist, he was far from neutral in either his philosophy or politics. In almost all his writings, it is clear which "regime of truth" he prefers; and he was for a time deeply committed to political activism. While he was working on *Discipline and Punish*, for example, he allied himself with French Maoists and spoke in positive terms about mob violence.[20] But Foucault had been reluctant to dictate the precise forms that postrevolutionary society should take. Indeed, toward the end of his life, he had specifically declared such a role inappropriate:

> The work of an intellectual is not to shape others' political will; it is, through the analyses that he carries out in his own field, to question over and over again what is postulated as self-evident, to disturb people's mental habits, the way they do and think things, to dissipate what is familiar and accepted, to reexamine rules and institutions and on the basis of this reproblematization (in which he carries out his specific task as an intellectual) to participate in the formation of a political will (in which he has his role as citizen to play).[21]

Many of the American intellectuals who took up Foucauldian ideas of knowledge and power had no such hesitation. It was not enough, as they saw it, simply to disturb mental habits so that rules and institutions could be reexamined. As a faculty member and graduate student at Duke University explained, merely teaching students to think critically would not bring them to "radical visions of the world." In order to bring that about, "the teacher must recognize that he or she must influence (perhaps manipulate is the more accurate word) students' values through charisma or power."[22] The 1960s intellectuals who came to dominate American campuses often saw their role very much as shaping the political will of others.

Thus the political activism being promoted on American campuses moved beyond Foucault, far enough beyond so that it even influenced a certain subset of Marxist intellectuals. The theoretical base of Marxist thought is diametrically opposed to the ideas Foucault advanced. The very opposite of skeptics, Marxist intellectuals believe in a real world that must be examined if we are to gain real knowledge—a fact that helps explain why a scholar like Eugene Genovese of the University of Georgia has been such a fierce proponent of academic freedom. But for Marxist ideologues, who are inclined to use the classroom for proselytizing, the activists inspired by Foucault opened the way. These activists invited politics into the classroom; and once that happened, it made no difference whether it was politics that had relativism as its rationale or politics based on class struggle. English Professor Richard Ohmann of Wesleyan University, whose Marxism has been part of the academic landscape for years, became particularly outspoken in the early 1990s. "Not to put too fine a point on it," he wrote:

> we work in whatever ways we can toward the end of capitalist patriarchy. No kidding. Not just canon reform or a dissident reading of *Paradise Lost*, but the transformation of society.
>
> Most of us don't expect it to happen with a bang, or indeed within our lifetimes, but what we're about is dismantling the corporate structure; taking away the money and power of those who own most of productive capital, and thus the right to determine the future of this beleaguered planet.[23]

ॐ

People who have not been in college in the last ten years or so are unlikely to understand how discredited ideas like truth and objectivity have become. This is especially the case in the humanities, particularly in English and art history (though not, interestingly enough, in philosophy). While fields like economics, where real-world information forces a certain discipline, are under some attack, they remain relatively unscathed; but many of the soft social sciences—sociology, for example—have been deeply affected.

Black studies, women's studies, and cultural studies departments have all joined in an assault on science and technology that is aimed at discrediting the objectivity and rationality at the heart of the scientific enterprise. As Paul R. Gross and Norman Levitt, who have written about this phenomenon, point out, this assault has been influential politically, despite its generally having been carried out by people who know little about science.[24] Andrew Ross of New York University, a professor of cultural studies and one of the leaders of the anti-scientific movement, prides himself on his lack of scientific training. He dedicated his 1991 book "to all of the science teachers I never had."[25] A recent book by two feminist professors is testimony to the low levels of scientific literacy in women's studies departments. The two professors, one from Wheaton College in Massachusetts and the other from California State University at Fullerton, approvingly quote a third feminist professor, Chinosole, from San Francisco State University, explaining "the multidimensional perspectives of feminist education in terms of the demise of the Copernican view of the earth as center of the universe."[26] The problem is that Copernicus did not place the earth at the center of the universe, Ptolemy did. It was Copernicus who uncovered the Ptolemaic fallacy and put the sun at the center—information of which all three feminists are blissfully unaware.

Also assailing science are the environmentalists—one of them very famous. Whenever I visit a college or university, I try to visit the campus bookstore to see what students are being assigned to read; and I almost always find Al Gore's *Earth in the Balance*. Like much environmental writing, the vice president's book (written when he was a senator) is about more than ecology, it is about how the great thinkers of the Enlightenment have led us astray. Overlooking the fact that these thinkers were a major source of inspiration for the founders of our country, Gore describes them as the source of almost everything that has gone wrong with the world. Their emphasis on reason and their insistence on objectivity—on standing apart from what is being studied and evaluating it disinterestedly—have caused us to become, Gore says, a "dysfunctional civilization," obsessed with consuming, prone to polluting, and deeply unhappy. As Gore describes it, the worldview that led to the scientific revolution has been responsible for everything bad (including "the atrocities of Hitler and Stalin") and nothing good, which does cause one to wonder what worldview the vice president imagines gave rise to anesthesia, polio vaccine, and—his pet project—the information superhighway.[27]

Gore singles out Francis Bacon, the seventeenth-century British thinker, as a primary villain and presents him as a man so intellectually separated from the world that he took up experiments with no thought of their consequences. Bacon, writes Gore, "was able to enthusiastically advocate vivisection for the pure joy of learning without reference to any moral purpose, such as saving human lives, as justification for the act."[28] But this is a warped and distorted version of Bacon, who saw—rightly—that the kind of knowledge that he and his contemporaries gained from vivisection would advance humankind. Through dissecting animals and cadavers, William Harvey, for example, was able to explain the circulation of blood. Bacon was simply not what Gore makes him out to be, a person who "defined human beings as disembodied intellects separate from the physical world."[29] To the contrary, Bacon insisted—as modern scientific method does—that we should study what is actually in the world rather than operate from mental prejudices and preconceptions; but this understanding of Bacon is not useful to Gore and others who see undermining science as a necessary part of the environmental project.[30]

Postmodern thinking has affected not only a range of disciplines, but also an array of academic institutions. Schools like Duke University, which have gained reputations as hotbeds of political correctness, are not the only places where the idea of disinterestedness has fallen on hard times. It has happened in public as well as private institutions, in small schools as well as large ones. Betty Jean Craige, whose prize-winning book *Reconnection* defends the idea of putting education into the service of politics, teaches at the University of Georgia. Paula Rothenberg, editor of a textbook, *Racism and Sexism*, that puts leftist thought at the center of freshman English instruction, is at William Paterson College in Wayne, New Jersey. Rothenberg is also director of "The New Jersey Project," which aims to transform curricula across the nation. At a 1993 conference organized by Rothenberg, more than seven hundred people, most of them from two-year colleges and state four-year institutions, gathered to discuss such matters as "Fourteen Weeks to Subvert Young Minds: Teaching Race, Class, Gender, and Sexual Orientation in Courses Fulfilling University Requirements" and "Looking Out, Looking Ahead: Prospects for a Post-Conservative, Feminist Agenda." At one session that I observed, "The Politics of Curriculum Transformation," conference attendees discussed their success at wresting control of their schools from more traditionally minded colleagues. One participant declared that it was sometimes easier for those bent on transforming curricula to prevail at nonelite colleges. "Being in a lower-prestige institution," she said, "we've been able to take over."

How is it that the idea of deliberately using education to promote political agendas has become so widespread? The key ideas that have become commonplace in recent years have been disseminated in many ways, some of them quite traditional, such as through books and journals. One does not have to sit at the feet of cutting-edge theorists in order to learn about politicizing scholarship; one can simply read *Proceedings of the Modern Language Association*, the prestigious journal of the Modern Language Association, an organization devoted to the study of languages and literature. A statistical study by scholar Will Morrisey shows that in the 1970s and 1980s, there was a striking increase in the number of *PMLA* articles advocating or displaying political commitment. Reports Morrisey:

> From 1930 through 1960, few articles are ideological (varying from 0 percent to 3 percent). . . . The percentage of ideological articles increased markedly in the 1970s and dramatically in the

1980s, until, in 1990 they made up 52.5 percent of all articles.

Morrisey also defines a second category of articles that he calls "tendentious": that is, "in which incidental political or social comment is so prominent it raises a question about whether the author's true motive in writing is not at least in part political." In 1990, nearly 20 percent of the articles in *PMLA* were tendentious by Morrisey's count. Thus, in 1990, nearly three-quarters of the articles had a political dimension, "and the ideologies represented," Morrisey writes, ". . . are predominantly of the Left, and often of an extreme Left."[31]

College English, the journal of the National Council of Teachers of English, edited during most of the 1970s by Marxist professor Richard Ohmann, frequently assumes an ideological tone at variance with its innocuous title. In recent years, its articles have offered advice on such matters as how teachers can "persuade students to agree with their values," overcome students' stubborn "insistence . . . on individualism," and "inculcate into . . . students the conviction that the dominant order is repressive."[32]

The number of journals amenable to such articles increased markedly during the 1970s and 1980s. One, *Radical Teacher*, founded in 1975 by Professor Ohmann and other members of the Modern Language Association's radical caucus, calls itself "a socialist and feminist journal on the theory and practice of teaching." According to a 1991 article in *The Chronicle of Higher Education*, contributors to the magazine used to keep their involvement with it off their résumés, but now, "many say they no longer need to play down the work."[33] Several journals founded in the last decade or so are in the recently conceived field of "cultural studies" (designated "left studies" by University of Chicago professor Gerald Graff[34]): *Social Text*, *Cultural Critique*, and *Cultural Studies*, to name a few. Feminist journals have proliferated: *Signs*, the *Women's Review of Books*, *Hypatia*, *differences*, *Genders*, the *National Women's Studies Association Journal*, *Gender and Society*. They not only offer examples of feminist scholarship—and it should be noted that in the early years of the feminist movement, when equality was still the goal, many of them were very good—but also have become a source of advice on such subjects as how to counter student resistance to feminism in the classroom.[35] *Transformations*, a nationally distributed by-product of Paula Rothenberg's New Jersey Project, offers readers the "information, resources and pedagogical strategies" needed to effect a feminist transformation of curricula from coast to coast. "A truly transformed curriculum," the fall 1992 issue advised, "wouldn't contain a Western Civilization course."[36]

Another staple of academic life—the convention or conference—has become a way of disseminating "transformative" ideas and practices. At the December 1992 convention of the Modern Language Association in New York City, Annette Kolodny of the University of Arizona described how she, as dean, had made sure that women and minorities were hired: Departments were required to put applications into two piles, one for women and minorities and another for white men; no one could be hired from the second pile if there was a qualified candidate in the first. Kolodny also described how she dealt with faculty members who might object to granting tenure to people who practiced politics in their scholarship and teaching. Scholars who had not embraced "the new forms of scholarly production," she explained, were declared professionally inactive and therefore ineligible to participate in promotion and tenure decisions.[37]

Other faculty members offered strategies for overcoming such so-called male values as hierarchy and objectivity and creating a new academic construct that properly valued so-called female values such as connectedness and subjectivity. Paul Heilker from Loyola University of Chicago presented a paper which argued that requiring students to write papers in which they present evidence to support a thesis "militates against academic freedom . . . [indoctrinates] students in obeisant attitudes toward authority, and [makes] them blindly revere and replicate the status quo." Heilker quoted a number of authorities himself, including one who urged composition instructors "to consider to what extent our teaching of the thesis/

support form forces students into an unconscious buttressing of the societal pyramid that has rich, young, able-bodied, highly educated, scientific, white, Christian, business-minded, materialistic, type-A males at the top and everyone else somewhere below them, trying to assimilate those values and become 'empowered'."[38]

At the same session, Lisa Jadwin of St. John Fisher College in Rochester, New York, talked about classroom strategies that offer "a way that serves our political convictions" and urged instructors to tell students "(or better yet, show them) that you permit swearing and slang to be used in the classroom; these words are also part of our language and deconstructing the sacredness of 'profanity' is a valuable intellectual exercise."[39] At a panel session entitled "Feminist Perspectives on Composition," Olivia Frey of St. Olaf College in Northfield, Minnesota, presented a paper in which she talked about her childhood identification with Scarlett O'Hara, her mother's menopause, and writer Robyn Davidson's menstrual period, all by way of rejecting "masculinist critical discourse" and illustrating the contextual and autobiographical ways that, according to Frey, are more natural to women.[40]

Less than two months after the MLA convention, the College Art Association, an organization devoted to the study of art and its history, met in Seattle, Washington, where its members discussed similar topics. At a session entitled "Curriculum Transformation in Art History," Susan J. Delaney of Mira Costa College in California noted the importance of seeing the art of the past in terms of the political concerns of the present. She and colleagues from Purdue University in Indiana, Hood College in Maryland, and the University of South Florida demonstrated how art so approached could be used to show students that women have been oppressed by everyone from textbook editors (who are apt to choose "less powerful" and "less threatening" pictures of goddesses with their "knees clasped tightly together" rather than an image of a goddess giving birth) to artists like Dürer (who, however much he may seem to be presenting a balanced presentation of Adam and Eve, is actually "working squarely within the misogynistic tradition").[41] At another session,

Frances Pohl of Pomona College in California took up objections to this approach to art history: specifically those made by art historian Stephen Polcari to politicized approaches that advance the "ideological agendas of the current . . . 1960s generation who now rules the university." As Pohl saw it, this objection was naive. "Art historical writing is, indeed, informed by political agendas . . . ," she claimed, sounding very much the disciple of Foucault. "Art history has to become engaged in the study of 'truths,' each of which has to be viewed not as objective, but as part of a changing discourse concerning power and specific historical relations."[42]

The National Women's Studies Association gathered a thousand teachers and activists together in June 1993 in Washington, D.C. At a plenary session entitled "Breaking/Making Paradigms: Feminism and Knowing," Elizabeth Minnich of Union Institute Graduate School in Cincinnati, Ohio, sounded a theme that echoed through the conference: "We are reuniting scholarship with action," she declared. The next day, Carol Wolfe Konek of Wichita State University declared teachers to be "agents for personal and social change." One of her fellow panelists, Berenice Fisher of New York University, extolled "politically engaged faculty members" who embody the "ideal of the radical professional." A third panelist, Sherry Gorelick of Rutgers University, exulted that she was "being paid by the state to subvert the state."[43]

All of this was prelude to the closing plenary session where the incoming NWSA president, Vivien Ng of the University of Oklahoma, declared, "I do political work, both inside the classroom and outside it." Noting that students often resist her efforts, Ng observed:

> That's to be expected. I'm doing political work. . . . I decided that I would make a good preacher. My students came around and I converted them. I have a great time realizing George Will's greatest fears.[44]

So uniform are the politics offered up at many academic conferences that meetings take on the air of solidarity sessions. Philosopher

Richard Rorty pronounced the 1988 conference in North Carolina that I described in the opening of this book "a rally of [the] cultural left."[45] Everyone at the conference had the same set of enemies—Allan Bloom, William Bennett, and myself.[46] Five years later, in 1993, at Paula Rothenberg's New Jersey conference, the Great Enemies list had grown to include people who are notably not conservative. Arthur Schlesinger, Jr.'s, name drew hisses because in his book *The Disuniting of America* he denounces multicultural projects that encourage ethnic separatism.[47] Even President Clinton was denounced as a "liberal," a political state of being that campus radicals regard with disdain, though it was noted, in the president's favor, that he is "malleable."

The lack of ideological diversity at these conferences means that ideas that should be challenged go unchallenged. At the Paula Rothenberg gathering, one panelist declared that worldwide economic conspiracies ("global structures" created by "global corporations") were oppressing everyone, that a "monopoly" was determining how "the resources of the world" are spent, assertions that no one in the audience seemed to find in need of evidence or exemplification. A speaker from a historically black college condemned "certain schools" that count "immigrants as people of color" and cited "white Cubans" as an example of a group that should not be accorded minority status—a view on which it would undoubtedly be enlightening to hear other perspectives.

Conferences and journals that encourage ideological scholarship and teaching do more than disseminate ideas, they advance the professional interests of participants. A paper published or presented helps build a résumé for tenure and promotion committees to consider. When enough papers have been presented or published, they can be gathered into a book, which helps build one's résumé even more. In 1991, for example, feminist professor Patti Lather of Ohio State University published *Getting Smart: Feminist Research and Pedagogy With/in the Postmodern*, a book that had its origins in numerous articles and convention speeches. A chapter discussing "student resistance to liberatory curriculum" had, for example, been presented at three different conferences (the annual meeting of the National Women's Studies Association, the Eighth Annual Curriculum Theorizing Conference, the annual meeting of the American Education Research Association Conference) and published in a journal (*Women's Studies International Forum*).[48] And so it is, thanks to the way that late-twentieth-century academic life is organized, that one essay can help generate five different résumé entries—and give academic standing to work that would not have been considered scholarly a decade or so ago.

In recent years, electronic mail has become an important supplement to the network of conferences and journals that offer information and advice on making scholarship and teaching effective political tools. Indeed, one of the primary activities of the Women's Studies List (WMST-L), carried on the Internet, is to advertise feminist conferences and journals. From the Women's Studies List, one could learn about the Feminist Ethics and Social Policy conference at the University of Pittsburgh, the Feminism and the Law conference at the University of Minnesota, and the sessions being organized by the International Association for Feminist Economics at the Western Social Science Association meeting in Albuquerque, New Mexico. One could learn that a publication called *Trivia: A Journal of Ideas* was seeking submissions from "radical visionary women," that *Women and Therapy* was seeking papers examining "the possible psychotherapeutic implications for women engaged in some aspect of feminist spirituality," that an anthology, *Daughters of the Sisterhood,* wanted people to write on such topics as "the gulf war—militarism and patriarchy."

Jobs are advertised on the Women's Studies List. The Futures Group in Washington, D.C., wants people with "demonstrated competence in gender issues" to work on its Agency for International Development–funded project on Women in Development. Clark University in Worcester, Massachusetts, wants someone to teach a course in Gender, Space, and Environment. The Department of Physical Education and Sport Studies of the University of Alberta is looking for someone to fill a tenure track appointment in the History of Sport and Leisure. The ideal candidate, the posting notes, will "have some knowledge and understanding of . . . marxism, FEMI-NISM, cultural studies."

Given the Women's Studies List's emphasis on putting scholarship and teaching into the service of politics, it is hardly a surprise to find it being used to rally support for specific political battles. When feminists at Pennsylvania State University were charged with theft for stealing copies of a campus newspaper that had attacked "incompetent teachers, politicized curricula and de facto censorship of student thought in the women's studies program," a notice was posted on the WMST-L asking people to write letters to the president and trustees of Pennsylvania State. Responses were posted on the network from colleges and universities across the country and around the world. A professor from Nova University in Florida promised support as did a faculty member at the University of Washington. Feminists from Canada to New Zealand let it be known that they stood in solidarity with their sisters at Pennsylvania State.

ß∾

Disseminating ideas costs money, and the fact that so many cutting-edge ideas in education today are on the political left means that they tend to be looked on with sympathy in the private foundation world, where the politics are often similar. An organization of professors called Teachers for a Democratic Culture (TDC) has tried recently to make the case that it is conservative foundations that unduly influence higher education, an argument that is at the very least counterintuitive when one takes into account the state of higher education today. The TDC has particularly cited the John M. Olin Foundation for financing academics of traditional bent,[49] but in point of fact the assets of the Olin Foundation (nearly $69 million in 1991) are small by comparison with the assets of organizations sympathetic to the ideas of the left. The Ford Foundation, for example, reported assets of more than $6 billion in 1991.[50]

In 1994, Althea K. Nagai, Robert Lerner, and Stanley Rothman published the results of a content analysis of grants made by private foundations. Looking at grants from 1986 and 1987, they determined that 225 foundations made at least one grant with a public policy dimension. Fifty-seven percent of those grants had political leanings, with 44 percent (nearly $170 million worth) tending to the left and 13 percent (nearly $43 million worth) to the right. The Ford Foundation awarded the most grants to projects of the left, 262, by the Nagai, Lerner, and Rothman count. Ford also made grants that the researchers designated conservative, but for every one of those, fifteen grants went to liberal causes. For every dollar that Ford spent on conservative grants, it spent over $28 on liberal grants.[51]

An example of the kind of grant many have come to expect from the Ford Foundation was made to Louisiana's Tulane University in 1990 "to bring multicultural perspectives to bear on all aspects of the curriculum."[52] The Tulane administration's explanation of how this would be accomplished began with a statement of assumptions:

> First, that racism and sexism are pervasive in America and are fundamentally present in all American institutions. Second, racism and sexism are subtle and for the most part, subconscious or at least sub-surface. Third, it is difficult for us to see and overcome racism and sexism because we are all a product of the problem, i.e. we are all the progeny of a racist and sexist society.

Having made a claim that could be neither proved nor disproved, the administration then used that assertion as a basis for requiring each department to hire a woman or person of color each year until "utilization goals" were met. Should any department fall short, the provost would have the power to overrule its hiring decisions and would be expected to use that authority "aggressively." The administration also recommended a university-wide course on racism and sexism, required sensitivity training, and "empowered" participants in sensitivity programs "to understand and identify elements of individual and institutional racism and sexism and provide us with tools to begin the process of removing racism and sexism from ourselves and our institution."[53]

Paul H. Lewis, chairman of the Tulane Political Science Department and a man who had been active in the civil rights movement as early as 1963, found these initiatives cause for deep concern. The way in which they encouraged faculty and students to report on one another he thought to be Orwellian; and giving Tulane's administration the power to overrule the hiring decisions of departmental specialists was, to his way of thinking, a gross violation of well-established academic procedures. Calling the initiatives "potentially the worst assault on academic freedom since Sen. Joe McCarthy's escapades in the 1950s," he went public with his concerns, writing a letter that appeared in the *New Orleans Times-Picayune*.[54] The letter, which Lewis terms "an act of desperation," aroused alumni interest in the matter and finally led, in April 1992, to the university's Board of Administrators (that is, its trustees) rejecting the initiatives. Reflecting on the year-and-a-half-long struggle at Tulane, Lewis notes the pivotal role that private foundation money played. "The Ford grant gave the initiatives legitimacy," he says.[55]

The study by Nagai, Lerner, and Rothman shows the John D. and Catherine T. MacArthur Foundation, with assets of more than $3 billion in 1991, awarding the second highest number of grants to the left, ninety-six of them.[56] Even before the Nagai, Lerner, and Rothman analysis, Joshua Muravchik, a resident scholar of the American Enterprise Institute, wrote in *The American Spectator* (TAS) about the distinct bias in MacArthur's grant-giving, citing as an example the foundation's most famous program:

> Of the 350 Americans from all walks of life who have won MacArthur Fellowships—better known as "genius awards"—no fewer than four are members of the editorial board of *Dissent*, the small quarterly devoted to what its principal editor, Irving Howe, calls the "steady work" of bearing the torch for democratic socialism. Roughly one out of every million Americans is a MacArthur genius; and one out of every ten members of the *Dissent* board. In comparison, the number of editors of *TAS*, *National Review*, and *Foreign Affairs* who are MacArthur fellows is zero. The *New Re-*

public and the *Atlantic* each have one (a contributing editor), the highest number I'm aware of for any political journal other than *Dissent*.[57]

In the 1980s and early 1990s, foundations with conservative agendas supported people that played high-profile roles in debates about American culture. The Olin Foundation, for example, supported Dinesh D'Sousa, Allan Bloom, Robert Bork, and Irving Kristol, and helped underwrite the *Public Interest* and *New Criterion* magazines. Conservative giving had impact chiefly because the money was effectively spent. But liberal foundations, with so much more to spend, still had an overwhelming advantage. Liberal scholars and projects are still far more likely to win private foundation funding and thus to influence not only higher education, but the course of the culture.

Public money also plays a role in supporting projects that aim to use education to achieve social transformation. The National Science Foundation funded a May 1993 conference at Williamsburg, Virginia, that brought instructors of introductory economics courses from across the nation together to learn how to achieve a race and gender transformation of their classrooms. They studied the suggestions of the ubiquitous Peggy McIntosh, who holds that "the traditional curriculum was designed for the education of white male Western leaders in a time of Western dominance" and who considers both competition and the idea of excellence to be dangers to civilization.[58] A June 1995 conference at Wellesley College in Massachusetts, where McIntosh is headquartered, was also sponsored by the National Science Foundation. It took up the same topic of classroom transformation and warned participants that they were "expected to teach their race- and gender-balanced principles [in] courses during the next academic year."[59]

The Upper Midwest Women's History Center in St. Louis Park, Minnesota, was founded with federal monies from the Women's Education Equity Act, and many of the materials the center distributes have been produced with public funds from other sources. One example is a manual intended to help organize workshops on *Wasted Resources, Diminished Lives: The Impact of Boy Preference on the Lives of Girls and Women.* Sponsored by the United States Agency for International Development, this manual cites research on the preference various cultures show for boys: a study in Bombay on the abuse of amniocentesis, in which all but one of eight thousand aborted fetuses were female; a study in Bangladesh showing girl babies suffering acute malnutrition at twice the rate of boy babies; a study in South Korea showing boys and girls being immunized against measles in equal numbers until an immunization fee was introduced: subsequently, only slightly over one-fourth of the children being immunized were female.[60]

To this point, the research is reasonably presented, but when the manual takes up the subject of the United States, politics supersedes scholarship. As is often the case with feminist research, the manual becomes intent upon validating the victim status of American girls—a necessary state of affairs to establish in order to justify policies that benefit girls alone, but one for which the evidence is weak. The author of the *Wasted Resources* manual equates a study showing the lives of girls in Third World countries to be endangered with a survey showing American girls to be short on self-esteem. Seeming to sense that this does not put young females in the United States in quite the same league as their peers in Bangladesh or India, the author goes on to make the case that in all nations girls are deprived educationally. "Worldwide and historically," she writes, "a son has usually been favored for advanced education if family resources are limited, even if a daughter is more gifted intellectually"; and in a note she adds that "a guidance counselor at Edina High School, an affluent Minnesota community," had reported to her "that he has many young women who tell him that they are discouraged from going to college because their brother is being sent and the family feels they can send only one child."[61]

Basing a case for the intellectual repression of young women in the United States on a single, secondhand report is unsound to begin with, but particularly so when there are relevant statistics that paint a very different picture. In 1992, 55 percent of those going to college were women. Fifty-four percent of those receiving bachelor's and master's degrees in 1991 were women. Since only 51 percent of the entire population is female, women are attending college and earning degrees in percentages that exceed their representation in the total population.[62]

Some of the materials distributed by the Upper Midwest Women's History Center are very well done. *Women on the American Frontier: Deferring Domesticity,* Volume 5 of *Women in United States History,* a series published by the center, is balanced and informative.[63] Avoiding the women-as-victims approach that characterizes so much revisionist history of the American West, it provides the kind of detail about women's lives that teachers should have available to them and that students should learn about. Its no-nonsense, set-the-record-straight approach is very much in the spirit of first-wave equity feminism. It is the kind of scholarship, I suspect, that many funders think they are supporting, when, in fact, they are increasingly underwriting a highly politicized feminism.

Consider, for example, the hundreds of thousands of dollars that the state of New Jersey, under both Democratic and Republican administrations, has put into Paula Rothenberg's curriculum transformation project.[64] My strong suspicion is that taxpayers who are aware of the project think that it has to do with opening up debate and broadening opportunities for learning. Doubtless they would be surprised to find out that the opposite is the case, to learn that people who try to debate the New Jersey Project's orthodoxy are, as in an Orwell novel, immediately assumed to be in need of reeducation. Their "resistance" is viewed as something to be cured with reading assignments from *Radical Teacher*.[65]

Several participants at the conference sponsored by the New Jersey Project explained that their work toward feminist curricular transformation was made possible by the United States Department of Education through its Fund for the Improvement of Postsecondary Education (FIPSE), and as some of these faculty members described it, their students were badly in need of the enlightenment that the FIPSE grant made possible. One professor from Towson State University in Maryland stereotyped her white, middle-class students in ways that would be totally unacceptable were they part of any other group. She referred to them as "preppie clones" and called them "Muffies and Chips." Another professor spoke of her "struggles to find humanity even in the smug products of the Baltimore suburbs."

Another FIPSE grant, this one to the Modern Language Association, is aimed at faculty members who are not yet on the cutting edge of ideas in their disciplines. In 1990, the MLA was awarded $294,000 by FIPSE to bring faculty members well acquainted with "new thinking" to institutions where "profound . . . developments in the discipline" were not so well known.[66] Professors from Duke University, for example, were dispatched to Northwest Missouri State University, to St. John Fisher College in New York, and to the University of Southern Maine. Professor Richard Ohmann of Wesleyan University, who has dedicated himself to working "toward the end of capitalist patriarchy" and to "dismantling the corporate structure," went to the State University of New York at Oswego, where he helpfully advised that "much could be done" to enrich the curriculum if the English Department's commitment to teach a Western Heritage course "ceased to exist."[67]

When disciplines become highly politicized, as has happened in the humanities, public monies that support them inevitably end up, at least some of the time, supporting a political viewpoint. National Endowment for the Humanities monies, I found to my dismay, helped support the Rothenberg curriculum transformation conference. An acknowledgment on the front of the conference agenda explained, "This program was made possible in part by grants from The New Jersey Committee for the Humanities, a state program of The National Endowment for the Humanities and The Pennsylvania Humanities Council, a statewide organization funded partially by the National Endowment for the Humanities."[68] The state organizations receive more than 20 percent of NEH monies in a direct pass-through. They decide how they will spend their percentage of the NEH budget, and while they have funded worthwhile projects, they also, as I discovered while I was chairman of the National Endowment for the Humanities, have supported efforts that have a strong political bias.

During my chairmanship of the NEH, I made it a goal to have the funds that I controlled support detached and balanced scholarship and teaching; and I was supported in this effort by the citizens and scholars who served on the presidentially appointed advisory board of the Endowment, the National Council on the Humanities. But despite this commitment, money sometimes went to projects with a decided political bent. The Folger Shakespeare Library in Washington, D.C., applied for a grant for a seminar that would give college teachers opportunities to learn about "New Directions in Shakespeare Criticism." How could such a project go wrong, combining as it did a highly respected cultural institution and an icon of Western civilization? But go wrong it did—at least according to a report from Marvin Hunt, a faculty member from Elon College in North Carolina who was one of the participants. "I'm suddenly aware of a creepy semiotics of place," he wrote of the experience of listening to a lecturer present "a Marxist deconstruction of Shakespeare, the Buddha of Conservative English-Speaking Culture, at a site a block and a half from the United States Capitol, the tabernacle of running dogs worldwide." Hunt went on to ask, "And who's footing his—our—bill? The duped capitalists themselves, of course."[69]

According to Hunt, "By tea time that afternoon, those of us not previously committed to politicizing Shakespeare seem to have been converted." And quite willingly, too. As Hunt explained:

Most of us are assistant professors, figures from the margins of mercantile society who came of age in the '60s, carrying a legacy of defeat and nearly a decade of Reagan-Thatcherism to our jobs. The discovery that as we inherit academia we have license to politicize our classes represents an irresistible temptation. To this group, the ideology of the left promises something like sweet revenge.[70]

But most disappointing of all were the National History Standards, described in the first chapter of this book. In 1992, shortly before I left the chairmanship of the NEH, I signed a grant for $525,000 (and the secretary of education signed a grant for $865,000) to fund this project. The award was made on the basis of an application from the History Center at the University of California at Los Angeles in which the directors of that center offered as a model of the work they would produce a highly regarded publication that they had previously done, *Lessons from History*. *Lessons* rightfully included Americans like Sojourner Truth, who were frequently overlooked in the past, while still emphasizing figures like George Washington. *Lessons* was frank about this country's failings without neglecting our many achievements.[71]

But the standards that were published in 1994 bore almost no relationship to *Lessons*. Instead they reflected the gloomy, politically driven revisionism that has become all too familiar on college campuses. They took the important principle of inclusion to such an extreme that a new kind of exclusion resulted. Harriet Tubman, who helped slaves escape from the South, is mentioned six times in the standards, while two of her white male contemporaries, Ulysses S. Grant and Robert E. Lee, are cited one and zero times, respectively.

In many ways the standards were the logical outcome of what I had observed during my six years at the NEH: the ever-increasing politicization of the humanities. As the 1960s generation of intellectuals assumed greater and greater power, scholarship came more and more to be the servant of social and political transformation. Applications to the Endowment reflected this shift; and when they did not, strategic maneuvering on the part of the applicant—rather than a commitment to disinterested inquiry—was sometimes the reason.

The Endowment had been founded in 1964 on the grounds that the humanities offered insight into such "enduring values as justice, freedom, virtue, beauty, and truth." The commision that authored these words and was chiefly responsible for the Endowment's original authorization had even paraphrased Matthew Arnold: "To know the best that has been thought and said in former times can make us wiser than we otherwise might be, and in this respect the humanities are not merely our, but the world's best hope."[72]

In thirty years, the world of the humanities had been so transformed that many of the projects that the Endowment was funding were contemptuous of the ideas on which it had been established. Indeed, what the commission had most sternly warned against, "a history politically controlled,"[73] was now—as the History Standards demonstrated—seen by some as the ideal. Three decades of government support had not brought improvement to the humanities. To the contrary, these years had witnessed their sharp decline; and while government support was not the only reason, it had played a major part in helping legitimate and disseminate ideas that would otherwise have been less influential.

The History Standards also drove home the point that no matter how committed an Endowment head might be to traditional scholarly standards, he or she could not succeed in upholding them when those most influential in the community of humanities scholars no longer thought them worthy. Asked in early 1995 to testify before the Congress about the future of the NEH, I felt compelled to say that it was time to do away with the Endowment, time to turn funding of the humanities—and the arts as well—back to the private sector.

ఈ *Chapter Four*

Justice Without
the Blindfold

"The Ministry of Love . . . maintained law and order."

—*George Orwell, 1984*

ALTHOUGH Rosalind Rosenberg's name does not usually appear in the annals of political correctness, she was one of the first to be disciplined for behavior inconsistent with reigning orthodoxy. Rosenberg's sin was to provide crucial testimony for the defense in a case that the Equal Employment Opportunity Commission (EEOC) brought against Sears, Roebuck & Company. Citing such evidence as the fact that 61 percent of those applying for sales positions at Sears were women, but only 27 percent of those hired for commission positions were female, the EEOC charged that Sears discriminated against women in hiring for commission sales jobs. Rosenberg, an associate professor of history at Barnard College, testified that the statistics did not prove discrimination because women often make different choices from men. Their "interests and aspirations regarding work" are different, she said; they are more attracted to jobs that are compatible with family life, less attracted to those like commission sales that require competitiveness and aggression.[1]

The feminist community erupted in anger, causing historian Carl Degler of Stanford University to warn:

I think criticism along those lines will hurt women's history, will make it seem to be simply a polemical subject and not a true historical subject. We still have to convince a lot of people that women's history is a real field of scholarly inquiry. If people have to follow a party line that will be fatal.[2]

But views such as Degler's did little to derail the condemnation of Rosenberg. At the 1985 annual meeting of the American Historical Association, the Women's Coordinating Committee passed a declaration declaring, "We believe as feminist scholars we have a responsibility not to allow our scholarship to be used against the interests of women struggling for equity in our society."[3] Sears's victory in the case a few months later served further to enrage feminists in academe.

Part of the anger no doubt came from Rosenberg's having exposed the vulnerability of an increasingly influential branch of feminist thought. Under the sway of thinkers like Carol Gilligan, a significant part of the feminist community had begun to emphasize exactly what Rosenberg had underlined in the Sears trial: the differences between men and women. Feminists in law, like feminists in other fields, often spoke of the two sexes as though they inhabited different universes. "Male and female perceptions of value are not shared, and are perhaps not even perceptible to each other," wrote University of New Mexico law professor Ann C. Scales. As Scales saw it, the values of women, being closer to "law's soul" and "law's duty" than those of men, should supplant the values of men.[4] Through the 1980s and into the 1990s, this gender-conscious approach continued to be an important part of feminist legal thinking. University of Chicago law professor Mary Becker argued that men were more comfortable than women with the formal requirements of contract law ("insisting that every 'i' be dotted and every 't' crossed"). Becker also maintained that men were more attuned than women to the notion of abstract rights that contract law emphasizes. "Under a more 'feminine' notion of justice," said Becker, "decision-making would be based . . . more on notions of connection, responsibility, and interdependence in a particular context."[5] Law professor Lani Guinier of the University of Pennsylvania argued that law schools need to be feminized. As they are, she maintained, they emphasize intellectual combat, a kind of competition that women often find alien; and in a law review article, she and several co-authors recommended that law schools "reconsider the value of the dominant pedagogy and the accompanying emphasis on adversarialism that presently permeates legal education."[6]

Feminists continued to pursue the idea of difference, but lurking behind their arguments was the problem that had surfaced in the Sears case: Emphasizing male/female difference might not always advance feminist interests. It was a dilemma that continued to vex— except for those who took the way out proposed by law professor Catharine MacKinnon. She resolved the problem by positing a new basis for legal differentiation between the sexes: male dominance rather than male/female difference.

Women live in a world dominated by men, MacKinnon argued. Their lives are dictated by male hegemony, "the most pervasive and tenacious system of power in history."[7] So complete is male dominance, MacKinnon claimed, that men define reality; and the purpose of law, she declared, was "to challenge and change" the world they had constructed. When that had been accomplished, when the foot of man had been removed from the neck of woman (to use a MacKinnon metaphor), then it would be time to talk about fundamental differences between men and women. Then, declared MacKinnon, "We will hear in what tongue women speak."[8]

This strategic shift allowed MacKinnon to argue for a gender-conscious law just as feminists who emphasized male/female difference did, but without the danger to feminist interests. Whenever women's differences from men resulted in the kind of choices seen in the Sears case, those differences should be seen as a product of male hegemony, whether or not the women involved saw it that way. If women choose less competitive positions than men, it is because male dominance creates a reality that encourages them to do so. Any employer—or so the argument goes—that participates in that reality, rather than trying to change it, is discriminating against women.

For purposes of restructuring society as feminists think it should be restructured, dominance theory offers a clear advantage; but it also requires an enormous amount of upkeep. With its claim that all of reality has been structured by men, it is all-encompassing. It has to be able to show male structuring in every aspect of experience—not only in the workplace, but also in the most deeply personal aspects of life. Sexual relations, in particular, have to be shown to be about inequality, about men having their way and women being forced to go along. Many women claim to enter sexual relations freely and to find pleasure in sex; but according to MacKinnon, what most of them are really enjoying is their own subordination.[9] Those who disagree with her on this—or, indeed, on any point—are, MacKinnon claims, simply misunderstanding their own experience.[10]

MacKinnon often works at the task of establishing the universality of her theory rhetorically. In describing the victimization of women, for example, she uses the pronoun "you" in a way that includes every female reading her words or listening to them. Thus, she begins a book published in 1993:

> You grow up with your father holding you down and covering your mouth so another man can make a horrible searing pain between your legs. When you are older, your husband ties you to the bed and drips hot wax on your nipples and brings in other men to watch and makes you smile through it. Your doctor will not give you drugs he has addicted you to unless you suck his penis.[11]

Characteristic of MacKinnon's work, this passage is a good example of the subjectivity that feminists who emphasize male/female differences say is natural to women, but too little valued in a male-dominated world. Andrea Dworkin, with whom MacKinnon frequently collaborates, is given to the same kind of specificity when she describes relations between men and women. "You exist," she told an audience in Chicago, "in order for him to wipe his penis on you."[12]

But dominance theory, by deferring such questions as whether objectivity is gender-linked, keeps all rhetorical possibilities open. Without being inconsistent, one can offer statistics as well as emotional accounts; and MacKinnon frequently does—though they are statistics of a most subjective kind. One database on which she has frequently drawn was compiled by Diana E. H. Russell in 1978. It consists of interviews with 930 randomly selected women in San Francisco. After interviewing the women at length (at least one interview lasted over eight hours), researchers concluded that 44 percent of the women had experienced either rape or attempted rape. They reached this conclusion even though *only* 22 percent responded in the affirmative when asked directly, "At any time in your life, have you ever been the victim of rape or attempted rape?"[13]

Interviewers with an expansive definition of rape decided whether or not those whom they were interviewing had been raped, a method that resulted in dramatic numbers; and they would become more dramatic still when MacKinnon used them. In one speech, the 44 percent from Russell's survey is transformed into "nearly half" of all women being the victims of rape or attempted rape. There is no mention of methodology nor any indication to the audience that the research was limited to one urban area in California. Instead, the impression left is that these are national statistics rather than local ones.[14]

So impressed was MacKinnon by Russell's survey that she asked the California researcher to derive from her data a figure indicating how many women had experienced "rape or other sexual abuse or harassment . . . noncontact as well as contact, from gang rape by strangers to obscene phone calls, unwanted sexual advances on the street, unwelcome requests to pose for pornography, and subjection to peeping Toms and sexual exhibitionists (flashers)."[15] So all-inclusive was the list, ranging as it did from wolf whistles to rape, that Russell reported only 7.8 percent of women had never experienced any of these things. In MacKinnon's hands, at a Harvard speech in 1984, this became "only 7.8 percent of women have never been sexually assaulted." Given the manipulations involved in such a statement, the context for it is particularly ironic: "Now why," MacKinnon asked, "are these basic realities of the subordination of women to men, for example, that only 7.8 percent of women have never been sexually assaulted, not effectively believed, not perceived as real in the face of all this evidence?"[16]

Establishing the victimhood of women and keeping it in the forefront is crucial in order to justify giving the cause of women precedence over the causes of other groups. President Clinton heralded the Violence Against Women Act, which became law as part of the 1994 Crime Bill, with dramatic statistics that are often cited by women's advocates. "The FBI estimates that a woman is beaten in this country once every twelve seconds," the president claimed. "Domestic violence," he said, "is now the number one health risk for women between the ages of fifteen and forty-four." When Ann Devroy of the *Washington Post* pointed out that some experts questioned such statistics, the White House admitted it could not substantiate the claim about the FBI estimate—and Devroy received angry calls from feminists. It was, she said, the most "abusive" reaction she had experienced "since John Sununu yelled at me on the White House lawn." A subsequent story in the *Post* pointed out that the figure about domestic violence being the number one health risk came from a study too small to have statistical significance.[17]

The president was not the only one to stumble in talking about the Violence Against Women Act. This legislation gives crimes of violence based on gender an added dimension so that they are not only assaults but also civil rights violations; and when Senator Orrin Hatch of Utah, a co-sponsor of the bill, tried to explain the difference between a rape based on lust, which, though a crime, would not be a civil rights violation, and a rape based on gender animus, which would be both, Eleanor Smeal of the Fund for a Feminist Majority castigated the senator's efforts as "ridiculous." "Rape is never an act of lust," she said. To feminists who think this way, rape is always an act of power, part of the system by which all men oppress all women, and the Violence Against Women Act codifies this view. By defining rape and other crimes against women not just as horrible offenses committed by some individuals against others but as a method employed by men to keep women from fully enjoying their status as citizens, the Act writes into law the theories of Catharine MacKinnon and Andrea Dworkin—a development that Dworkin found somewhat amazing. "The only possible explanation for it," she said, "is that senators don't understand the meaning of the legislation they pass."[18]

Grossly exaggerating the plight of women is also useful for justifying other changes in the law, such as those pertaining to free speech. MacKinnon and Dworkin use the theory of male dominance and female subordination to argue for increased censorship. They base their case on an expansive definition of pornography. It is, they say, "the graphic sexually explicit subordination of women." Writes MacKinnon:

> Pornography is not harmless fantasy or a corrupt and confused misrepresentation of an otherwise natural and healthy sexuality. Along with the rape and prostitution in which it participates, pornography institutionalizes the sexuality of male supremacy, which fuses the erotization of dominance and submission with the social construction of male and female.[19]

On the grounds that pornography helps construct the reality in which men dominate, it becomes a practice of sex discrimination, a violation of women's civil rights. Legislation based on this idea has been proposed at the local, state, and national levels. In 1985, in Indianapolis, Indiana, an ordinance inspired by MacKinnon and Dworkin actually became law for a time before it was overturned by a court of appeals. In 1992, a bill embodying their theory passed out of the U.S. Senate Judiciary Committee, but was never voted on by the full Senate. MacKinnon and Dworkin's most important victory has been in Canada where the Supreme Court has embraced their definition of pornography. In 1992, upholding the conviction of a pornography store owner, the court declared, "If true equality between male and female persons is to be achieved, we cannot ignore the threat to equality resulting from exposure to audiences of certain types of violent and degrading material."[20]

Commenting on the Canadian decision, MacKinnon, who had filed a brief with the court, made clear her disdain for the principle of free expression. The Canadian court's deliberations occasioned none of the "free speech litany" invariably used to counter efforts at censorship in the United States, she observed; nor was there any of the nonsense about "the marketplace of ideas" that Justice Oliver Wendell Holmes, Jr., espoused. Declared MacKinnon:

> Maybe in Canada, people talk to each other, rather than buy and sell each other as ideas. In an equality context, it becomes obvious that those with the most power buy the most speech, and that the marketplace rewards the powerful, whose views then become established as truth. We were not subjected to "Let [Truth] and falsehood grapple; who ever knew Truth put to the worse, in a free and open encounter." Milton had not been around for the success of the Big Lie technique, but this Court had.[21]

MacKinnon is correct to note that the free and open competition of ideas does not always work perfectly. Sometimes, for a while, the Big Lie does prevail; but not so often or long in a free society as in a totalitarian regime, where competing ideas are suppressed. It was Hitler, after all, a dictator who seldom allowed truth and falsehood to grapple, who gave us the concept of the Big Lie—and plentiful examples of it.

In going after what they consider to be the Big Lie—namely, the male version of reality—MacKinnon and Dworkin often sound like tyrants themselves, Big Sisters so certain of their views that they are anxious to impose them on everyone else. Under their regime, not only would magazines and films that might be widely agreed to be pornography be banned, so would works of art such as William

Butler Yeats's poem "Leda and the Swan," which clearly and graph-
ically depicts the sexual subordination of a woman. Also at risk
would be one of the most famous works of Artemisia Gentileschi, a
seventeenth-century painter of great interest to twentieth-century
feminists not only for her talent but also because of a trial in which
her teacher was charged with raping her. Gentileschi's *Susanna
and the Elders* shows two men conspiring in the degradation of a
young, naked woman and thus would qualify for banning. This is a
price that MacKinnon is perfectly willing to pay. "If a woman is
subjected, why should it matter that the work has other value?" she
asks.[22]

Some feminists oppose MacKinnon's and Dworkin's efforts. Susan
Estrich, Betty Friedan, and Adrienne Rich were among those who
filed a court brief opposing the Indianapolis ordinance that MacKinnon and Dworkin helped bring about. But MacKinnon is undeterred
("House niggers who sided with the masters," she has reportedly
called feminists who oppose her);[23] and within the community of
legal academicians, pro-censorship forces inspired by her seem to be
growing. A 1993 conference held at the University of Chicago, sponsored by the MacArthur Foundation, and starring MacKinnon and
Dworkin, brought together more than a thousand legal scholars and
activists to discuss not *whether* there should be incursions on the
principle of free expression in order to end practices like pornography, but *how* most effectively to bring those incursions about. The
time has ended, Dworkin declared, for dealing with materials that
subordinate women in the way that a "liberal political culture" usually does: that is, through reason and persuasion. "We're not trying
to convince them," Dworkin told her audience. "We're trying to
move society around so that they have to change or die."[24]

One might expect such ideas to be coolly received in a law school
setting; but instead, as a sign of the times, they were cheered. Nadine
Strossen, president of the American Civil Liberties Union, notes that
the unanimity of opinion exhibited at the Chicago conference is not
unusual.[25] Andrew J. Kleinfeld, circuit judge of the Ninth Circuit
Court of Appeals, writes that "groups holding considerable power"

in the nation's law schools "loathe speech with the wrong content about topics important to them." The result, says Kleinfeld, is "an infusion into the legal system of personnel who have learned to devalue [freedom of speech]."[26] The growing favor with which censorship is regarded in law schools, where the next generation of judges and litigators is being trained, may well foreshadow changes in American law about what citizens can read or watch or say.

Indeed, in one area, MacKinnon has already effected a change. She has been a primary force—*the* primary force, many would say—in broadening the definition of sexual harassment so that it includes more than *quid pro quo* behavior (such as the demand for sexual favors in exchange for advancement in a job). In a key case brought before the U.S. Supreme Court in 1986, MacKinnon was part of a team arguing that sexual harassment also includes the creation of a "hostile" work environment. The Court decided in *Meritor Savings Bank, FSB v. Mechelle Vinson et al.* that an "abusive work environment" could be actionable under Title VII of the Civil Rights Act. The Court used words like "severe" and "pervasive" in describing what would constitute a hostile environment[27] and reaffirmed in a 1993 decision that sexual harassment is more than merely offensive behavior, but lower courts have allowed a wide range of conduct to fall within the definition of what can constitute a hostile environment.

In *Robinson v. Jacksonville Shipyards, Inc.*, a Florida judge found in favor of the female plaintiff, a welder, who described a "visual assault" on her sensibilities caused not only by numerous pinup calendars, photographs, and grafitti of nude and seminude women around the shipyard, but also by "a magazine containing pictures of nude and partially nude women in the possession of a pipefitter . . . who was reading it in the engine room of a ship." As evidence of the pervasiveness of the harassing behavior, the court cited the testimony of a female machinist who testified not only to "comments, pictures, public humiliation and touching by male coworkers and supervisors," but to "men's adult magazines, such as *Playboy, Penthouse, Cheri, Chic,* and foreign titles, kept in trailers and carried by male employees in their back pockets." By basing its ruling of sexual harassment on "the totality of the circumstances" at the shipyard, the court left open the possibility that simply possessing or looking at a men's magazine in the workplace is harassing behavior.[28] It seemed for a time that the Supreme Court might deal with the issues raised in this case, but it was settled in 1995, leaving unanswered many questions about what does and does not go into the creation of a hostile environment.

In another case, *Tunis v. Corning Glass Works*, a New York district court found against the plaintiff, but only because the company had responded so swiftly to her complaints of nude pictures of women in the workplace. The company manager had even ordered a post-card taped to the inside cover of a maintenance employee's toolbox removed. Management was also sympathetic and responsive to her complaints about other employees using job descriptions like "tank man" and "cullet man" that were not gender neutral.[29] As Kingsley Browne, a law professor at Wayne State University, notes, the court's decision in this case leaves open the possibility that the use of words such as "foreman" and "draftsman" (rather than "foreperson" and "draftsperson"), in the absence of a strong employer response to complaints about them, is a violation of Title VII.[30]

Because sexual harassment law under Title VII can make employers liable for the speech and conduct of their employees, and because there are no constitutional constraints on what a private entity can do to regulate speech (the First Amendment constrains only the public sector), the result of cases such as these is a chilling effect of considerable magnitude. Writes Kingsley Browne:

> The employer receives little gratification from its employees' free speech, but it faces litigation costs and damage awards if its efforts to regulate such speech are deemed inadequate. The rational employer, therefore, does not prohibit merely the expression of actually prohibited language; it prohibits, and punishes, all expression that could even arguably be viewed as impermissible.[31]

The rational employer will also institute training aimed at increasing employee sensitivity on issues of gender and race. Thoughtfully presented, such training has a contribution to make not only to an enlightened workplace, but to the financial well-being of companies that must operate in an increasingly diverse society. But all too often, training sessions are not thoughtful. They deal in stereotypes about gender: "Women tend to manage by consensus and men by hierarchy," says one manager quoted in a packet of diversity materials.[32] And training sessions deal in stereotypes about race. Diversity consultant Dianne Sutton has a chart listing Anglo-American characteristics on one side and those of "other ethnocultural groups" on the other. Anglos seek "mastery over nature," while others seek "harmony with nature." Anglos like "competition" and practice "materialism," while others prefer "cooperation" and "spiritualism/detachment."[33] Everything bad comes to be associated with those who are male and those who are white, and the result is not a peaceable kingdom. Writer Andrew Ferguson, who attended a Washington, D.C., diversity workshop, reports one facilitator's comments:

> Sharing power is not something a male-dominated culture naturally gravitates towards, is it? . . . Sometimes force is necessary. If more won't do this on their own, then a force situation *will* become necessary.[34]

A white male administrator in an Ohio sheriff's office left a training session run by a white female and two black males feeling he had been blamed "for everything from slavery to the glass ceiling." Said the administrator, "I became bitter and remain so."[35] At a California utility, a number of senior executives stormed out of a diversity training session when as part of a simulation exercise they were instructed to sit on the floor so they could experience what it was like to be part of an "oppressed group."[36]

We have in the United States arrived at a consensus that racial and sexual harassment are wrong, and we should take great pride in having advanced to this conclusion. But in trying to make the workplace harassment-free, we often proceed in ways that exacerbate tensions of race and gender. The problem seems obvious: If our goal is to get employees to stop using race and gender to humiliate and disparage one another, then we cannot start by using race and gender in humiliating and disparaging ways.

And there is another, even more important point. We will not achieve either an enlightened workplace or an enlightened society if in the process of trying to do so we violate overarching principles—such as the principle of free speech—that have served us well. Robert Bolt makes this point in his play *A Man for All Seasons* when he has Sir Thomas More, the play's protagonist, describe the dangers of destroying agreed-upon laws in order to accomplish a certain end. "What would you do?" he asks William Roper, "Cut a great road through the law to get after the Devil?"

ROPER: I'd cut down every law in England to do that.

MORE: Oh? And when the last law was down—and the Devil turned round on you—where would you hide, Roper, the laws all being flat? . . . D'you really think you could stand upright in the winds that would blow then?[37]

An apt illustration of More's point occurred in January 1993 when Canadian customs seized two books on the grounds of obscenity. Both were by Andrea Dworkin.

る

Like many activists on campus today, Catharine MacKinnon disdains deconstruction as self-indulgent, politically useless intellectual activity;[38] but like those activists, she nonetheless owes a great deal to the deconstructionists and other French theorists of the 1960s who introduced into contemporary conversation ideas on which she depends: that reality is indeterminate; that what is real is only what the powerful say is real; that a redeployment of power can result in a redeployment of reality.

These ideas are set forth in their purest form in critical legal studies (CLS), a movement utterly familiar to anyone who knows Derrida or Foucault—or to anyone who has spent time in an English Department lately. Cutting-edge views in the humanities have so influenced this approach to law that one finds English professors quoted as authorities in books associated with CLS—and even invited onto law school faculties. According to his *curriculum vitae*, Stanley Fish's degrees are in English; but since 1985, he has been not only a professor of English but also a professor of law at Duke University, teaching courses ranging from Contracts to Twentieth-Century Legal Theory. Conversely, law professors can occasionally be found in English classrooms, though probably studying more often than teaching. A professor at Harvard Law School explained why he was auditing a literature course this way: "More and more lawyers these days recognize that law can be read the way one reads literature, and they are using works of literature and the techniques of modern literary theory to explain and analyze their subject."[39] The law, in other words, is no more definitive than a poem or play. Indeed, one of the primary purposes of CLS is to destroy any illusions that might exist about stability and objectivity in the law by deconstructing its arguments.

Insofar as the practitioners of CLS focus simply on destabilizing the law (or "trashing" it, to use a term some in CLS prefer), they are practicing Foucault's "relativism without recourse."[40] They, like him, however, find a position of total nihilism hard to maintain, and their preferences quickly begin to come through: for horizontal organizations rather than hierarchical ones and for progressive rather than conservative thinking.[41]

The heirs of CLS, such as those in the critical race theory movement, take a giant step further. As feminists have done, critical race theorists not only attack the notion that law is disinterested, they advocate using the law to promote their own interests. The goal is not to make the law strive for neutrality (indeed, the whole idea of neutrality is thought to be a snare and delusion), but to change the law so that it takes race into account. Like Catharine MacKinnon, critical race theorists argue for removing the blindfold from Justice.

The vicissitudes of politics have made Lani Guinier the most famous of those associated with critical race theory. In writings that became widely publicized when President Clinton nominated her to head the Justice Department's Civil Rights Division, she proposed ways to restructure the voting process to ensure "authentic" black representatives (a black person elected with white votes would not be authentic).[42] She recommended that supermajorities be used in legislative decision-making in order to ensure a black legislative veto. She emphasized that equal opportunities were not sufficient: "Roughly equal outcomes, not merely an apparently fair process, are the goal."[43] Guinier claims that her views were and continue to be misrepresented, and it is true that the positions she advocates are less radical than those of the leading proponents of critical race theory. Nonetheless, her writings as they originally appeared leave the clear impression that it is not equality before the law regardless of race that she seeks, but legal and legislative systems so regardful of race that they parcel out results on that basis.

Critical race theory has many similarities to feminist legal theory. Just as Carol Gilligan and the law professors influenced by her argue for a distinctive female voice, so critical race theorists argue that there is "a voice of color." Indeed, the critical race theory movement had its origins at Harvard in the early 1980s when a white professor was assigned to teach a course in the law school on race relations. Inspired by the arguments of Professor Derrick Bell, who has maintained that there is a "special and quite valuable perspective on law and life in this country that a black person can provide,"[44] a group of students organized an alternative course in which academics of color were invited to lecture.

Mari J. Matsuda, one of the original participants in the alternative course and now a law professor at Georgetown University, has become the most prominent advocate of the "distinctive voice" theory; and she has expounded on this idea in a way that brings her to the same strategic ground that MacKinnon occupies: She locates the reason for distinctiveness in victimization. "Those who have experienced discrimination," Matsuda writes, "speak with a special voice."[45] If we listen to victims, if we hear their experiences, Matsuda maintains, we will understand the importance of using the law to advance their interests. Justifying this claim—just as justifying the claim that law should be used to advance the interests of women over men—requires seeing oppression everywhere. In an introduction to a recent book, *Words That Wound*, Matsuda and three other proponents of critical race theory write that a key element of their work is conceiving racism "not as isolated instances of conscious bigoted decisionmaking or prejudiced practice, but as larger, systemic, structural, and cultural, as deeply psychologically and socially ingrained."[46]

Richard Delgado, a law professor at the University of Colorado at Boulder and one of the leading figures in critical race theory, has written that in addition to substantive racism, in which nonwhite persons are treated as though they are actually inferior to whites, our society has periods of procedural racism:

> In these periods, there are fewer images, stories, and laws conveying the idea of black inferiority. That idea is banished, put underground. Instead, we promulgate narratives and rules that invalidate or handicap black claims. We erect difficult-to-satisfy standing requirements for civil rights cases, demand proof of intent, and insist on tight chains of causation. . . . We insist that remedies not endanger white well-being; "reverse discrimination" is given a wide berth. We elevate equality of opportunity over equality of result and reject statistical proof of lack of the former.
>
> There is change from one era to another, but the net quantum of racism remains exactly the same, obeying a melancholy Law of Racial Thermodynamics: Racism is neither created nor destroyed.[47]

None of the progress that has been made in the United States in the last thirty years, in other words, amounts to anything. There is as much racism today as there was then—and anyone who wishes evidence need only mark the words of those who argue against reverse discrimination or for equality of opportunity. They may not believe themselves to be advancing racist views, but that, to Delgado's way of thinking, merely reflects their naïveté. Just as Catharine MacKinnon and "dominance" feminists claim to understand the motives of individuals better than they do themselves, so, too, do Delgado and other critical race theorists.

Critical race theory has attracted its share of academic criticism. In a lengthy 1989 article, Randall L. Kennedy of Harvard Law School questioned the thesis of distinctive voice, noting that writers like Matsuda suggest "that victimization breeds certain intellectual and moral virtues" and that this generalization simply is not true in all instances. It is also unjustified, he wrote, to assume that all members of a racial group have the same experience—or respond the same way to the same experience. "My central objection to the claim of racial distinctiveness propounded by Professor Matsuda and others of like mind," he concluded, "can best be summarized by observing that it *stereotypes* scholars."[48]

In a 1993 article analyzing Lani Guinier's nomination and the subsequent White House withdrawal of it, Kennedy argued that many of the ideas currently being propounded on the left allowed Guinier's opponents to picture her views as more radical than they are. Wrote Kennedy:

All too many intellectuals on the left have loudly embraced, or quietly accepted, such notions as the claim that *nothing* substantial has changed in race relations since slavery, that the very idea of merit is a racist myth, that it is impossible for blacks to be racist, that it is better for orphaned black children to be raised in institutions than for them to be adopted by white adults, that only indifference to racial justice can explain refusals to censor speech hurtful to members of racial minority groups, that only racism can explain opposition to affirmative action.[49]

All of these ideas, Kennedy concludes, helped Guinier's opponents fuel anxieties about her nomination.

Despite such criticism, the ideas of critical race theorists have had an impact, most notably in providing a rationale for restricting speech. Like feminists of the MacKinnon/Dworkin school, critical race theorists claim that allowing people to express themselves freely helps perpetuate society's inequalities. Institutions that do not restrict the kind of speech that conveys messages of inferiority toward racially oppressed groups are, as critical race theorists see it, guilty of discriminating against those groups. In at least one of its forms, this argument results in a double standard of immense proportion. While restraining the speech of dominant group members, it would leave members of historically oppressed groups—such as Professor Leonard Jeffries of the City College of New York or Khalid Abdul Muhammad, Louis Farrakhan's deputy, free to propagate hate speech. "Hateful verbal attacks upon dominant-group members by victims is permissible," Mari Matsuda writes.[50]

A recent survey showed more than a third of public colleges and universities have speech codes.[51] Numerous challenges have been brought to these codes, some with notable success. The University of Michigan's and the University of Wisconsin's speech codes were found to constitute First Amendment violations. The University of Pennsylvania decided to do away with its speech code after the "water buffalo" case, which I discuss in Chapter 2, received negative national attention. The speech code at Stanford University was struck down by a California court.

But in spite of all this and in spite of a 1992 U.S. Supreme Court ruling that abusive expressions cannot be selectively punished according to the topic they take up, the impulse to censor speech on the basis of its content remains strong. The latest effort, undertaken by the U.S. Department of Education, draws inspiration from Catharine MacKinnon's notion of "hostile environment" as well as from critical race theorists. Instead of going after speech directly, the department announced on March 10, 1994, that when investigating discrimination, it would look for "a racially hostile environment— i.e., harassing conduct (e.g., physical, verbal, graphic, or written)." The announcement set forth various ways in which the department would determine whether an environment is hostile. One is that harassment must be "severe, pervasive or persistent," but another requires only that the harassment adversely affect "the enjoyment of some aspect of the recipient's educational program [in the view of] a reasonable person, of the same age and race as the victim." The latter requirement, specifically linking judgment to race, represents the kind of thinking that has come to characterize critical race theory. Instead of everyone having a single standard, each victimized group will determine when there is discrimination; and whether or not anyone outside the group thinks the complaint is justified is of no consequence at all. The Department of Education's announcement also holds a college or university responsible for hostile environment no matter who might be guilty of harassment ("a teacher, a student, the grounds crew, a cafeteria worker, neighborhood teenagers, a visiting baseball team, a guest speaker, parents, or others") and thus comes close to mandating that institutions of higher education promulgate restrictions on expression for anyone who sets foot on campus—not as a First Amendment matter, since those efforts have been discredited, but in order to discourage harassment.[52]

The suppression of speech on campus has received a great deal of attention—much more than the suppression of speech in the workplace, although the latter is at least as severe as the former.[53] Kingsley Browne suggests that elitism is the explanation:

It is difficult to avoid the conclusion that some who would protect the speech of students and faculty but not the speech of workers possess an elitist perspective that simply values the former group of speakers more than the latter. The lack of value of the speech of workers seems to be based upon one or more of the following opinions: (1) when workers speak they do not convey ideas; (2) ideas are not important to workers; (3) the ideas of workers are not important to us.[54]

There is a slightly softer conclusion that one might draw about why the suppression of workplace speech has occasioned so little outcry, which is that those whom our society expects to cry out—intellectuals and journalists—simply are not very familiar with worklife in the bank or shipyard or factory. They write about the workplaces they know, the campus and the newsroom—which is one off-campus workplace that has received significant attention. When the *Los Angeles Times* put out nineteen pages of "Guidelines on Ethnic, Racial, Sexual and Other Identification," columnists across the country wrote about the newspaper banning words such as *crazy* ("vague and stigmatizing," the *Times* declared) or *gyp* (offensive to gypsies).[55] When a *Boston Globe* reporter was fined $1,250 for using a crude phrase for *henpecked* in conversation with a male colleague (a woman reporter nearby overheard and objected), his travails were reported by publications as diverse as *The New Yorker* and *National Review*.[56] Eventually the *Globe*'s management rescinded the fine. Articles have also appeared about the anxiety that white males feel in the many newsrooms where there are now preferences for hiring and promoting minorities and women.[57]

ße

Justice wears her blindfold so that neither race nor sex makes a difference. The aim is equal treatment no matter who we are. I do not mean for a moment to suggest that this has always happened. Our history is replete with instances of injustice, with examples of minorities and women receiving different treatment from the majority group and men. Imperfect as we are, we may never be able to establish a rule of law that is always and ever indifferent to race and gender, but it should be our goal. And we made admirable progress toward it with the Civil Rights Act of 1964, which reads in part:

> It shall be an unlawful employment practice for an employer—(1) to fail or refuse to hire or to discharge any individual or otherwise to discriminate against any individual with respect to his compensation, terms, conditions, or privileges of employment, because of such individual's race, color, religion, sex, or national origin.

But in the thirty years since the original civil rights legislation, we have managed again and again to turn it on its head, to move from trying to make race and gender not count to giving them a position of preeminence. Examples abound across society, but there is a particularly dramatic one from the schools of Cincinnati. Because of enormous discipline problems, the school district introduced a new discipline code that allowed administrators to suspend students whose disruptive and violent behavior was making education impossible for everyone. Teachers overwhelmingly supported the new policy, and so, according to a poll, did the public,[58] but it had to be abandoned when it turned out that there were racial disparities among those disciplined. A court settlement that went into effect in January 1995 requires that records be kept of the race and gender of students being suspended and the race and gender of the teachers recommending them for discipline. The records will be considered when decisions are made about which teachers are to be retained and promoted and which are to be let go. Albert Shanker, president of the American Federation of Teachers, points out the questions raised by this settlement:

> Will it be OK for a black teacher to refer a black child for disciplinary action but not for a white teacher—even if it's for the same offense? . . . Will kids of different races who break the same rules be dealt with differently? Might a quota system be set up that establishes how many kids in different race groups can be disciplined for a given offense in a given year?[59]

Both Democrats and Republicans have moved us away from gender-blind, race-blind law,[60] but the Clinton administration has attempted to do so in unprecedented ways. The health care proposal that the president sent to the Congress in 1993, for example, would have resulted in much sought-after slots for training for medical specialists being parceled out on the basis of race. Exactly how many members of each racial and ethnic group would be allowed to become specialists would be determined by the degree to which that group is "under-represented" not only among medical specialists but also in the field of medicine generally. In 1990, Asians and Pacific

Islanders comprised only 3 percent of the population, but 11 percent of those in the field of medicine. Thus, because of race, it would be very difficult for someone of Asian or Pacific Islander heritage to be accepted for specialist training.[61]

The idea so common on campuses, that individual merit should give way to group entitlement, has now become commonplace in Washington. On a single day on a single page of the *Washington Post*, two stories were reported. The first explained that the reason for the delay in filling positions at the Equal Employment Opportunity Commission was that the administration was looking for a Hispanic—specifically a Puerto Rican—to head the EEOC and an Asian to serve as vice chair. The second story reported on a memo that Roger Kennedy, head of the National Park Service, sent in an effort to find a job for one John Trevor. After listing Trevor's assets, Kennedy wrote, "Unfortunately, Mr. Trevor is white, which is too bad."[62] On the same day that these stories appeared in the *Washington Post*, the *Chronicle of Higher Education* reported a change at the Department of Education that would permit colleges and universities to award "race-exclusive" scholarships to some minorities but not others. According to the new policy, there could be scholarships for African-American or Hispanic students but probably not for students of Armenian or Italian descent.[63] The dubious constitutionality of this policy and others based on race was underscored when in May 1995, the U.S. Supreme Court let stand a lower-court ruling that a scholarship program intended only for African-Americans was unconstitutional.

Because our society has had a long history of denying opportunities to persons of color and women, it is reasonable to think that special efforts might be required before we achieve a time when equality before the law translates into true equality. But it is one thing to cast an employment or college recruitment net widely—and to ask sharp questions about whether it has really been cast widely enough if time and again women and minorities fail to appear in it—and quite another to place certain employment and educational opportunities off-limits to certain races. Jack Nelson, the head of the

Washington bureau of the *Los Angeles Times*, is reported to have declared that he will bring no more white males into the bureau on the grounds that there are too many of them and too few minorities and women.[64] What else is this but a violation of the spirit, if not the letter, of the original civil rights legislation that made it unlawful to refuse to hire someone on the basis of that individual's race or sex?

The reason that Martin Luther King, Jr.'s, "I Have a Dream" speech appeals so universally is that it, like the original civil rights legislation, puts individuals in charge of their lives. They are to be judged by the content of their character—by whether they work hard and persevere, by whether they are honest and trustworthy. They are to be judged by things that are in their control—rather than by factors like race and gender over which they have no control. In any frank discussion, the practices described above—setting aside jobs or scholarships for certain races or regarding an individual's race as "unfortunate" when he is seeking employment—arouse indignation because they put individuals at a disadvantage for which there is no remedy. One's fate comes to depend on accidents of birth.

But frank discussions of these issues have become more and more difficult. Such is the temper of our times that anyone who brings up these issues risks being branded racist and sexist. The critical race theorists who wrote *Words That Wound*, for example, equate debate over affirmative action with "an emerging and increasingly virulent backlash" against women and people of color. "The code words of this backlash," they write, "are words like merit, rigor, standards, qualifications, and excellence."[65]

In Chapter 2, I pointed out how risky it can be for undergraduates to express doubt about ideas such as affirmative action. In law schools, this phenomenon is also pronounced. On certain issues, says Provost Geoffrey Stone of the University of Chicago, "Anyone who disagrees or raises doubts runs the risk of being thought of as racist or sexist or homophobic."[66] He or she is also likely to be booed and hissed. "It happens an awful lot," says a New York University law student:

When the subject [of affirmative action] arose in my constitutional law class, a few students raised questions concerning its validity and constitutionality. These students were almost immediately attacked—being hissed in the classroom, and later, away from class, by being called "fascist," "racist," or "Nazi."[67]

In a 1991 survey conducted through the American Bar Association's General Practice Section, 60 percent of the student respondents stated that there were professors at their law schools who did not tolerate beliefs that differed from their own. Fifty-one percent of the students said that they did not feel free to register disagreement with their professors' political perspectives either in class or on examinations or papers. While a few of the students surveyed felt that their professors weren't sufficiently sympathetic to feminist causes, it was for the most part "politically incorrect" views that they reported they did not dare discuss, believing that if they did they were likely to be graded down or publicly humiliated. Wrote one student, "Rather than engaging in a dispassionate examination of the issues at hand, [some professors] often will engage in what amounts to gross personal attacks on the moral character and integrity of the person with whom they disagree."[68] Concluded Steven C. Bahls, then at the University of Montana Law School, who conducted the survey, "Law schools would do well to attack the problem of intolerance with the same vigor with which they attacked the lack of gender diversity and the lack of racial and cultural diversity."[69]

The fact that law schools have become places where students are afraid to express their views on certain issues is deeply troubling not only for people who believe in free speech, but for those who believe that education is incomplete unless a variety of arguments is heard and a diversity of approaches considered. When legal education becomes narrow, it is clearly cause for concern.

And when legal education becomes nonexistent, one begins to despair about the future. Both feminist legal theory and critical race theory are changing the pedagogy of law schools in ways that make the law itself irrelevant. Since the corpus of the law is constructed on outmoded notions like objectivity and rationality, there is little point in making that corpus the subject of the classroom—or so the thinking goes. Instead, the classroom should be used to help students value subjectivity, intuition, and the knowledge that comes from personal experience. One law review article describes a required course in introduction to law at the University of New Mexico that begins with the singing of a Woody Guthrie song. Write the professors who invented the course:

> Song defies the voice of domination—the voice that affirms its version of reality as reality, its way of knowing as knowledge, its way of being in the world as human destiny. . . .
> Song liberates what we have repressed. . . .
> To law's message of hierarchy, song answers with all the regenerative power of trust in human creativity.
> So we sing because we want this class to *be* a song. . . . We want this machine to kill the fascist in us.[70]

In another law review article, a professor at Osgoode Hall Law School in Canada describes his attempt to turn a course on legal research and writing ("a paradigm of training for hierarchy") into a class on sexual politics. His device was to have the class debate over a period of weeks whether or not the film *9½ Weeks* was pornographic according to Andrea Dworkin's and Catharine MacKinnon's definition and further to decide if it was necessary to see the movie in order to judge it. Although the vast majority of the students who expressed an opinion said the movie should be shown, the professor, concerned with the minority who believed that showing the film would "threaten any security and trust that women might have felt they had within the law school community," chose not to show it and instead to have a discussion of the issues led by Catharine MacKinnon. Sensitivity is not always rewarded, however, particularly when displayed by a member of a dominant group. In an ironic turn of events, several women in the class sought counseling at the school's sexual harassment center for the "high level of pressure" they had experienced "from dealing with an assignment based on pornography," and the professor was warned that should a similar situation occur, a sexual harassment investigation would be called.[71]

Consciousness-raising is a common activity in law courses taught by feminists and critical race theorists, and the primary vehicle for accomplishing it is the personal narrative. Students are encouraged to tell their stories whether or not they relate to the material at hand. Professors join in, telling their own stories in order to emphasize the personal, the subjective, the nonhierarchical. Victimization is a favored theme because, as a feminist group from DePaul University College of Law writes, "We need to uncover and identify our oppression before we can begin to combat it."[72]

Many law students wish to learn the law; and when instead they learn about the personal experiences of their professors and classmates, they sometimes complain. In her book *The Alchemy of Race and Rights*, law professor Patricia J. Williams, then at the University of Wisconsin, describes a class in which she told stories of her encounters with homeless people. After the class, Williams reports:

> My students rush to the dean to complain. They are not learning real law, they say, and they want someone else to give them remedial classes. How will they ever pass the bar with subway stories?

The dean warns Williams that her teaching style is "inappropriate," but apparently to little effect since at the end of the year student after student complains that what she is teaching is "not law." Williams is comforted, however, by two students who see the complaints as racist and sexist, as having to do "with the perceived preposterousness of the authority that I, as the first black woman ever to have taught at this particular institution, symbolically and imagistically bring to bear in and out of the classroom." Writes Williams, "That, I tell them in a grateful swell of unscholarly emotionalism, feels like truth to me."[73]

When Derrick Bell, the inspirational spirit of critical race theory and a man who is famous for his classroom parables and tales,

141

taught an introductory course in constitutional law at Stanford in 1986, students complained they were not learning the subject and began auditing other classes. These circumstances led to a series of public lectures on constitutional law, but it was quickly called off when the Black Students Law Association deemed the dissatisfied students and the lecture series racist. Their interpretation was accepted widely, including by Bell himself, who seemed to have forgotten that five years earlier, students he had inspired had boycotted a course taught by a white professor and organized the lecture series that gave birth to critical race theory.

As postmodern thinking has moved the law away from principles to redefine it in terms of group power, our fate has become less the result of what we do and more of who we are—a situation that ought not to give anyone much comfort. Former City College professor Kenneth B. Clark recently explained to the *New York Times* that to try to remedy the exclusion of blacks by providing preferential treatment that has the result of excluding whites is to promote the idea of exclusion—and thus to make us all vulnerable. "I am afraid of exclusions," Clark said. "And I'm afraid of exclusions, of blacks or whites."[74] In law, as in other aspects of civic life, we can feel secure in the future only to the extent that we know that the same principles will apply to all of us—no matter the group to which we belong.

*ठ** *Chapter Five*

Museums, Moving Images, and False Memories

'Just pronounce the magic word 'art,' and everything is OK. Rotting corpses with snails crawling over them are OK; kicking little girls on the head is OK."

—*George Orwell, "Benefit of Clergy: Some Notes on Salvador Dali"*

THE progress of postmodernism can be seen in a range of institutions, from museums, to cinema, and even including the practice of therapy. It accounts for many of the grotesqueries of our time, including those recently encountered by visitors to the New Museum of Contemporary Art in New York City:

• A painting by Sue Williams entitled *Try to be more accommodating* that showed penises being inserted into a woman's eyes, ears, nose, and mouth.

• A large color photograph of a doll of Jasmine from the movie *Aladdin* being stuffed up a man's crotch so that his testicles draped around the doll's head like a turban. The photograph was entitled *Jasmine Swami*.

• A wall arrangement of seven hundred varnished bars of soap, each of which had a crude word or phrase (*cunt* was one of the least objectionable) painted on it.

The New Museum has a reputation for trying to shock. Its director, Marcia Tucker, talks about it as a countercultural institution,
bent on throwing "a grenade into the idea of exhibitions."[1] But even
august and venerable museums now sometimes have an edge of
anti-culture to them. Consider what visitors to the Smithsonian
Institution have encountered:

- Etiquette of the Undercaste, an installation entered by lying
down on a morgue drawer. The exhibit attacked the American
belief in upward mobility by portraying poor people striving to
enter the American middle class as misguided fools who had
bought into a myth benefiting white male elites. At a discussion
held in conjunction with the exhibit, a panelist called on artists
to "belong to activist organizations . . . [and] develop forms
that are appropriate vehicles for revolutionary ideas."[2]

- In the Museum of Natural History, a cage holding two "un-
discovered aborigines," a male wearing a feathered headdress
and leather boots and a female with face-painting, a grass skirt,
and black sneakers. Urged on by docents stationed near the
cage, museum visitors asked for native dances and stories from
the pair—which resulted in listless swaying and lengthy gib-
berish. The so-called aborigines were actually performance artists making a comment about Western cultural imperialism—a
point that the Washington Post reported escaped many museum
visitors.[3]

Museums used to be places that invited visitors to learn about
great works of art, to understand their society, and to know more
about the course of history. Today, like so many other cultural
institutions, they are apt instead to be in the business of debunking
greatness, Western society, and even history itself. This has come
about partly because of a recognition that what has in the past gone
on in museums has often been flawed. The idea of greatness was
associated mostly with men of European descent. The roles played

by women and minorities in history were often ignored. In 1992, installation artist Fred Wilson created an exhibit at the Maryland Historical Society that made this point very skillfully. One part of his display was a gray room with a silver trophy labeled "TRUTH" at its center. On the right side of the trophy were three white marble pedestals with busts atop them of Andrew Jackson, Henry Clay, and Napoleon Bonaparte. On the left side were black marble pedestals, empty except for labels bearing the names of Harriet Tubman, Benjamin Banneker, and Frederick Douglass. As the empty pedestals most eloquently indicated, museums have often missed the truth of our society's complex heritage.

Unfortunately, many museum professionals, under the sway of ideas current in the academic community, have leaped from this observation to the conclusion that there is no such thing as truth. Consider how the staff of the Maryland Historical Society saw Fred Wilson's gray room. In a handout given to the exhibit's visitors, they explained:

> People often come to historical museums looking for the "truth" about history. By putting the Advertising Clubs' "truth trophy" on display and surrounding it with empty plastic mounts, the artist is ironically questioning this attitude. After all, doesn't everyone interpret history in his own individual way?[4]

In this view, there is no truth (indeed, the handout's authors are unable to use the word without surrounding it with scare quotes). Everyone has his or her own interpretation of the past and none is better than any other. None could be better, according to senior curator Jennifer Goldsboro, because, as she declared in a radio interview, "there's no such thing as objectivity"—and thus no way to judge one interpretation superior to another. For museum visitors, declared Goldsboro, "The exhibit is whatever it means to them."[5]

Goldsboro gives us what Michel Foucault called "relativism without recourse" and at the same time illustrates how foolishly this position is sometimes put forward. If she were pressed, Goldsboro would surely deny that any visitor should take away from Wilson's installation the idea that a view of American history that excludes African-Americans is as accurate as one that includes them. Museums have in the past often operated on this assumption, but when they did, they were in error. The truth is (and it is a truth that we understand better today than we have before) that African-Americans, like Latinos and Asian-Americans and the members of many other groups, have contributed mightily to our society and that those contributions should be recognized.

But the idea of truth, like ideas of beauty and excellence, is not very well received within the postmodern museum community. People in charge of our cultural institutions tend to move with amazing rapidity from the observation that truth has often been imperfectly represented to a conclusion that truth does not exist. Robert Sullivan, associate director of the Smithsonian's Museum of Natural History, expressed a widely held view when he declared, "All truths including anthropological and scientific ones are now viewed as contingent, contextual, and relative."[6]

A corollary to the idea that there is no truth is that there are no standards, no intellectual standards and no aesthetic ones either. The 1993 Biennial Exhibition of the Whitney Museum of American Art in New York City illustrated this notion at every turn. Its catalogue advertised it as an attack on the very notion of excellence, "a deliberate rejection of all the emblems of successful art: originality, integrity of materials, coherence of form."[7] Sue Williams's work was a case in point. On the right hand side of one of her paintings was a cartoonish drawing of a masturbating man; at the left and center, horses with elongated penises; scattered around, anuses large and small. Wherever there weren't pictures—and sometimes where there were—Williams had scrawled stream-of-consciousness graffiti: "I've got to paint assholes—just *tell* me it doesn't hurt anyone." "I'm stymied—I can't produce any shit!" "Why horses? I don't know."

Another of Williams's works, "The Sweet and Pungent Smell of Success" was on the floor of the Whitney where it required a strategically stationed guard to keep visitors from stepping in it. A commentary on women and bulimia, it consisted of a large, "mixed-media" puddle of vomit.

Janine Antoni struck a similar note with her display of a large block of chocolate on which she had gnawed as well as lard that she had chewed and spit out. In a photographic display, Kiki Smith and David Wojnarowicz featured various parts of their blood-coated bodies. Matthew Barney's video installation starred a man made up as a satyr who had a penchant for flaying his own skin.

Although critics denounced the Biennial, the show was, in fact, typical of what is esteemed today. Selected to represent the United States in a recent international exhibition in São Paulo, Brazil, for example, was an American artist who displayed turkey carcasses being devoured by beetles. The display ran into some difficulty when the turkey carcasses became rancid. The exhibit's organizers tried baking them to cut down on the stench, but the beetles, it turned out, were uninterested in cooked meat. Or consider three artists who have worked under the imprimatur of the National Endowment for the Arts. Photographer Joel-Peter Witkin has substituted a baby's corpse for the dead pheasant that is a traditional centerpiece of still lifes. His photograph of the result, called *Feast of Fools,* shows the dead baby artfully arranged amidst prawns, grapes, pomegranates, and severed human limbs. Andres Serrano has recently been showing (and selling) photographs of corpses taken in an unidentified morgue. Performance artist Ron Athey slices designs into the flesh of a fellow performer. When Athey displayed his expertise at the Walker Art Center in Minneapolis, Minnesota, in 1994, by carving a design into the flesh of another artist, he also had two female assistants weave acupuncture needles through his scalp and assist him with putting some two dozen hypodermic needles in his arm. He in turn pierced the women's cheeks with what the *Minneapolis Star Tribune* described as "slender steel spikes."[8]

Thus, the Whitney Biennial was part and parcel of the art of our time; and it made clear the academic influence on what is happening. The Biennial's vocabulary might have come straight from a faculty convention. Maureen Connor, who exhibited female tongues

147

and larynxes made from what seemed a familiar material, explained in a wall label that she was illustrating "the contingency of the female body, the cultural construction of femininity and the silencing of women through the use of a specifically gendered material—lipstick." Catalogue essays and wall labels cited the German philosophers Nietzsche and Heidegger as well as French thinkers such as Foucault and Derrida who took up and brought to this country the effort begun by their German predecessors of undercutting the defining principles of the modern world.

Time and again, Biennial artists adopted the reigning notions of today's academic establishment. "I have come to think of history as a dysfunctional idea," wrote artist Jimmie Durham on one of the labels for his work. "We believe whatever our situation causes us to believe and it may or may not be true." A film playing at the Biennial picked up the theme. "The truth," according to the film, "is what is believed."

Just as what we think is true does not reflect reality, neither does who we think we are. In the postmodern view, the self, like truth, is a social construct—a point made by Cindy Sherman's photographs of constructed women: a female figure, for example, legs akimbo, draped with a bib of oversized breasts and displaying gigantic pink plastic genitalia. Hillary Leone and Jennifer Macdonald used the metaphor of branding to talk about the social construction of identity. Their room-sized presentation included a row of branding irons and a free-verse explanation: "We started to brand/ To think about how we've been branded as people/ as gendered subjects/ as sexual subjects in culture."

The process by which "truth" is constructed and identities are created, the Biennial made clear, depends on power, on the ability of one group (white males, to be specific) to foist its ideas upon others and thus advance its interests at the expense of others. Those who are repressed have but one recourse: to seize power themselves so that their version of reality will dominate, "to fully deconstruct the marginality-centrality paradigm," as the academese of the Biennial catalogue put it, so that "marginality, in effect, becomes the norm while the center is increasingly undefinable and perhaps irrelevant."[9]

And this will not likely be a peaceful undertaking, as the Biennial presented it. At the entrance to the show five unsmiling young black men stared out from a photomural, the words WHAT YOU LOOKN AT spraypainted across them. In another installation, huge cut-out letters read, "In the rich man's house the only place to spit is in his face." Visitors to the museum were given tin admission buttons to wear. Each contained a part of the sentence: I CAN'T IMAGINE EVER WANTING TO BE WHITE.

When I visited the 1993 Whitney Biennial, I observed two distinct reactions to it. There were, on the one hand, people determined to invest significance, even profundity, into every aspect of the show. Coming upon the work of an artist who seemed to have transported his desk together with several months of untouched detritus upon it directly to the exhibition, a well-dressed docent informed the crowd gathered around her, "There are enough objects in the world, so [the artist] creates images dissected from his own home, anti-aesthetic junk gathered together [to make] an archeology of a life."

A museum guard with whom I fell into conversation represented the second, skeptical reaction: "If you were a great painter, you couldn't be in a show like this unless you were making a certain type of statement," he said. "If it's political, that's enough. The aesthetic isn't important." The guard described how visitors to the Whitney were frequently disappointed with what they found on display. Where, they asked, were the distinguished works of American art the museum holds in its collection? "Everyone asks for the [Edward] Hoppers. They come in here and that's what they want to see."[10]

These people still think of museums in terms of quality—a concept that many museum directors and curators now hold in contempt. The idea that art should offer insight, virtuoso workmanship, and creative genius is regarded as not only naive, but sexist, racist, and imperialist. According to Benjamin H. D. Buchloh, a professor at the Massachusetts Institute of Technology, "The central tool which bourgeois hegemonic culture (that is, white, male, Western culture) has traditionally used to exclude or marginalize all other cultural practices is the abstract concept of 'quality.' "[11]

Thus at museums like the Whitney, curators see themselves undertaking an important political mission when they display works that are deliberately ugly and off-putting. Perhaps the artist who best epitomizes this trend is John Miller, who is represented in the permanent collection of the Whitney. A catalogue produced for a recent show there pointed out (rather unnecessarily) that Miller's "coprophiliac sculptures . . . resemble piles of shit or fecal sticks." "Miller seems determined," the catalogue went on, "to undermine idealizing notions of the sublime and the beautiful."[12] When curators choose works that exemplify victimization and rage, politics is again at work. The aim is not only to remind visitors that traditional notions of beauty and excellence are a cover-up, but to show the racism, sexism, and imperialism that were supposedly hidden—and thus justify social and political transformation.

The idea that artistic choices ought to be made on the basis of politics rather than aesthetics is not exclusively the product of East Coast museums. Wilma Webb, head of the Denver, Colorado, Mayor's Commission on Art, Culture and Film, has suggested that the main criterion for choosing a work of art ought to be the race of the artist, with the percentage of grants awarded to any group for the creation of public art being guided by that group's percentage of the population.[13] If the guidelines were met, Hispanic and African-American artists would receive more grants than they now do in Denver and Caucasian artists fewer. But Native Americans would also receive fewer, almost four times so, an ironic result for a system premised on the belief that social justice can only be achieved by emphasizing group membership over individual merit.

Replacing the idea of quality with the goals of group politics does not mean that revered art and artifacts have to be abandoned; but when they are displayed, it will be in order to expose the oppressive views supposedly reflected in and fostered by them. This has often been the strategy at the Smithsonian Institution:

• In 1991, the Smithsonian displayed the works of such artists as Frederic Remington and Charles Russell in an exhibit called The West as America. By way of revealing "hidden agendas and ambitions,"[14] wall captions accompanying the paintings concentrated on racism, sexism, and xenophobia, even when it required extraordinary leaps of logic to do so. According to one wall caption, cowboys fighting off Indians at a water hole in a Remington painting represent the beleaguered feeling that Eastern industrialists were beginning to have because the labor force they had imported to work in their mills and factories was beginning to challenge them.

• In 1991, the Smithsonian mounted an exhibit of World War I aircraft. Entitled Legend, Memory, and the Great War in the Air, it set out to unmask romantic views of World War I aviation and reveal the "scientific murder" that airplanes had made possible. An accompanying catalogue, suffused with antimilitarism, conveniently ignored important historical facts, from the profound sentiment against war that came out of World War I to the massive U.S. reductions in nuclear armaments that have followed the end of the Cold War.[15]

• In 1994, in preparation for the fiftieth anniversary of the end of World War II, Smithsonian curators decided to bring the *Enola Gay,* the B-29 that dropped the atomic bomb on Hiroshima, out of storage; and they proposed surrounding it with an exhibition that depicted the bombing as an act of needless violence motivated by racism and the desire for vengeance. Only after considerable public protest did the museum agree to show that Americans also suffered grievously in World War II. Even then, curators remained so intent on debunking the idea that dropping the bomb was justified that the interpretive part of the exhibit finally had to be scuttled.[16]

Although the Smithsonian is a national institution, heavily dependent on taxpayer dollars, some of those in charge of its museums seem remarkably disdainful of the citizens who come through the doors. When Robert Sullivan accepted the position of associate director of the Museum of Natural History, he wrote that museum visitors "don't want to be engaged, empowered, or even educated, they just want to be distracted for a moment from the dailiness, the tedium, the fear of their lives."[17] In Sullivan's view, museum directors have bigger fish to fry, such as de-privileging a view of man as "rational-logical, scientific, technological [and] Western."[18]

This is, of course, the goal of many on our campuses, and it is the desire to be approved of by the academic establishment that seems to motivate Smithsonian curators. The only ideas they present uncritically are those of the universities from whence they came. Even the growing anti-scientism of humanities departments has made its way into Smithsonian museums. From a permanent exhibition at the National Museum of American History entitled "Science in American Life," one might well conclude that in the last 125 years, the main accomplishments of science have been the bomb, birth control pills, pesticides, and the ozone hole. In the interest of making sure that we understand how misguided we are "to identify science with progress," as a booklet accompanying the exhibition puts it,[19] such scientific advances as penicillin are tucked away in a corner to make room for large displays of the devastation wreaked at Hiroshima. Although the exhibit is ostensibly about hard science, curators have gone out of their way to make sure that museum visitors do not for a moment forget about social oppression. They manage to include information on the federal government's Indian removal policies, on people who had to beg for work during the Great Depression, and on segregation in the armed forces during World War II.

People who object to the latest trends in art and culture—and particularly to government funding of them—are often portrayed as know-nothing philistines who lack the sophistication to realize that art should be difficult and challenging. But there are legitimate intellectual and cultural concerns to be raised when art is judged by the views it advances rather than by its excellence. Helen Frankenthaler, one of the most accomplished artists of our time and a member of the advisory council of the National Endowment for the Arts at the end of the 1980s, wrote about the decline she was witnessing:

Despite the deserved grants, I see more and more non-deserving recipients. I feel there was a time when I experienced loftier minds, relatively unloaded with politics, fashion, and chic. They encouraged the endurance of a great tradition.[20]

In the summer of 1995, a film dramatically underscored how government funding of the arts has sometimes played into art world decadence. An NEA grant-sponsored book of photographs that is almost impossible to obtain— probably because no one wants to admit possessing child pornography—lies behind the highly controversial *Kids*, a film about underage teenagers doing drugs and having sex. In the 1970s, *Kids* producer Larry Clark was awarded an NEA grant on the basis of his previous work—a collection of photographs of underage teenagers, as well as himself (well overage), shooting and sniffing amphetamines and other substances. Between various arrests for beating up a variety of people, knifing one and shooting another, NEA grantee Clark continued his photography; and while the grant money itself—$5,000—went to lawyers to try to keep him out of jail, the project was finished in the early eighties and published under the title *Teenage Lust*. Clark's photographs show, among other things, a close-up of a prostitute performing oral sex on a teenager and a teenage boy raping a drugged-out teenage girl while one of his friends awaits his turn. A picture captioned "brother and sister" shows a naked boy with an erection pointing a gun at a naked, tied-up girl.[21]

These photographs—the dissemination of which would be illegal in twenty states—made Clark an art-world celebrity. With the imprimatur of the NEA and one-man shows across the country and around the world, he gained sufficient clout and connections to enable him, at age fifty-two, working with a nineteen-year-old writer, to put together a deal to produce *Kids*—a film version for the nineties of *Teenage Lust,* including another rape of a drugged-out teenage girl. This version can be distributed, however, since, according to the producers, the stars of the film only *look* underage. Some film aficionados have praised *Kids* for being powerful, gritty, and relentless; but surely there are other issues that should be considered, such as whether the film legitimizes the activities it depicts. Even though the specter of AIDS hovers over *Kids,* the film nevertheless depicts drugs, drunkenness, random violence, and particularly casual sex as the whole point of growing up in the nineties. Clark's shots of adolescent foreplay linger too long and lovingly: He clearly doesn't think these kids would be better off abstinent. And with the hype surrounding the film—a fashion shoot in *Details* magazine of the kids from *Kids,* for example—adolescent sex becomes unquestionably glamorous. Even if one could somehow manage to defend this message (an accomplishment hard to imagine), surely it is impossible to justify the way in which taxpayer dollars helped make it possible. One hardly has to be a philistine to be concerned about government funding of the arts.

❧

Many people have written about the way in which moving images undercut the idea of an enduring, stable tradition.[22] They have noted how rapid movements from image to image and from one unrelated topic to another undermine rationality.[23] At the same time that moving images have weakened notions of transcendence and truth, they have bestowed enormous power on the characteristic postmodern form of expression—narrative. That, in turn, has brought into focus the kinds of stories we use moving images to tell. Shouldn't we be worried that on prime-time television there is a sexual act or reference every four minutes?[24] Isn't it the role of the responsible citizen to protest—to censure, though not to censor—when violent films like *Pulp Fiction* have become part of the cultural landscape? "The medium," S. Robert Lichter of the Center for Media and Public Affairs observes, "isn't the only message."[25]

Political scientist Jean Bethke Elshtain suggests a variation on this theme by exploring the way in which violent film narratives lead to false beliefs. They convey, for example, erroneous notions about the likelihood of women being victims. Many believe that women are the most likely to be victimized, when, in fact, black males are. Many believe that violence against women is surging sharply, when, in fact, says Elshtain, compared to other crimes it is not. Women have internalized these ideas, Elshtain contends: "They have assumed an ide-

154

ology of victimization that is startlingly out of proportion to the actual threat." And film narratives have helped that happen. Writes Elshtain:

> For example, in 1991, half of the 250 American movies made for television depicted women undergoing abuse of one kind or another. This could give television viewers the impression that women have a 50 percent chance each week of being victims of a violent crime. Often such trashy programs are given a feminist gloss, but by portraying women in peril in the home, the workplace, and the street, they ill serve women or any feminism worthy of the name.[26]

A recent *TV Guide* supports Elshtain's observation. Saturday night offered only one prime-time movie, an obscure comedy, but on Sunday night, one could watch Kathleen Turner "as an emotionally battered wife suing for divorce"; on Monday, a Danielle Steel melodrama in which a woman's first husband blames her for the accidental death of their child and her second uses her as a broodmare; on Tuesday, a crime story "linking disturbed teens to the murder of their friend, a popular high-school beauty"; and on Wednesday a film about a woman who is the object of an obsessed lothario who undertakes a plot against her daughter. Thankfully for the sanity of women, there were no prime-time network movies on Thursday or Friday.[27]

These narratives of victimization are powerful reinforcement for other stories being told—by the American Association of University Women, for example, about how girls are victims; by Catharine MacKinnon about female suffering in a system of male dominance; by Sue Williams about the way women's lives are distorted and damaged by male-imposed standards of beauty. Similarly, film narratives about American history provide a mighty impetus to revisionist ideas that are making their way in schools, colleges, and cultural institutions.

One would sometimes think from reading today's textbooks that the founders of this country were a most singularly flawed group of men; and a 1995 film, *Jefferson in Paris*, produced by Ismail Merchant and directed by James Ivory, certainly reinforces this idea. It gives prominent place to an affair between Thomas Jefferson and Sally Hemings, one of his slaves, a relationship for which there is no proof. In Jefferson's day, rumors about Jefferson and Hemings were circulated by a bitter enemy of his. More recently, historian Fawn Brodie, on the basis of circumstantial evidence, concluded that a relationship existed; but other historians, including many more knowledgeable about Jefferson than Brodie, have argued that no such conclusion is justified. As far as the film and much of the promotion for it are concerned, however, there is no question: Thomas Jefferson was a randy fellow who engaged in the most exploitive kind of sexual relationship possible: one between master and adolescent slave.

Even before the film, many people believed the story of the Jefferson-Hemings affair. Douglas L. Wilson, writing in *Atlantic* magazine in 1992, noted that many students accept it as fact, though, ironically enough, fail to understand that it is supposed to make them admire Jefferson less. For some, Wilson writes, the supposed affair "actually seems to work in [Jefferson's] favor, showing him to have been not a stuffy moralist but a man who cleverly managed to appear respectable while secretly carrying on an illicit relationship."[28] The confusion involved in using the views of today, when rectitude is considered a bore, to frame a figure like Jefferson, for whom words like *duty* and *honor* were freighted with meaning, is perpetrated by the Merchant-Ivory film, which shows Jefferson taking up with Sally Hemings with an untroubled conscience and, once having discovered her sexual delights, blithely making plans to enjoy them for the rest of his life. This particularly bothered a black woman in the audience with whom I watched the film—as well it should have. As Jefferson was shown (in an invented scene) promising Sally Hemings, who is pregnant for the first time with his child, eventual freedom for herself and *all* the children she should bear, this woman, who clearly thought that what she was watching was historical, could not contain herself. "He *planned* on it!" she burst out. And so it is that people come to believe that Jefferson was the man that his enemies made him out to be.

Oliver Stone's films have been dedicated to insuring that people see more recent American history in the gloomiest light possible. To be sure, there are many grim episodes for him to work with, Vietnam being one of them; but with invention and distortion, he adds to our failures until they seem sure signs of systemic collapse. In his 1989 film, *Born on the Fourth of July*, Stone places wheelchair-bound Vietnam veteran Ron Kovic at a student strike at Syracuse University where he is among those attacked by police in full riot gear with clubs and tear gas. But in the book on which the movie is based, Kovic makes no mention of being at Syracuse; and an eyewitness who was there testifies that no force was used against the strikers. Indeed, according to a member of the police department at the time, the police were never even called.[29] Stone also showed Kovic being removed from the 1972 Republican convention in Miami, thrown from his wheelchair, and roughed up. Kovic was indeed removed from the convention when he and two other demonstrators began shouting during Richard Nixon's acceptance speech; but, as Kovic's book makes clear, this was not done violently. Kovic was once dumped from his wheelchair and roughed up, but it was in Los Angeles, not Miami Beach; and the incident resulted from his resisting arrest after having wheeled himself into oncoming traffic on Wilshire Boulevard.[30]

Stone's 1991 film, *JFK*, was even more inventive. In a skillfully filmed, very realistic scene shot in black and white (as is the documentary footage that almost directly precedes it), a Lyndon Johnson look-alike declares to various members of the military-industrial complex, "Just get me elected. I'll give you your damned war." In another scene, a character named David William Ferrie does something he never did in real life—confesses that Lee Harvey Oswald had ties to the U.S. government.[31]

While Stone's penchant for twisting history and inventing things that never happened has been often remarked upon, the many ways in which he has reinforced the idea that his films are true have been less noticed. *Born on the Fourth of July* claimed to be a "true story" in its advertising. Given an opportunity by the *Los Angeles Times* to describe this film as a meditation on war or a broad cultural commentary, Stone chose to emphasize its literal truth: "I'm obviously telling Ron's story. I'm not screwing with the facts."[32] District Attorney Jim Garrison, the hero of *JFK*, declared in the film, "Truth is the most important value we have," and *JFK* was dedicated "to the young in whose spirit the search for truth marches on." Perhaps most remarkable of all are the study guides to *JFK* that were distributed to schools around the country. Providing information selectively and urging students to use it to reach the same conspiratorial conclusions that animate *JFK*, the guides characterized Oliver Stone as a truth-teller: "The very questions that compelled Oliver Stone to make 'JFK' also made him determined to insure that the facts, as known, would be presented accurately."[33]

Why is it that Stone, actively involved in inventing details and presenting them as facts, insists on presenting his work as true? Remarks that he made at a panel in New York City sponsored by the Nation Institute and the Center for American Culture Studies of Columbia University, in association with Writers Guild, East, offer a hint. Stone presented himself to the audience as a thoroughgoing skeptic, doubtful of all history:

> I have come to have severe doubts about Columbus, Washington, the Civil War being fought for slavery, the Indian Wars, World War I, World War II, the supposed fight against Nazism and/or Japanese control of resources in Southeast Asia. I've doubted everything. I don't even know if I was born and who my parents were. It may be virtual reality.

But if the truth of the past cannot be known, political convictions can, and they become the lodestar. "Even if I am totally wrong . . . ," Stone said to a New York panelist who challenged his facts, "I am still right. . . . I am essentially right because I am depicting the Evil with a capital E of government."[34]

Stone is the Hollywood incarnation of the postmodern academic notion that it is political utility—not some naive idea of accuracy—that determines a historical presentation's value. He is a West Coast version of two University of Pennsylvania scholars who proclaim,

"We are all engaged in writing a kind of propaganda. . . . Rather than believe in the absolute truth of what we are writing, we must believe in the moral or political position we are taking with it."[35] But "the repressed and ignorant masses," to borrow a phrase that Stone used in his New York presentation,[36] have not necessarily reached this awareness. For them, it is important to portray the politically useful narrative as a well-supported argument because its effect will be diminished unless they believe it is true.

Stone is hardly the only one to put the moving image into the service of politics. Linda Bloodworth-Thomason's characters in the television program *Designing Women* have taken stands on any number of controversial political issues, including the nomination fight over Supreme Court nominee Clarence Thomas. "This man does not belong on the Supreme Court," proclaimed Julia Sugarbaker two weeks after Clarence Thomas was confirmed. Mary Jo threatened to go to the center of America, climb a tower, and shout, "Who the hell do you men think you are?"—which is, of course, exactly what Bloodworth-Thomason did with this particular episode of her show. A longtime supporter of President Clinton (she wrote and produced the film that introduced him at his party's 1992 convention), Bloodworth-Thomason is not the least embarrassed by the political editorializing in her show. "I have my own column on TV," she has said, "and I take it as seriously as does Mike Royko or David Broder." Similarly, Diane English, the creator of *Murphy Brown,* declared shortly before the 1992 presidential election that the liberal Democratic bent of television shows like hers provided balance to "twelve years of Republicans."[37]

But all of this is minor compared to Oliver Stone's work, which passes beyond scoring partisan points to distorting the past in order to present a vision of American civic life as fundamentally corrupt— and which does so with remarkable effect. After seeing *JFK,* a film that presents the assassination of President Kennedy as the work not only of the Mafia and anti-Castro Cubans, but also the CIA, the FBI, high-ranking military men, and even Lyndon Johnson himself, a Maryland high school student declared, "It really makes sense." A high school art teacher coming out of the movie theater said that the film made her feel almost embarrassed to be an American. "I'd be surprised if it wasn't true," she said.[38] "Of course, that's what happened," said a student at Duke University Law School. "We knew that. Why is this such big news?"[39] More than three years after the film's release, a student from Washington, D.C.'s, Banneker Academic High School told C-SPAN viewers that the film had convinced her—and her history teacher as well.[40] After the bombing of a federal building in Oklahoma City in April 1995, an Arizona sheriff, asked on CNN's *Crossfire* whether he really believed that the U.S. government assassinated JFK, replied, "Well, I reminded some people about the JFK movie which showed—Oliver Stone clearly showed governmental corruption."[41]

In 1995, Melvin Van Peebles justified the film *Panther,* which shows the FBI conspiring with the Mafia to create a drug epidemic to destroy the Panthers and the black community, by pointing to Oliver Stone's work. Said Van Peebles, who wrote the book on which the film was based and whose son, Mario, directed *Panther*: "With *JFK* I'm in pretty good company." Added Mario Van Peebles:

> For example, Oliver Stone didn't get into any of Kennedy's personal life in *JFK*. He focused specifically on the conspiracy to take out a president and commit a coup d'etat.

Like Stone, whose movie he seems to have believed, Mario Van Peebles worked to convince young people of the political message of his film, which not only demonizes the U.S. government but also makes heroes of the Black Panthers, many of whose leaders were deeply implicated in drugs and violence. On the weekend before the film's opening, Van Peebles held youth forums in Washington, D.C., "bringing along former Panthers," as the *Washington Post* described it, "and stressing the party's positive side."[42]

Oliver Stone's films—and their offspring—have a particularly pernicious civic effect, but distortions of truth can be harmful even when the intent behind them is to strengthen the body politic. In

1993, a public television film, *Liberators,* told the story of a black tank battalion's liberating the Nazi concentration camp at Buchenwald. This particular tank battalion—the 761st—had an admirable record. It had distinguished itself at the Battle of the Bulge and helped to liberate Günskirchen, a concentration camp in Austria. But the historical record indicates that the 761st was sixty to one hundred miles away when Buchenwald was liberated. Thus, one of *Liberators'* most affecting scenes is also one of its most deceptive. The beginning of the film, set some fifty years after World War II, describes how "two veterans of the 761st Tank Battalion returned to Buchenwald with Benjamin Bender, who had been imprisoned there as a boy."[43] As Bender remembers the family he lost at Buchenwald, he is overcome with emotion; and the two veterans, E. G. McConnell and Leonard Smith, offer comfort. The problem is that neither McConnell nor Smith had ever been to Buchenwald before the filming of *Liberators.* "I first went to Buchenwald in 1991 with PBS, not the 761st," McConnell told Jeffrey Goldberg, who was writing for the *New Republic.*[44]

How did this error happen? Given its magnitude, it seems improbable that it was an accident. More likely, rather significant license was taken for dramatic effect. Names like Buchenwald have acquired a horrible resonance that compels attention, and shouldn't as much attention as possible be focused on African-Americans helping free Jewish prisoners? If one considered nothing else but the 1991 violence that occurred in Crown Heights, Brooklyn, and the anger and tension it spawned, wouldn't that person conclude it was time to underscore black soldiers reaching out to Jewish men and women, time to emphasize African-American and Jewish brotherhood? Said one of the co-hosts of a screening of the film at New York's Apollo Theater, "What we're trying to do is make New York a better place for you and me to live." As she saw it, the fact that the 761st Tank Battalion had not been at Buchenwald was of little importance: "There are a lot of truths that are very necessary. This is not a truth that's necessary."[45]

But others saw it otherwise. Veteran E. G. McConnell of the 761st says that he warned the film's producers that they were going too far with their claims. When they went ahead anyway, he tried—futilely, it turned out—to warn then Mayor David Dinkins and the Reverend Jesse Jackson before they attended the Apollo showing. Said Mc-Connell, "We had been stripped of our history in our slavery, and I didn't want to come up with anything that could tarnish our record."[46]

Kenneth S. Stern of the American Jewish Committee prepared a carefully researched background report on *Liberators*. While emphasizing that black soldiers did help liberate concentration camps and that all-black units distinguished themselves in many ways in World War II, Stern makes clear the serious factual errors that plague *Liberators*, chief among them being its claim about the 761st and Buchenwald.[47]

Stern's report was the death knell for the film, and New York public television station WNET pulled it from PBS. Shortly before that happened, one of the film's producers, Nina Rosenblum, lashed out angrily, saying that the film's critics were racist (though, in fact, some of those who complained were black) and accusing those who criticized *Liberators* of sharing the worldview of Holocaust deniers. "These people are [of] the same mentality that says that the Holocaust didn't happen," she said.[48]

Rosenblum had it exactly backwards. Critics of *Liberators* were seeking truth. Using standards of evidence and verification, they were doing exactly what those who claim that the Holocaust never occurred fail to do—indeed, cannot do, because their case depends on falsification and distortion.

And the critics of *Liberators* had compelling reasons for insisting on truth. Any discrepancy in the account of Nazi attempts to annihilate the Jews becomes an opening for deniers to question the entire account. Moreover, those who are indifferent to distortions of the past when they seem beneficent lose the moral authority to combat the twisting of history when it is done with pernicious intent. As Jeffrey Goldberg told the *Washington Post*, "No matter how noble the purpose, you just can't make up facts."[49]

ॐ

In Oliver Stone's *JFK*, David William Ferrie's confession is corroborated by a character named Willie O'Keefe. As I have pointed out, however, there never was a Ferrie confession; and, as Edward Jay Epstein has indicated, neither was there a Willie O'Keefe. The witness for whom Stone substituted O'Keefe in the film was Perry Raymond Russo, who waited until four years after the assassination to tell his story, and then, as Epstein describes it, "only after he had been rendered semiconscious by sodium pentothal and instructed by a hypnotist to imagine he is watching an important discussion 'about assassinating someone.' "[50]

Oliver Stone was no doubt motivated to create a substitute for Russo because he suspected that *JFK* audiences might have doubts about such testimony. Moreover, District Attorney Jim Garrison is meant to be a sympathetic figure in *JFK*; and the public, Stone may well have concluded, was unlikely to think it a positive thing for prosecution forces, led by Garrison, to rely on evidence obtained through drugs, hypnosis, and suggestion.

It is one of the small ironies of history that in the 1990s, as Oliver Stone was covering up Garrison's methods, the very techniques used by the New Orleans district attorney some three decades before were gaining acceptance in a major part of the therapeutic community in the United States. In the late 1980s and early 1990s, many therapists encouraged people who came to them seeking relief for symptoms as diverse as bulimia, eyebrow-pulling, and fear of dentists to look upon their difficulties as indications of child abuse. And if the patient had no memory of abuse, therapists would help recover it through sessions that often involved drugs, hypnosis, and suggestion.

Consider the case of Jennifer, as related by psychologist Michael D. Yapko. Unhappy in her personal life, Jennifer went to a therapist who suggested that her troubled relationships with men, her constant anxiety, and her low self-esteem were classic symptoms of having been abused. Because she did not remember any abuse, he suggested that he hypnotize her. In the first of the sessions, as the therapist asked her leading questions, Jennifer remembered her father sexually abusing her when she was a baby. In following sessions, the therapist asked if any of the abuse she remembered had been part of a ritual. Jennifer subsequently recalled being raped in a room lit by candles by men who chanted about Satan while her father and mother watched.

Confused and frightened, Jennifer was told by her therapist to write a letter to her parents setting out what she remembered and to prepare to cut off all contact with them. They would only deny what she said, he told her, thus undermining her belief in the memories she had recovered. Jennifer wrote the letter and told her parents she would neither talk to them nor see them. "I have no forgiveness in me for what you did to me," she wrote.[51]

Sexual abuse is a despicable crime, one that happens much more frequently than we used to think. But precisely because it is abhorrent, encouraging people to charge sexual abuse on the basis of doubtful or limited evidence is a very serious matter. Dr. Yapko, who treated Jennifer's parents, writes, "I hate to think of the pain of all the families I have seen who have been devastated by this phenomenon."[52] Says Dr. Pam Freyd, the executive director of the False Memory Syndrome Foundation, an organization founded in support of those wrongly accused, "If incest is the worst crime, just imagine the devastating impact on parents who are falsely accused."[53]

The trauma of being accused of child abuse is not only deeply personal, but economic and social. People lose their jobs and become pariahs, things they richly deserve if they are guilty; but what if they are not? Ethan Watters, a journalist who has written at length on recovered memory, notes that patients often express surprise at the memories that surface because they are entirely incompatible with conscious memories. Moreover, writes Watters, "Patients are often troubled that their recovered memories don't feel like normal memories, but are dreamlike and nonsensical."[54] Patients are frequently encouraged not to worry too much about their doubts—indeed, even to regard them as evidence that the memories are accurate. According to one popular book, "The existence of profound disbelief is an indication that memories are real."[55] The same book advises that when an individual decides to disclose to family members what therapy has uncovered, she should "avoid being tentative about your repressed memories. Do not just tell them; express them as truth. If months or years down the road, you find you are mistaken about details, you can always apologize and set the record straight."[56]

As I began to read the literature on recovered memory, I found myself astonished that people were being urged to make charges about sexual abuse when they were not absolutely sure that anything had happened. But I probably should not have been surprised, for what more predictable outcome could there be to the view that there is no external reality, no way of looking outside ourselves to establish the truth of an event, than an approach that tells us not to bother to try? It is symptomatic of our times that *The Courage to Heal: A Guide for Women Survivors of Child Sexual Abuse*, a best-selling book of the late eighties and early nineties, advises: "Assume your feelings are valid. . . . If you think you were abused and your life shows the symptoms, then you were."[57] One of the most thorough exposés of the recovered memory movement, Mark Pendergrast's *Victims of Memory*, contains example after example of therapists saying that the literal truth of an accusation is not important. The following quotation, from a therapist who is talking about "accepting a client's truth," is typical:

> We have to accept it whether it existed in objective reality or not. How is that truth playing out in the client's life? It's the *dynamic* past, not the *content* past, that is important.[58]

A number of therapists have spoken out about what they see happening in their profession. This is no easy task since those who express doubt about recovered memory often find themselves accused of setting back the recovery of thousands of people, mostly women, who have actually experienced sexual abuse. "I hate, I *hate*, the idea that there are genuine survivors of sexual abuse out there feeling like I'm re-victimizing them," says psychologist Elizabeth Loftus of the University of Washington.[59] She stresses that her concern is not focused on situations in which people wait many years to talk about childhood abuse: "We know that many tortured individuals need time to bring the dark secret of their abuse to light."[60] Rather she is concerned with the uncritical acceptance of memories recovered in therapy, some of them going back to the first months of life, by patients who before therapy had absolutely no memory of abuse, even when it had supposedly spanned many years. Recovered memories should not be rejected out of hand, in Loftus's view, but we should be skeptical about them, particularly in light of the role that therapeutic suggestion might play. There is a rich literature in which researchers have demonstrated susceptibility to suggestion. In one project, for example, Loftus and an associate easily convinced several people that when they were around five years old, they had been lost in a department store or mall for a lengthy period.[61]

Even more outspoken about the recovered memory phenomenon than Loftus is Richard Ofshe, a professor of sociology at the University of California at Berkeley. In an article co-authored with Ethan Watters, Ofshe notes the lack of empirical evidence for the concept of repression, on which the recovered memory movement relies: "Sixty years of experiments that would demonstrate the phenomenon have failed to produce any evidence of its existence." He argues that the "warning signs" of abuse listed in the popular books to which patients are often referred are "so general that they could apply to almost anyone—difficulty in maintaining a relationship, general feelings of dissatisfaction, liking sex too much, lack of career success, and fear of dentists." And he points out how susceptible to suggestion people can be, under hypnosis in particular, but generally as well: "Research . . . documents that entirely false memories can be created with minimal pressure or suggestion."[62]

Ofshe demonstrated how open some people are to suggestion when the police asked him to advise them on the case of Paul

Ingram, a deputy in the sheriff's department in Olympia, Washington. Ingram's troubles began when his daughters attended a church camp where they and others were addressed by Karla Franko, a charismatic Christian from California.[63] After Franko told her audience that she sensed one of them had been molested as a child, a number of the young women present claimed to have been abused, including Paul Ingram's twenty-two-year-old daughter, Ericka. (In a slightly different version of events, the one told by Franko herself, she prayed over Ericka and announced to her, specifically, that she had been molested and that her father had done it.)

Ericka and her eighteen-year-old sister, Julie, who also said she had been abused, reported their father to the police. He was arrested and confessed, though in a very strange way. He was guilty, he said; but he had absolutely no memory of the events he was guilty of. Gradually, pressured and plentifully supplied with suggestions by sheriff and police officials and a psychologist, Ingram confessed to assaulting both girls over a number of years. A minister was added to the group interrogating him, and his confession expanded to include other family members as both victims and perpetrators and to implicate almost a dozen friends and acquaintances in abusive activities. Two men with whom he played poker were arrested.

Then Ingram began, as did his daughters, to describe elaborate satanic rituals. Ericka Ingram, during the same summer that she had first begun to talk about sexual abuse, had read a book about satanic rituals. A month before the Ingram daughters went to the police, the Ingram family had watched a Geraldo Rivera special: *Devil Worship: Exposing Satan's Underground*. Now they told authorities about hundreds of rituals, many including human sacrifice (more than two dozen babies, according to Ericka). When the stories that poured out from various members of the Ingram family turned out to be internally inconsistent and when police could not turn up corroborating evidence, the prosecution called in Ofshe. Was it possible, they wanted to know, for some kind of cult mind control to have scrambled the Ingram family's memories?

Ofshe suspected that something unusual might be going on when one of the detectives on the case told him of Ingram's habit of confessing to his crimes as though he were an observer watching himself participate in them. The detective also described the conditional language ("would've," "must have") that characterized Ingram's accounts. After Ofshe interviewed Ingram and heard him describe how he would imagine himself in a warm white fog and how he would wait in that fog for the images of the abuse he knew he was guilty of to materialize, Ofshe decided to run a test. He invented a scenario—that Ingram had forced his children to have sex with one another—and asked Ingram to tell him about it, assuring him—although this was not the case—that the Ingram children remembered this happening. A few days later, Ingram produced an elaborate account of the scenario Ofshe had suggested.

Believing it highly likely that a number of innocent people were about to be put on trial, Ofshe began to side with the defense. Charges were eventually dropped against the two Ingram friends who had been arrested, but since Ingram himself had confessed, he was sentenced to twenty years in prison. Today, still in prison, he says he is convinced that he only imagined the crimes to which he confessed.

Ofshe maintains that there are serious questions about whether Ingram is guilty of the crimes for which he is imprisoned. Two recent books—one by Ofshe and Watters and another by Elizabeth Loftus and Katherine Ketcham—argue convincingly that the same is true in another case. George Franklin was convicted of murder in 1990 on the basis of his daughter's testimony that she had suddenly remembered his raping and murdering an eight-year-old friend of hers some twenty years earlier; and while Franklin seems to be a thoroughly unsavory character, Loftus and Ketcham note that "not one piece of forensic or scientific evidence" connects him to the murder.[64] Ofshe and Watters point out that during the trial the fact that the accusing daughter had been undergoing recovered memory therapy when the rape and murder came back to her was not "fully appreciated."[65] Indeed, in 1990, few people knew what to make of the idea of recovered memory or how to challenge the claims made in its name. Shortly after the publications of Loftus and Ketcham's and Ofshe and Watters' books, a judge overturned Franklin's conviction on a technicality, leaving open the possibility that in a new trial the matter of whether recovered memory constitutes reliable evidence can be thoroughly aired.

Those who believe that traumatic events—even ones occurring over long periods of time—can be so completely suppressed that a traumatized person will be unaware of them for decades might well point to the case of Frank Fitzpatrick. A Rhode Island insurance adjuster, Fitzpatrick was lying on his bed one day feeling anguished, although he was unsure why, when he began to remember the sound of heavy breathing. Over the next two weeks he recalled in detail having been abused twenty-six years before by a priest in Massachusetts. More than a hundred other people, a few of whom did not recall their experiences until they heard of Fitzpatrick's, have since come forward to say that the same priest abused them.[66]

But cases like Fitzpatrick's do not indicate that all recovered memories are accurate, and it would seem highly dangerous to encourage blanket and uncritical acceptance. A few years after Fitzpatrick's charge, a Philadelphia man accused Chicago Cardinal Joseph Bernardin with having abused him when he was a teenager. After the charges received worldwide publicity, the accuser recanted. He had recalled the abuse while under hypnosis, and he said he now realized that "the memories of sexual abuse by Cardinal Bernardin which arose during and after hypnosis are unreliable."[67]

There are dozens of others who have now recanted charges of sexual abuse that they have brought, often against family members. Some have sued therapists whom they blame for having created false memories. In the spring of 1994, a California father accused two therapists of implanting in his daughter's mind false memories that he had sexually abused her. He charged that they told her that the bulimia for which she had sought treatment was usually caused by sexual abuse ("70 to 80 percent of women with eating disorders were incest victims," the *New York Times* reported the daughter was told[68]). It was only after being questioned under sodium amytal, a witness for the father pointed out, that the daughter identified her father as her abuser. The jury awarded the father $500,000.

It seems only common sense to say that when people claim to

recall events that they have not remembered for a long time, we should not rush to judgment about whether what they recall is true. And we should be particularly wary about charges that spring from circumstances in which suggestion could play a role. But in an important part of the therapeutic community, what seems common sense is viewed as heretical. The prevailing orthodoxy is that people who say that they are victims of abuse are to be believed. Particularly since we are a society in which guilt has long been thought to be something that must be proved, it is well worth asking: How did we arrive at such a pass?

Freud—or rather reaction to him—is part of the answer. When, during the course of therapy, his female patients recalled tales of how they had been seduced as children, usually by their fathers, Freud at first believed them. He presented what they said as true. But he subsequently changed his approach and argued that these tales, which his patients had repressed until they came to him for analysis, were fantasies. They were not about real events, but about his patients' own incestuous desires.

Twentieth-century feminists, rightfully angered that Freud and his followers tended to look upon female claims of childhood sexual abuse as fantasies, have gone to the other extreme. *The Courage to Heal* puts the feminist reaction to Freud succinctly, *"No one fantasizes abuse."*[69] But in trying to walk away from Freud, feminists and others in the therapeutic profession may have, instead, fallen into lockstep with him. As Frederick Crews has observed, the key question to be asked about Freud is not "Were those stories true? but rather, *What* stories?"[70] As Crews and others have noted, Freud was very aggressive about getting his patients to recall childhood sexual incidents or fantasies that they had no notion of before coming to him. Assuming that the sexual tale was there, waiting to be uncovered, he would suggest what its nature was, sometimes to patients under hypnosis—precisely as many therapists do today:

- An Oregon woman reports that the therapist from whom she sought help for depression and anxiety suggested that sexual abuse might lie behind her problems. Since first making that suggestion, she says, "He has become more and more certain of his diagnosis." She has not been successful at producing the memories he wants, but not for lack of trying. "For the past two years I have done little else but try to remember. I've tried self-hypnosis and light trance work with my therapist. And I even travelled to childhood homes . . . in an attempt to trigger memories."[71]

• A Colorado attorney reports that the therapist from whom he sought help in dealing with his father's suicide told him that something else lay behind the pain he was experiencing. Unable to figure out what that "something else" was, the attorney became more and more depressed. Finally one day, the attorney says, the therapist offered this suggestion: "I don't know how to tell you this, but you display the same kinds of characteristics as some of my patients who are victims of Satanic ritualistic abuse."[72]

• A computer specialist from Reno, Nevada, says that the therapist she visited told her that her depression and anxiety were common symptoms of child abuse. Trying hard to come up with memories of being molested, the computer specialist thought she remembered her father raping her, but she wasn't sure. Assuring her that certainty was not important, the therapist encouraged her to confront her parents and urged her to read *The Courage to Heal*. The computer specialist joined an incest survivors group, underwent hypnotherapy, and recovered more and more memories of abuse, some so fantastic that she finally concluded that her recovered memories were false memories. She subsequently started a newsletter called the *Retractor*.[73]

The therapists in these incidents would doubtless recoil at the observation, but there are striking parallels between what they are doing and what the misogynist Freud did. "Freud," writes Frederick

Crews, "is the true historical sponsor of 'false memory syndrome.' "[74] Richard Ofshe and Ethan Watters call recovered memory therapies "pumped-up versions of the core Freudian speculation," and they warn against regarding this kind of treatment as a passing fad. Recovered memory therapy and the ideas on which it is based are being institutionalized, they observe, "taught in university psychology graduate programs, education school psychology programs, psychiatric residence programs, doctoral programs in clinical psychology, and at schools of social work."[75]

Judith Herman, a Harvard psychiatrist who is one of the leaders of the recovered memory movement, explains that so many people are now recalling long repressed memories of sexual abuse because of the supportive atmosphere that feminism provides: "To hold traumatic reality in consciousness requires a social context that affirms and protects the victim," she writes.[76] Indeed, there are many parallels between the recovered memory movement and feminism as it has come to be practiced on campuses. The encouragement—even the requirement—in feminist classrooms to confess personal views and traumas establishes an environment very much like the one that exists in victim recovery groups. A report on women's studies at Oberlin College says, for example, that the classroom atmosphere "often is searing."[77]

The emphasis on subjective experience and feminist solidarity leads on campuses—as in recovered memory therapy—to an ethos in which the objective truth of an accusation takes on secondary importance. In her book *The Morning After*, Katie Roiphe tells of "Take Back the Night" marches—events that have become common at many colleges and universities—where women students progress through campus, stopping at strategically placed microphones to tell about the sexual violence they have experienced and survived. At Princeton, one detailed accusation of rape turned out to be false. Declared the accuser, "I made my statements . . . in order to raise awareness for the plight of campus rape victims." Roiphe also notes a case at George Washington University where a student explained a false accusation of rape she had made by saying, "My goal from the beginning was to call attention to what I perceived to be a serious safety concern for women."[78]

One idea common to both campuses and the recovered memory movement has to do with the potential of all males to be sexual predators. When several male students at Vassar were found to be innocent of charges of date rape that had been lodged against them, the assistant dean of students, Catherine Comins, declared:

> They have a lot of pain, but it is not a pain I would necessarily have spared them. I think it ideally initiates a process of self-exploration. "How do I see women?" "If I didn't violate her, could I have?" "Do I have the potential to do to her what they say I did?" Those are good questions.[79]

At the University of Maryland at College Park, nine female students enrolled in a class called "Contemporary Issues in Feminist Art" put up posters headlined "POTENTIAL RAPISTS" on which were listed all male-sounding names in the student directory. The professor of the class, apparently not at all troubled that the posters amounted to a false accusation, pronounced the project "wildly successful."[80]

Mark Pendergrast, who wrote his book, *Victims of Memory*, after his two daughters' therapy led them to accuse him of abuse that they had not previously remembered, notes in passing that the daughters had taken women's studies courses.[81] A father who lives in the Midwest wrote a long and moving story in the *Chicago Tribune* about losing his daughter when she recalled memories of his having abused her as a child—a charge that he writes left him dumbstruck as well as completely alienated from his wife, whom the daughter eventually accused of abuse as well. The memories had returned while the daughter was in therapy; but he had sensed the estrangement beginning earlier, during a Christmas vacation when his daughter announced that she had "changed her college major from English to 'gender studies'" and began carrying around a book by Andrea Dworkin.[82] When one notes the rising numbers of women who claim to have recovered memories of abuse and considers what has happened with feminism on our campuses, it does not seem unreasonable to suspect a connection, to see therapy-assisted recovered memory as a natural extension of women's studies courses and consciousness-raising activities. It is one more way in which what happens on campuses has an impact on the larger world.

Many people have noted that what is happening today with recovered memory resembles what happened in seventeenth-century Salem. In a sense the comparison with witch trials is flawed because we know that childhood sexual abuse exists, while there are grave doubts about witchcraft as our Puritan forebears thought of it. Sexual abuse is a real and severe social problem that we must continue to combat.

But with that caveat, and it is a crucial one, the comparison can be instructive. It brings attention to careless accusations followed (even when no court is involved) by the most intense punishment. It brings attention to the way this phenomenon can feed upon itself and grow in a situation where truth and evidence are not esteemed. The irrationality of Salem occurred as Enlightenment values of reason and objectivity were making their way in the world. In our time, the irrationality of the recovered memory movement is a measure of the degree to which Enlightenment ideas are no longer thought to matter.

The Press and the Postmodern Presidency

"All words grouping themselves round the concepts of objectivity and rationalism were contained in the single word *oldthink*."

—*George Orwell, 1984*

MICHEL Foucault would have been fascinated by late-twentieth-century presidential campaigns. To him they would have seemed examples on a massive scale of what he had observed in miniature in nineteenth-century France. In his book *I, Pierre Rivière*, discussed in Chapter 3, he focused on various efforts to gain control of the narrative describing the brutal 1835 murder of Pierre Rivière's mother and his siblings. Rivière had one narrative or "discourse," the neighbors another, some of the medical men a third; and these discourses competed with one another as each of the various interests involved tried to impose its own particular regime of truth.

Since the late 1960s, as Foucault might have described it, presidential elections have been in part about whether the press or the politicians would control the campaign narrative. After Richard Nixon's loss to John F. Kennedy, Nixon advisor Ray Price wrote, "It's not what's *there* that counts, it's what's projected—and . . . what the voter receives."[1] From thence forward, as candidate and president, Nixon set in place organizations aimed at creating the perceptions that he wanted rather than letting the press tell the story. Ronald Reagan, relying on advance men, media consultants, and his own skills as an actor, became so adept at controlling the narrative that even his admirers worried from time to time that an emphasis on perception was replacing a concern with reality. Wrote Peggy Noonan, who had worked as a Reagan speechwriter, "Decisions were made with TV so much in mind, from the photo op to the impromptu remark on the way to the helicopter, that the president's top aides who planned the day, were no longer just part of the story—it was as if they were the producers of the story. They were the line producers of a show called *White House*, with Ronald Reagan as the President."[2]

To the press, the 1988 campaign carried this tendency further still. As they saw it, George Bush and those around him succeeded in turning the campaign against Michael Dukakis into stories about Willie Horton and the pledge of allegiance; and these were irrelevancies. "We looked back at the last campaign and asked what prison furloughs and flags had to do with the real world," said Gloria Borger of *U.S. News & World Report*.[3] David Broder wrote an influential article in which he lamented the way in which candidates and their consultants emphasized issues that would help them win but had little to do with the real problems of the country. It was no wonder that voters were cynical, he wrote. "They have caught onto the fact that they are being conned." Broder recommended that his fellow journalists "challenge the operating assumption of the candidates and consultants that the campaign agenda is theirs to determine." His idea was that the press could find out what voters were concerned about and make that the centerpiece of the campaign.[4]

In some ways the mainstream press was in a very powerful position to create the campaign story. From 1968 to 1988, the average sound bite for a presidential candidate on the network evening news had plummeted from 42.3 seconds to 9.8 seconds.[5] In the 1992 campaign the length of time would become shorter still: 8.4 seconds. Meanwhile, the portion of the news taken up by correspondents' comments rose to 71 percent, with candidates sharing the remainder of the time with voters and political experts.[6] A study of the *New York Times* showed a similar trend. From 1960 to 1992, the average continuous quote or phrase from a candidate in a front page story fell from fourteen lines to six lines.[7] In both television and print, reporters increasingly had power to turn the candidates' words and deeds into illustrative material for the stories they wanted to tell.

Broder's piece led the mainstream press to make some impressive resolutions. NBC vowed to keep its top reporters off the campaign trail so that they would not succumb to press availabilities or to photo opportunities of the kind that the 1988 Bush campaign had staged. The *Washington Post* began polling and interviewing to find out what voters cared about. But hardly had the campaign gotten under way when the tabloids seized control of the narrative. Three weeks before the New Hampshire primary, the *Star*, a supermarket tabloid, broke the story of Gennifer Flowers; and soon the networks and major newspapers, albeit with embarrassment, were following the *Star*'s lead.

According to some media observers, the press never did get back on track. Instead of redirecting the narrative toward what voters perceived to be the real problems of the day, journalists fell into a familiar pattern of coverage, the campaign as horse race, in which journalists focus on who is ahead, who behind, and what strategies got them there. Political scientist Thomas Patterson writes that the horse race was the focus from New Hampshire until after the Democratic nomination was settled. Then, during the summer, Patterson says, "the Clinton-Gore bus caravan got extensive coverage, particularly on network television. It was a staged photo-op that exceeded anything Bush had produced in 1988, but the press went for it without hesitation."[8] Perhaps most telling are the statistics from the Center for Media and Public Affairs showing that in the fall campaign, the horse race was a more important topic than it had been in 1988 (35 percent of the stories on ABC, CBS, and NBC focused on it as opposed to 25 percent in 1988) and policy issues were less important (32 percent of the stories as opposed to 40 percent in 1988).[9] Observes Darrell West, a media researcher at Brown University, "It's almost as if the media got hijacked by Gennifer Flowers and never recovered."[10]

Others thought that the press did redirect the narrative. Media critic Edwin Diamond declared that in some respects network coverage was the best of the last forty years.[11] Most of the media insiders surveyed by the Freedom Forum Media Studies Center of Columbia University said that the press had done a better job in 1992 than in 1988. "There was a lot more emphasis on what these guys really stood for," said Roger Smith, political editor of the *Los Angeles Times*. "I think overall this was the best year I've ever seen for issue coverage," said Ron Cohen, executive editor of Gannett News Service. Top campaign correspondents agreed. John King, political writer for the Associated Press, said, "We did a better job this year of avoiding event manipulation, such as flag factories, and giving ads a more thorough analysis."[12]

There was a third view as well: that the press, rather than controlling the campaign narrative, participated in Bill Clinton's telling of it. In 1992, said a number of journalists, members of the press crossed over a line into advocacy. In August, before the general election began, Evan Thomas of *Newsweek* magazine declared, "The Republicans are going to whack away at the press for the next couple of months as being pro-Clinton, and you know what? They're right. The press is pro-Clinton."[13] As the fall campaign started, Howard Kurtz, media critic for the *Washington Post*, asked, "Has the press gone soft on Bill Clinton?" He quoted a number of journalists who had made that case and himself observed that "a favorable tone sometimes creeps into daily coverage."[14] After the election, Tom Rosenstiel of the *Los Angeles Times* asked, "Was there bias in the press?" and answered, "Yes," though he emphasized that "the media's ideological slant is not a manifest conspiracy to harm Republicans, but a failure to understand some of their arguments."[15]

That journalists tend to be liberal is a long-established phenomenon. It appears in surveys of journalists' party affiliations and candidate preferences, one of which goes back more than two decades.[16] But a liberal tendency, or a tendency of any kind—for change, for a generational shift—is of marginal importance unless it is apparent in what journalists report, which is exactly what many journalists and media observers say happened in 1992. That a liberal bias became evident then suggests that the kind of thinking so common on campuses—the idea, for example, that objectivity is an illusion that only the foolish value—was beginning to have a significant impact on journalism, just as it had had on other professions, such as law. Press commentary on this topic did bear strong resemblance to explanations given on campuses for subjectivity in research and teaching. Just as academics had been saying they were "no longer believers in 'objectivity',"[17] so, too, now were journalists.

Joann Byrd, then ombudsman for the *Washington Post*, wrote that through most of the campaigns of her lifetime, journalism had been ruled by the convention of objectivity, "a sort of bias police," as she described it, that "corrected for having humans do the nation's journalism." Journalists had come to see, however, that objectivity was impossible to achieve and limiting to strive for: "We wised up and dismissed objectivity as a pretentious fantasy that made stenographers of reporters and produced irresponsible journalism." But as she looked at pictures, headlines, and news stories in her paper for the concluding seventy-three days of the campaign and calculated that nearly five times as many were negative for Bush as for Clinton, she had to conclude that no good replacement had come along: "Fairness—which was supposed to substitute for objectivity—is, it turns out, a very subjective successor."[18]

Apparently a number of *Washington Post* readers did not regard throwing out objectivity as any sort of journalistic advance and wrote in to say so. "Most readers who liked objectivity," Byrd wrote in a second column, "liked it because it didn't tell them what to think. They are worried." She tried to make clear that when she dismissed objectivity, she wasn't suggesting that reporters shouldn't be "disinterested, detached, and fair." She had just been trying to say that the kind of journalism that simply passed along the claims of people in power was no longer thought to be responsible. The McCarthy era had demonstrated this, and so had Vietnam: "Voices inside and outside journalism thought the press still too wedded to objectivity when the early days in Vietnam were reported by parroting the official U.S. government version of events." Byrd concluded with suggestions about how the needs and desires of readers might be met without returning to the bad old days of "authorized versions" and "rephrased news releases and accounts."[19]

Media critic Howard Kurtz offered a similarly negative view of objectivity in his post-election book, *Media Circus*. "The conventions of objectivity," Kurtz argued, led journalists to quote experts when what they should be doing was crusading. These conventions led to the quoting of opposing views ("Pierce Says Housing Shortage Nonexistent, Critics Disagree") even when one of those views was clearly wrong. "The shackles of objectivity," Kurtz wrote, kept journalists from pointing out when television ads were inaccurate; and it was only by breaking those shackles that journalists were able to critique campaign ads, as they did for the first time in a presidential campaign in 1992.[20] Max Frankel, writing in the *New York Times Magazine* more recently, maintains that reporting "just the facts" can amount to "objective misrepresentation." What is needed, he says, is "disinterested interpretation": that is, for journalists to contextualize and analyze the pronouncements of public figures rather than letting them speak for themselves. "*Aggressive* interpretation," Frankel writes, is necessary "for accuracy and fairness."[21]

As a rule, postmodern thinking does not withstand logical analysis very well, and these versions of it, common in the journalistic profession, are no exception. To quote experts and public figures is not necessarily to be objective. If there are facts that contradict what a powerful person has to say, it is certainly not in the interest of objective truth to ignore them. Nor does analysis have to be totally subjective. Indeed, if it does not strive for objectivity, it is unlikely to be disinterested or detached. These ideals are all connected; and delinking them, as these explanations tend to do, permits the troubling conclusion that without even trying to be objective, one can nonetheless be fair. As Joann Byrd noted, this is not an idea that works very well in practice, nor should we expect it to, since it is riven by contradiction. If we cannot get outside ourselves to be objective, where are we to find a standard by which to judge if we are fair?

But logical or not, these views are in the journalistic air, as are fuller blown forms of postmodern skepticism. Richard Harwood, writing in the *Washington Post,* describes the "radical critique" of objectivity being carried out in newsrooms by women and minorities "on grounds that the dominant perspectives of white males are both limited and distorted."[22] Michael Lewis, a senior editor at the *New Republic*, defends a photographer who staged a photograph by observing that journalism never delivers "an unadulterated slice of reality." Why then, asks Lewis, should the photographer, who was only indulging in a minor form of what everybody else always does anyway, be punished?[23]

Added to this mix is the idea that even to attempt objectivity is to be part of a tired and hopelessly old-fashioned enterprise. In a March 1992 article in *Rolling Stone*, Jon Katz drew a distinction between two kinds of news: Old News and New News. The first, the straight news product traditionally associated with major newspapers and television networks, is, Katz wrote, "pooped, confused and broke." Its readership and audiences are declining and its advertising revenues drying up. Meanwhile, New News is evolving, "dazzling, adolescent, irresponsible, fearless, frightening and powerful." As Katz described it, the New News is "a heady concoction, part Hollywood film and TV movie, part pop music and pop art, mixed with popular culture and celebrity magazines, tabloid telecasts, cable and home video." Its creators, from rapper Chuck D to filmmaker Oliver Stone, do not concern themselves with balance, moderation, and objectivity. Instead they provide a sharp contrast to the Old News:

> Consumers can have a balanced discussion, with every side of an issue neutralizing the other, or they can turn to singers, producers and filmmakers offering colorful, distinctive, often flawed but frequently powerful visions of their truth. More and more, Americans are making it clear which they prefer.[24]

Katz's article was widely read and widely quoted. "Old News" and "New News" entered the journalistic lexicon, converged with various forms of the idea that objectivity is an oppressive myth, and helped form the backdrop for the press coverage of the presidential election of 1992, the "year the restraint was gone," as Fred Barnes, then of the *New Republic,* described it. Barnes worried, as well he might, that a historical shift had occurred. "I hope," he wrote, that "campaign coverage isn't permanently changed."[25]

ૢૺ

Journalists were not the only ones carrying on postmodern conversations; so were those they covered. Bob Woodward's book *The Agenda* depicts Mrs. Clinton explaining to the Clinton cabinet and White House staff during a retreat at Camp David in the early days of the Clinton presidency the importance of having well-constructed narratives in place. Woodward paraphrases her saying that it was crucial to have "a simple story, with characters, with an objective, with a beginning, middle, and end. And it all had to come from a moral point of view." Not having had a story had cost Bill Clinton the Arkansas governorship after his first term, she explained; having one had helped him win it back. The story they had used back in those days, she told the group, had been about the poor state of education in Arkansas and about how the Clintons would reform it; and, realizing that a narrative needed enemies as well as heroes, they had chosen the teachers' union, formerly a Clinton ally, to play the villain. "You show people what you're willing to fight for when you fight your friends," Mrs. Clinton is quoted as saying.[26]

According to *The Agenda,* Paul Begala, who played a key role in the 1992 campaign, was the one most in tune with what Mrs. Clinton was saying. As Woodward tells it, Begala's first rule of politics was a quintessentially postmodern one: "Define and create the reality that you want."[27] When it came to identifying villains for President Clinton's economic plan, Begala preferred "the greed and short-sightedness of the past," as did Mrs. Clinton, who, according to *The Agenda,* urged the president and his key advisors to describe the economic plan as a values document, an attempt to reverse the greedy 1980s.[28]

Begala and Clinton's decision to make the 1980s the adversary was no doubt influenced by their experience in 1992, when the 1980s had proved such an exploitable villain. The Clinton narrative in the 1992 campaign had been about a country in deep economic trouble that needed a leader who would disrupt "the old arrangements" that "serve the rich and powerful."[29] He would fight the "corrupt" values of the 1980s, when "the rich cashed in, [and] the forgotten middle class—the people who work hard and play by the rules—took it on the chin . . . [and] the working poor had the door of opportunity slammed in their face." He would move the country from a time when there was no economic vision and no economic growth to an era of expansion by "putting people first."[30]

This was the story, the value-filled narrative, that served as context for the centerpiece of the campaign: the Clinton economic plan. Like most such plans, this one did not bear close scrutiny. As Elizabeth Drew has noted, its numbers did not add up: "They relied on very optimistic assumptions and evaded some of the hard questions."[31] To cite just one example, the Clinton economic plan treated health care reform—which after the election would be assigned a hundred billion dollar price tag[32]—as though it could be accomplished at no cost.

But whatever its drawbacks, the Clinton plan had a huge advantage in that many journalists were inclined to accept its controlling narrative. Although the stereotype of the 1980s as an era when only the rich benefited has been disputed by liberal as well as conservative economists (Isabel Sawhill, whom Clinton appointed to the Office of Management and Budget, has flatly declared it "not true"),[33] in 1992 it was an article of faith with many members of the press. In just a single month, May 1992, *Philadelphia Inquirer* reporter Alexis Moore talked on C-SPAN about current problems as "the result of the past ten, twelve, fifteen years of . . . putting selfish[ness] and greed ahead of the needs of us all"; Marc Levinson in *Newsweek* described the 1980s as a "second Gilded Age—a time when, amid prosperity, many Americans became worse off"; and John Greenwald in *Time* described the Reagan era as a time when "the rich got bigger yachts, the middle class foundered, and many of the poor

183

went under."[34] To have journalists presenting the same version of history as the candidate—and often with the same rhetorical enthusiasm—was clearly a benefit in terms of public perception.

And it may have affected press perceptions as well. As the 1992 campaign progressed, the economy was getting better. Many people, including economists, did not realize this at the time; and one could hardly expect the press to have done so. But neither would one have expected that absent evidence that things were getting worse, the press would paint an increasingly bleak picture. That is, however, exactly what happened. During the general election, as Bill Clinton hammered home his message of greed, excess, and economic failure, press reports on the economy grew more negative. Thomas Patterson, pointing to a pattern that he says "strongly suggests" partisan bias (though of a kind that journalists may unconsciously exhibit), notes that before the fall campaign started, 75 percent of references to the economy on the network news had been negative; during the general election, the number rose to 90 percent. Writes Patterson, "*The networks' portrayal of the economy got worse as the economy improved.*"[35]

Nixon advisor Ray Price once observed, "Historical untruth may be a political reality."[36] One startling sequence of events from the 1992 campaign illustrates the converse of this rule: Historical truth can be political unreality. On October 27, 1992, the Department of Commerce reported that the Gross Domestic Product had grown at a rate of 2.7 percent in the third quarter of 1992, a healthy pace. News reports in the *Washington Post* and the *New York Times* quoted President Bush and his advisors trumpeting the figures as evidence that things were getting better and the Clinton camp debunking the news. A week before the election, none of this was surprising; but the *Post*'s and the *Times*' use of outside experts certainly was. It was to them that the ordinary reader might look to break the impasse of competing claims—and all of the quotes from outside experts were negative. Typical was the comment by Donald Rataczjak of Georgia State University in the *Post*: "Anyone who says that 2.7 percent is now our new growth rate is crazy."[37]

NBC's Tom Brokaw described the 2.7 percent growth rate as "an economic number [President Bush] can brag about." But ABC's Peter Jennings said it was "more than economists had projected, but in many cases, less than meets the eye." ABC correspondent Bob Jamieson declared that "many economists say the report is not proof the economy is taking a sharp turn for the better" and underscored the point with an economist who talked about the "divergence between this report and underlying reality."[38]

CBS's Dan Rather introduced the 2.7 growth rate by saying, "There is some doubt about the accuracy of the figures," and CBS correspondent Susan Spencer reported that "some economists warned that rate may not hold." CBS took up the subject again the next evening, October 28, in a segment entitled "Reality Check" in which correspondent Eric Engberg called the 2.7 figure a "quarterly bump" and "a notoriously volatile number" that economists say "does not necessarily mean a trend." He then presented four negative statistics, all more narrowly focused than the GDP estimate, and concluded by declaring that for most voters "the highest of the measurable economic indicators is anxiety."[39]

Within a month after the election, all of these news organizations would be reporting that the third quarter figures were even stronger than the 2.7 number. Revising its estimate upward, the Commerce Department said that the economy had actually expanded at 3.9 percent during July, August, and September. The new figure dramatically underscored how skewed earlier reporting had been. That so many had so thoroughly discredited a number that showed the economy improving had not merely been an error, it had been eloquent testimony to the way that accepting a certain view of the world—a certain narrative—can keep one from seeing what is really going on.

The focus that Bill Clinton chose for the campaign of 1992—the economy—certainly related to voter concerns more closely than did the flag factories of 1988, but he did not always deal with those concerns in ways that reflected reality. While one can certainly fault journalists for failing to press and challenge him as vigorously as they might have, who—given the progress of politics in our time—can fault Clinton? As Kathleen Hall Jamieson, dean of the Annenberg

School for Communication at the University of Pennsylvania, has pointed out, it is when candidates engage with reality rather than construct stories that citizens are most likely to be enlightened; but real engagement is dangerous for candidates, "suicide," Jamieson quotes Bush advisor Roger Ailes calling it.[40] With winning as the goal, better to go with stories, and most effective of all, if one has the wit and nerve to bring it off, to construct tales that seem to be more than they are, narratives that offer the illusion of substance without exacting the price.

What Bill Clinton may have done in 1992 is establish a new principle for the narrative-driven world of presidential campaigning. Yes, the story is important; but it must, above all, not seem like one. This is, of course, a task infinitely easier to accomplish if members of the press take up the narrative as their own.

ॐ

It is not uncommon for politicians to try to paint situations to their advantage, nor, if the circumstances seem to require, to reverse today what was said yesterday. It was during the Nixon administration that the public first learned that explanations that had become embarrassing could be declared "inoperative." Ronald Reagan regularly had to retract "facts" he used in speeches that turned out not to be factual. Surely one of the highest-profile 180 degree turns ever executed was the one that occurred between George Bush's 1988 nomination speech ("Read my lips: No new taxes") and the Bush administration tax increase of 1990. But when Bill Clinton reversed himself, he often made it sound as though his previous positions had never existed. During the New Hampshire primary, he had repeatedly declared a middle-class tax cut to be central to his economic plan. When pressed in June on his having backed off this position, he declared, "The press and my opponents always made more of the middle-class tax cut than I did." During the spring of 1992, he promised that when he became president, there would be "an explosive hundred-day action period," "the most productive period in modern history."[41] As his inauguration day actually neared, however, the following exchange took place:

REPORTER: We were originally led to believe that you'd have an outline to Congress even before the inauguration and present it on day one or shortly thereafter. When will it be ready?

CLINTON: I don't know who led you to believe that, but I'm the only one who's authorized to talk about that.[42]

During the campaign, Clinton's reconstructions of reality sometimes caused him trouble. His evolving stories on the draft, for example, received a good deal of press attention. But his reversal on the middle-class tax cut excited relatively little interest,[43] and it was mainly the *American Spectator* that gave notice to his changing account of his first hundred days.[44]

The pattern of shifts and revisions continued into his presidency. During the campaign, he had condemned the policy of shipping Haitian refugees back to Haiti as heartless and immoral;[45] as president-elect, he had declared that the refugees had to be shipped back because it was too dangerous for them to be at sea "in homemade boats made from wood they take off the roofs of their houses."[46] After he became president and activist Randall Robinson went on a hunger strike to protest the repatriation of Haitians who had fled their country, Clinton sided with Robinson ("He ought to stay out there"), as though his administration's policy had been none of his doing.[47]

As his presidency progressed, there were more and more such reversals; and they became an object of high anxiety among the press. In early 1994, columnist Bob Herbert wondered if the president was someone who could be trusted. He wrote about "Mr. Clinton's more or less fluid conception of what's real" and suggested that the White House staff "make a concerted effort to heighten Mr. Clinton's regard for the objective truth."[48] Herbert cited flip-flops on Bosnia and continuously revised explanations about state troopers, Whitewater, and what happened after Vincent Foster's suicide. He could also have mentioned Somalia, where the president's statements sometimes seemed to come out of different universes. In June 1993, he had declared that the goal of the U.S.-led United Nations operation was "to make sure that the United Nations can fulfill its mission there and continue to work with the Somalis toward nation building." In October 1993, he reported to the Congress, "The U.S. military mission is not now nor was it ever one of 'nation building.' "[49]

After a campaign in which he had enjoyed the support of many members of the press, Bill Clinton now found journalists treating him in an extraordinarily negative way. One measure of how critical they had become was a survey showing that only 38 percent of the evaluations of him on the three networks were positive during his first eighteen months in office. George Bush, during approximately the same period of his term in the White House, had had 49 percent positive evaluations.[50]

A theme that ran through many critical stories was disregard for truth. After the White House gave successive explanations about Hillary Clinton's commodities trading, Joe Klein of *Newsweek* wrote, "With the Clintons, the story *always* is subject to further revision"; and he and other journalists began to try to understand Bill Clinton's relationship to truth and reality. "The president truly likes people— his personal affection, and attention, is authentic—but he likes them indiscriminately," Klein wrote. "This wanton affability . . . ," he continued, "leads to a rhetorical promiscuity, the reckless belief that he can talk anyone into anything (or, more to the point, that he can talk his way *out of* anything), that he can seduce, and abandon, without will and without consequence."[51]

Michael Kelly, writing in the *New York Times*, noted Clinton's "chameleonesque habit of becoming whoever he was with, his talent for losing himself in the moment." Wrote Kelly:

> The President's essential character flaw isn't dishonesty so much as a-honesty. It isn't that Clinton means to say things that are not true, or that he cannot make true, but that everything is true for him when he says it, because he says it. Clinton means what he says when he says it, but tomorrow he will mean what he says when he says the opposite. He is the existential President, living with absolute sincerity in the passing moment.[52]

Kelly tried to explain Clinton's character by looking at his past. He suggested that the president might owe to his mother "the char-

acter trait that was perhaps the essential determinant of his political success—an unusually large need for adulation." It was a trait
that served him well as a politician, but also made him "peculiarly
vulnerable to the universal temptation of political life—to tell people what they want to hear." Moreover, Kelly noted, Clinton's
mother had been intensely present-oriented. He quoted from her
autobiography. "I've always felt the past is irrelevant," she had
written. "I've always maintained that whatever's in someone's past
is past, and I don't need to know about it." And when she thought
of the future, she said that she had trained herself "not to worry
about what-ifs, either. . . . And when bad things do happen, I
brainwash myself to put them out of my mind." Writes Michael
Kelly:

> Her world view taught, ultimately, that people are not to be
> judged by their actions, but are endlessly free to reinvent them-
> selves, to be whatever the moment demands. . . . Since the "irrel-
> evant" past does not really exist . . . the actions of the moment
> cease to exist once the moment becomes the past, and cannot be
> held against one later.[33]

People are influenced by their parents, of course; but they are also
influenced by their times; and another way of understanding Bill
Clinton is to see him as the incarnation of a personality type that the
present age has brought to full flower. In 1976, early in the postmodern era, Professor Richard Lanham of the University of California at Los Angeles labeled this type *Homo rhetoricus*:

> Rhetorical man is an actor; his reality public, dramatic. His sense
> of identity, his self, depends on the reassurance of daily histrionic
> reenactment. . . . He thinks first of winning, of mastering the rules
> the current game enforces. He assumes a natural agility in chang-
> ing orientations. He hits the street already street-wise. From birth,
> almost, he has dwelt not in a single value-structure but in several.
> He is thus committed to no single construction of the world;

much rather, to prevailing in the game at hand. . . . Rhetorical man is trained not to discover reality but to manipulate it. Reality is what is accepted as reality, what is useful. . . . Rhetorical man does not ask, "What is real?" He asks, "What is accepted as reality here and now?" He is thus typically present-centered. Past and future remain as possibility only, a paradigm he may some day have to learn.[54]

The rhetorical view of life, Lanham observed, was coming into increasing favor. Now almost twenty years later, we can see how profoundly influential it has been in fields ranging from the humanities to art to law. Given how widespread this way of thinking is, we should not be surprised to see it demonstrated plainly in a national leader, particularly when he is a man whose adult years have been almost perfectly co-extensive with the era of postmodern thought.

Unlike his opposite, *Homo seriosus*, or Serious Man, as Lanham labels him, *Homo rhetoricus* does not include in his thinking the idea of "a central self, an irreducible identity."[55] This is a difficult notion to do away with, as postmodern thinkers have frequently acknowledged. Foucault dramatized the trauma of recognizing that there is no true self by writing that this realization causes "man [to] be erased, like a face drawn in sand at the edge of the sea."[56] Philosopher Richard Rorty has noted the feeling of loss that comes with "the sense that there is nothing deep down inside us except what we have put there ourselves."[57] Mrs. Clinton may have had in mind the difficulties of doing away with long-established notions of identity when she told a commencement audience in Texas, "It is not going to be easy to redefine who we are as human beings in this postmodern age."[58]

Seen from this perspective, much of the criticism being directed at President Clinton is beside the point. When Michael Kelly writes of a "hollowness to the Clinton Presidency, a sense that it lacks a center because the man at its center lacks one of his own,"[59] he is looking for a true self, expecting something that a postmodernist would say never was and never can be. When NBC's Gwen Ifill reports that people ask about the president, "Where is your core? Where is your soul?"[60] she is, or so a postmodernist would have it, participating in mythmaking since such things do not exist.

An enthusiast of postmodern thought might well say that we are in a time of transition, that journalists have learned some of the lessons—that objectivity is foolish delusion, for example—but not all of them; and that as members of the press become more knowledgeable, they will understand the futility of expecting consistency and of trying to know who anyone really is, deep down. Others—and I include myself among them—worry about the impact of postmodern thinking on our political culture. How can a democracy hope to choose its leaders wisely if time and again what their campaigns offer us are artful fictions? Indeed, what can it mean to choose a leader if those who would lead us reject the idea of a core self with core beliefs and see the endless reinvention of personality as the way of the world? These concerns lead to a hope that the criticism of Bill Clinton is not the sign of a transition, but of an important reassessment, a new understanding on the part of the press that in our political life, as in other aspects of our existence, there is something called truth. Imperfect as we are, we can never hope to know it fully or possess it completely; but beyond the spin of the moment, it exists for us to pursue.

Living in Truth

"There is some hope, therefore, that the liberal habit of mind, which thinks of truth as something outside yourself, something to be discovered, and not as something you can make up as you go along, will survive."

—*George Orwell, "As I Please," 4 February 1944*

On the wall of the Whitney Museum of American Art hangs a large canvas on which strands of color twist and turn, red crossing over yellow, green metamorphosing into gold. Brice Marden's *Muses (Hydra Version)* is a serious work by a serious artist; and after many years in which painting has been discredited as an imperialist form of art making, it is significant that this painting appears in the 1995 Biennial Exhibition. Even though there are other artists in the Biennial whose work is driven by politics (Sue Williams is represented again), and even though there are those who say that the inclusion of serious painters like Marden is simply an attempt on the part of the Whitney to avoid the kind of criticism the 1993 Biennial brought, Marden is nonetheless here. A few months later, so is Edward Hopper. In June 1995, the Whitney put fifty-nine haunting, memorable paintings by this American master on display, a hopeful sign for those who think that art is about more than victimization and rage.

On the other side of the continent in California, two professors from the University of California at Berkeley are working to refocus civil rights efforts on the overarching principle of justice for all rather than on the political idea of group preference for some. Their goal is passage of an initiative that would forbid discrimination on the basis of race and gender—just as the Civil Rights Act of 1964 did. The regents of the University of California, following the lead of one of their members, who is African-American, have voted to end racial preferences in the state university system. Meanwhile, Supreme Court decisions on subjects ranging from college scholarships to government contracts hold that awards based on race must have specific justification. These are hopeful signs for those who think that merit is more than a code word for oppression.

Governor Christine Todd Whitman of New Jersey has become widely admired not only for her preelection promise to cut taxes, but for actually cutting them once she was in office. She thereby established a pattern that the Republicans in Congress, particularly in the House of Representatives, built on spectacularly in 1994. The Contract with America was a device for setting out specific preelection promises that, after the election, could be fulfilled to the political benefit of the promisers. One does not have to agree with either Governor Whitman or the substance of the Contract (in fact, a poll taken not long after voting on Contract items was complete showed the country evenly split on its policies, 44 percent approving and 43 percent disapproving)[1] in order to find it a good sign that politicians are paying attention to delivering on what they say.

Some members of the one hundred and fourth Congress have shown a heartening determination to deal with troubling issues, from large ones such as affirmative action to much smaller but still significant matters such as the National History Standards. The ninety-nine senators who voted on January 19, 1995, for a sense-of-the-Senate resolution denouncing the History Standards were taking an important step toward stopping the teaching of distorted versions of the past in our schools. And so were the thousands of people who wrote to their congressmen and senators and to anyone else they thought could help keep the standards out of classrooms. My office received more than three thousand letters, many of them emphasizing that their writers didn't want to go back to history as it was taught many years ago. "I don't think anyone wants to return to those outdated views which often failed to give any credence to women and minority achievement," wrote a history teacher. But time and again, letter writers stressed the importance of what a State University of New York professor emeritus called "an ACCURATE account of what made this nation what it is." A correspondent from California wrote, "Whatever else the writing of history should be, it should be accurate and objective."

The proposed *Enola Gay* exhibition also inspired an outpouring of letters. *Smithsonian* magazine heard from twenty thousand of their subscribers.[2] Surely it is reason for optimism that so many citizens are intent on reclaiming the past—and better understanding the present. They are looking for and finding in talk radio and on cable television points of view often missing in the mainstream press. Like other forms of New News, these were at times "dazzling, adolescent [and] irresponsible," to borrow Jon Katz's words; but at its best, talk radio enlarged the marketplace of ideas in a worthy fashion, and cable television—C-SPAN, in particular—gave people a chance to see what was happening for themselves so that they no longer had to depend on filtered news.

But for all these hopeful signs, we are far from having restored what George Orwell called "the liberal habit of mind, which thinks of truth as something outside yourself, something to be discovered, and not as something you can make up as you go along." The History Standards illustrate the problem. Although they have been widely condemned, there are twenty thousand copies of them in circulation, put there at government expense; and in the early months of 1995, their influence could be seen in curricular proposals in a number of states. It is also important to pay attention to the claim of the standards developers that hundreds of academics and educators across the country helped in this project. The developers say this to demonstrate that their project is mainstream; but, in fact, it helps show how far many people in academia and education have drifted from the mainstream. There would not be great cause for concern if only a few people had been involved in developing a document in which the Seneca Falls

Declaration of Sentiments, an important feminist text, is cited nine times and Lincoln's Gettysburg Address only once, or in which Thomas Edison isn't mentioned at all, but Joseph McCarthy and Mc-Carthyism come up nineteen times; but when hundreds of people who have influence on the schools are involved, it makes clear how large the problem of politicized history is.

That there are no true stories, but only useful ones, no overarching principles, but only the interests of the moment, are ideas now deeply embedded in our culture. We are not the first society in which this has happened; and damaging as the consequences are for us, they have been far more destructive in other places, in the Soviet Union and in Soviet-dominated Eastern Europe, for example. Bad as it is when powerful groups within a democracy insist on fealty to their views, it is far worse when a totalitarian government forces its orthodoxy upon a population. Nonetheless, there are things that we can learn from the experience of others; and first and foremost among them is the relationship between truth and freedom. As journalist David Remnick points out in his book *Lenin's Tomb*, it was the return of history, the return of truth about the past, that was the beginning of the end of the Soviet empire. For decades, people who called themselves historians produced the dogma that undergirded the Soviet regime. Schoolchildren were forced to memorize it; intellectuals to pay homage to it. When Mikhail Gorbachev began to speak tentatively about what many people knew but dared not talk about—the cruelties and repressions of the Stalinist state—the dogma began to crumble, as did the totalitarian superstructure it supported.[3]

Václav Havel—a man who lived under totalitarianism, fought it, and after its failure served as an elected leader—calls dissent from orthodoxy "living in truth"; and he illustrates this idea with a story about a Czechoslovakian greengrocer, who during the years of Soviet domination of Eastern Europe decides one day *not* to display in his shop window a party slogan in which neither he nor anyone else really believes. It is a decision with consequences, as Havel tells it. The greengrocer will likely lose his managerial job and be assigned to work in a warehouse. His children may find it hard to get into college. His superiors will harass him. But that is only one kind of result. The greengrocer's action, as Havel describes it, also shatters the world of appearances and helps all around him to see the reality that lies behind the facade of the system. By throwing into relief the orthodoxy being enforced, the greengrocer's action casts light on the entire society. "His action went beyond itself," Havel writes, "because it illuminated its surroundings."[4]

In writing this book, I discovered many examples of people who are illuminating some aspect of American life, from citizens like Sandra Stotsky and Robert Costrell in Brookline, Massachusetts, who have stood up against letting their local schools succumb to anti-Western faddishness, to psychologist Elizabeth Loftus at the University of Washington in Seattle, who was one of the first to object when some in her field began to urge patients to explain all manner of adult behavior with "recovered memories" of childhood abuse. The cost for speaking out in our society is not nearly what it was for Havel's greengrocer; but usually there is a price. As often happens when citizens protest what is happening in schools, Stotsky and Costrell found themselves denounced as "censors"—by, among others, the Massachusetts state council of the National Endowment for the Humanities.[5] Loftus has been accused of further victimizing people who are already in pain.[6]

Moreover, it requires effort to go against the grain, "to live in truth," as Havel puts it. It is easier to go along and save one's energy for family or for the quiet kind of work that has not become politicized. Thus, while our society does not make us pay nearly as much for living according to truth as Havel's society once did, I still find myself extraordinarily grateful when I come across men and women who won't put the sign in the window, who won't go along, who won't ignore the evidence their reason provides, and who will speak out about it. They are the models for the rest of us. When we find ourselves faced with situations that violate good sense—whether it is how our children are being taught or how our legal system is abandoning the principles that have long undergirded it—we should, each of us, speak out about what we see. We should not let ourselves be intimidated by seemingly sophisticated statements about how there is no reality and thus no truth. As philosopher John Searle has observed, "Once you state the claims and arguments of the anti-realists out in the open, naked and undisguised, they tend to look fairly ridiculous."[7] Nor should we bow down to heavyhanded assertions about how there is no objectivity and thus no way to judge whether one way of doing a thing, be it educating the young or choosing a leader, is better or worse than any other. Complete objectivity may be beyond our reach, but we can achieve a significant degree of it, certainly enough to understand that social arrangements are mutable and to make reasoned judgments about how the ones our society has chosen measure up. Faced with demands that those arrangements change, citizens of a democracy should demand reasoned argument and make clear that invective and name-calling do not fall into that category. Meanwhile, within the arrangements we have, it is quite possible to seek evidence, examine it, and arrive at conclusions about all manner of things, from whether we should encourage the habit of hard work to whether a society benefits when people in professions that range from education to filmmaking, from law to psychotherapy, are encouraged to pursue the truth.

Nor need we—to return to a point with which this book started—accept the idea that literature, history, and philosophy are about nothing more than politics, nothing more than social power. While it is surely the case that there have been and are societies in which Shakespeare's poems and plays do not resonate, that does not mean that they are not transcendent—only that they are not absolutely transcendent. Prospero's words, "We are such stuff as dreams are made on," speaks to many, perhaps even to most, of life's glory and briefness. How impoverished our world if we accept the idea that *The Tempest* is about nothing more than the impact of European imperialism on native societies. There is a wisdom about things that really matter to be found in the humanities—a sense of how life could be different and why it is like it is; a sense of what greatness is, and excellence, and how these qualities have ennobled the world;

a sense of where we stand in the progression of time and of how those who came before us delighted in the joy and dealt with the sorrow our own journey will surely bring. It can be intimidating to listen to those who have sparkling credentials and prestigious positions proclaim that the humanities are about none of these things, but generations have found otherwise. And isn't it odd, we should ask, that today's academics have discovered a truth that has eluded humanities scholars for centuries—particularly when the defining characteristic of today's generation is lack of belief in truth.

In concluding this book, I want to focus on three people in the academic world, surely one of the venues in our society where it is hardest to seek the truth and speak one's mind about it—and one of the most important places for truth-seeking to continue. As I have tried to show, it is from our colleges and universities that messages radiate—or fail to radiate—to schools, to legal institutions, to popular culture, and to politics about the importance of reason, of trying to overcome bias, of seeking truth through evidence and verification. Colleges and universities are the wellspring of the ideas around which we organize ourselves, and while many in these institutions have of late, particularly in the humanities, turned against reason and truth, there are also men and women associated with our campuses who refuse to subscribe to current dogma and who, like Havel's greengrocer, remind us by their refusal of the way things could be and should be.

One of them is Frank M. Snowden, Jr., a man in his eighties now who taught for half a century at Howard University in Washington, D.C. Snowden received his Ph.D. from Harvard in the days when doctoral dissertations were still written in Latin; and for most of his career he has focused on discovering and revealing the role played by blacks in the ancient world. He has traveled to libraries and museums around the world, reviewing manuscripts, examining artifacts from antiquity, and trying always to understand these things objectively, to see them as they were created—not as later prejudices and preferences would have us see them.

Snowden first encountered the distorting effects of scholars' reading the present into the past when he observed the way that some researchers brought their own prejudices against black people to their observations of the ancient portrayal of blacks. They would see ugliness, caricature, or comedy in places where none of these things existed and where the renderings were, in fact, fine and sympathetic.[8] Snowden's latest encounter with researchers who impose an agenda on the past is with Martin Bernal, the author of *Black Athena*, and the Afrocentrists. Although Bernal usually couches his assertions in ways that make him hard to pin down, his work is seen by many as supporting Afrocentric claims, such as the notion that Egypt was a black nation. This is an idea that Frank Snowden, the meticulous scholar, simply could not let pass without notice. Pointing out that Bernal places a great deal of weight on Herodotus's having, in Bernal's words, "thought the Egyptians and some Libyans were black," Snowden used his knowledge of ancient languages and cultures to dispute Bernal's interpretation of Herodotus and dismiss the larger claim about the population of ancient Egypt.[9]

Since Snowden is *emeritus* now, the enemies he makes in such encounters can do nothing to affect his university career. Instead they go after his scholarly reputation, charging that he is the dupe of white scholars and white scholarship.[10] But Snowden is undeterred by the attacks. He continues to describe ancient Africa in the way that a lifetime of scholarship has taught him is accurate and to emphasize that the world of antiquity is not one to which we should bring our prejudices, but a place to which we should come objectively, dispassionately, and in the true spirit of inquiry.

If we do this, we can learn an important lesson, according to Snowden. "Scholars have painstakingly examined the entire corpus of classical literature and hundreds of portraits of blacks from the workshops of ancient artists," he told University of Maryland graduates in 1993. "The overwhelming conclusion is that the color of the skin never acquired in the Greco-Roman world the dreadful importance it has assumed in some modern societies, where it poisons the self-image of many peoples, and rationalizes the denial of equality to minorities."[11] If truth rather than politics is our goal when we study ancient history, Snowden teaches, what we will learn is that racism is an *un*necessary part of the human condition.

Elizabeth Fox-Genovese founded Emory University's women's studies program in the mid-1980s with the idea that women's studies could be an academic discipline: that is, a field of study in which knowledge of women, gender, and feminist theory is the goal.[12] She determined that the program she headed would be ideologically open. There would be no correct positions and no incorrect ones. It should be possible, as she saw it, for someone who opposed feminist theory to feel at home in Emory's program. She even imagined that someone with a pro-life position on abortion might have a contribution to make as a student or teacher.

By the fall of 1991, the program had eight core faculty members, dozens of associated faculty, many satisfied students—and a growing number of opponents. There was criticism of the program's introductory course, which was taught by a classicist who took up themes of marriage and motherhood in texts that ranged from Euripides' *Medea* to Toni Morrison's *Beloved*. As some saw it, the course was too demanding and Eurocentric besides. There were also complaints that Emory's women's studies program was not sufficiently "nurturing." That is, it did not spend enough time on the confessional, consciousness-raising activities that have become the hallmark of campus feminism.

During the fall of 1991, Fox-Genovese refused a request that she send a telegram to the Senate Judiciary Committee putting Emory's women's studies program on record opposing the nomination of Clarence Thomas. "I don't take political positions for the program," she explained. She also spoke to a group in Rochester, New York, called Feminists for Life, sparking reports that she herself was pro-life, though, in fact, she believes that abortion should be available during the early months of pregnancy. Pressures against her continuing to serve as director of the Emory program became severe; and feeling that she no longer had the support of the administration, Fox-Genovese resigned. Women's studies, she said, "faces an internal struggle":

The battle against the conservatives was much easier to win. . . . But the battle against the radicals is much harder, it's pervasive. The tendency in women's studies is towards politicization. It isn't necessary, but it's natural. It's the path of least resistance, and it's fairly widespread throughout the country, because it's so easy to assume that women's studies is really going to be feminist studies, that its main purpose is ideological, not intellectual.[13]

But her resignation was not the end of the story. Like others who have offended feminist activists, she found herself the target of a sexual harassment suit, this one focusing on supposed demands for personal services (picking up dry cleaning, according to campus gossip) and a putative request for a hug. The National Association of Scholars, of which Fox-Genovese is a member, declared that the charges "trivialize the very notion of sexual harassment."[14]

None of this forced Fox-Genovese into conformity. She went on to endorse the right of the Virginia Military Institute and the Citadel to remain all-male institutions—and to defend these schools from a feminist perspective. Since single-sex education is an option that women should have, it must also be defended for men, she argued. By ensuring that every individual regardless of gender has the right to attend any academic institution, "it accordingly follows," she said, "that the countless individuals who might seek a single-sex education would have nothing left to choose."[15]

With the sexual harassment suit dragging on, Fox-Genovese describes many of her experiences of the last few years as "painful," but she appears to have no regrets for the path she charted for the women's studies program. Never having doubted the value of intellectual honesty, she says she is not about to start now. "Middle age is no time *not* to say what you think," she advises, "because if you don't say what you think, you won't say anything well."[16]

Alan C. Kors began teaching at the University of Pennsylvania in 1968, when his Ph.D. in history from Harvard was brand-new. Lyndon Johnson was president and his Vietnam policy was the target of massive demonstrations. As Kors describes it, he, too, was a Johnson critic, but from the right rather than from the left, where most of his colleagues were. "People said don't worry about it. No one will hold your politics against you. [If I were starting out] now, I'm convinced I couldn't get a job."[17]

It's not just Kors's politics that would make him unwelcome on many campuses, but also his outspoken opposition to the politicization of campus life. He hates the idea of dividing up the curriculum on racial or ethnic lines. "Growing up Jewish in Jersey City, I really thought of Plato as *our* philosopher and Dante Alighieri as *our* poet. It's criminal to tell black kids that Plato isn't their philosopher."[18] Kors has done more than anyone else to call attention to the way that various "student life" activities have assumed authority "over the souls and private consciences" of students.[19] Diversity education in particular, undertaken in orientation sessions and dormitory seminars, has as its goal, Kors says, "the political indoctrination and New Age moral reformation of moderate undergraduates deemed to be the benighted products of a benighted society."[20]

When Eden Jacobowitz of "water buffalo" fame decided to contest the charges of racial harassment that had been lodged against him, Kors counseled him, urging him, when the university was unresponsive, to call media attention to the situation. Kors has also proved to be a tough combatant on his own behalf. In 1992, he was nominated to be a member of the National Council on the Humanities, whereupon the *Chronicle of Higher Education* identified him as a "vocal opponent . . . of left-wing scholars."[21] In a letter to the editor, he denounced the charge as "outrageous," and wrote:

> Some of the deepest influences on my intellectual and personal life, and many of the scholars I admire most, academically and humanly, are "left-wing." I am opposed to tendentious scholarship, period, and to hiring or promotion on the basis of political affiliations. I would oppose these with equal fervor if they came from right, left, or center.[22]

In a contentious time, Kors managed to get himself confirmed by the United States Senate.

Kors, who reads Aleksandr Solzhenitsyn's *Gulag Archipelago* every three years, says that his fellow academics frequently tell him that it is brave of him to take the stands he does. "I say, 'how absurd.' The only price you pay is that you're blackballed by other history departments. That drives pay, and so you end up being underpaid."[23] Compared to what dissidents in the Soviet Union and Eastern Europe sacrificed for speaking out, Kors maintains, reduced pay is a matter of hardly any consequence at all.

He is right, of course; and his modesty is admirable. But he is also correct when he observes that it would be hard, if not impossible, for him if he were starting out now to get a job at a major American university. This is an intolerable situation—and we should not lose sight that it is so. Almost as important as holding truth as a goal for ourselves is maintaining a healthy level of indignation at the behavior of those who do not, whether it is search committees that pose ideological tests; professors who will not pay heed to what their composition or law students quite sensibly want to learn; or a film director who distorts history in the most pernicious way, all the while claiming to be a truth-teller. Repeatedly bombarded with the idea that there is no truth, but only various fictions that must be enforced, one can all too easily decide to adapt, to go along in order to get along. Encountering postmodernists at work, we must not lose sight of how offensive their assumptions are, how condescending to those who seek knowledge, only to find that they are supposed to be content with ideology.

As I look back over this book, I am struck by the high level of arrogance that often exists among those who maintain that there is no truth except the one they would have us believe. They redefine our words and our lives for us, and expect us to go along. They rewrite the past and are shocked when we object. And this arrogance is often combined with an amazing lack of thought to the consequences of what they are preaching. It does not require great insight, for example, to see a connection between the idea that one's truth is defined by one's group and the resegregation and racial hostility that have become all too common in our society. Nor should we overlook the moral consequences of insisting that reality is nothing more than what we create. If history is only an invention, then we never have to account for what we have done. We never have to admit to even the most grievous error; we can simply revise it out of existence.

The well-known case of Paul de Man, a Yale professor and a leader of the deconstructionist movement, is an apt illustration. After his death in 1983, it was discovered that de Man had been the author of anti-Semitic writings during World War II; and although his followers tried mightily to deny a connection, one can easily see why a man who wanted to escape responsibility for such acts would spin out a philosophy that allows one constantly to rewrite the past. The idea of responsibility—of being accountable for one's actions—has no meaning in a world where there is neither truth nor reality, but only endless interpretation.

Nor is there a place in such a world for other moral concepts that many people increasingly believe must play a role in our lives and our society. What can it mean to say we should treat one another fairly when there is no external reality in which we can seek a standard that would allow us to know whether we are doing so? What can it mean to say that we should have compassion for one another? That assumes a real world in which the pain of others, hurting them as much as our own does us, deserves our sympathetic understanding.

In late spring 1994 an incident in Philadelphia provided a chilling vision of life without such qualities. Forty-nine-year-old Mohammad Jaberipour was working a route in South Philadelphia in a Mister Softee ice cream truck when a sixteen-year-old tried to extort money from him. Jaberipour refused to give the sixteen-year-old what he demanded, and the youth shot Jaberipour. As the father of three lay dying, neighborhood teenagers laughed at him and mocked his agony with a rap song they composed on the spot—"They Killed Mr. Softee." Another ice cream truck driver and friend of Jaberipour, who came on the scene shortly after the shooting, described what he saw. "It wasn't human," he said:

> When I got there people were laughing and asking me for ice cream. I was crying. My best friend was killed. They were acting as though a cat had died, not a human being.[24]

Accounting for such behavior is no simple matter. People who behave this way have obviously become desensitized to violence, probably because they have seen so much of it. Columnist Bob Greene suggests that their insensitivity reveals a contemporary confusion of entertainment and reality. "We [have] increasingly become a nation of citizens who watch anything and everything as if it is all a show," he writes.[25]

But however it has come about, people who laugh at a dying man have no sense that a stranger can suffer just as they do, that his death creates sorrow for someone just as would the death of someone close to them. They have lost the animating perception of compassion, the awareness, as Josiah Royce described it, that another person is "just as real . . . as actual, as concrete, as thou art:"

> His life [is] as bright a light, as warm a fire, to him, as thine to thee; his will is as full of struggling desires, of hard problems, of fateful decisions; his pains are as hateful, his joys as dear.[26]

Without the idea that we live in reality with other people who are as real as we are, compassion is impossible and so is any other virtue one could name. Nothing beyond the gratification of the moment matters in such a world, not fairness, not justice, not responsibility, not honor. None of them matters because in such a world none of them exists.

The pathology involved in the murder of Mohammad Jaberipour and the behavior of the crowd afterward runs so deep that it is clear there is no single explanation for it and no easy remedy. But it is also evident that intellectual elites do no one a favor by sending through society messages that there is no external reality in which we all participate, that there is only the game of the moment, the entertainment of the day. Outside the protective environment of the campus, these ideas have real and devastating effects.

The virtues that we have increasingly come to believe we must nurture if we are to be successful as a culture simply make no sense if we turn away from reason and reality. Thus, whether we as a society find the will to live in truth is more than a matter for idle speculation. The answer may very well determine whether we survive.

ɞ Notes

Introduction

1. Richard Bernstein, "Academia's Liberals Defend Their Carnival of Canons Against Bloom's 'Killer B's,' " *New York Times* (25 September 1988), Sec. 4, p. 26.
2. Lynne V. Cheney, *Humanities in America: A Report to the President, the Congress, and the American People* (Washington, D.C.: National Endowment for the Humanities, September 1988), 11–12, 14.
3. Matthew Arnold, "The Function of Criticism at the Present Time," *Poetry and Criticism of Matthew Arnold,* A. Dwight Culler, ed. (Boston: Houghton Mifflin, 1961), 257. Lecture first delivered at Oxford University, 29 October 1864.
4. Lynne V. Cheney, *Telling the Truth: A Report on the State of the Humanities in Higher Education* (Washington, D.C.: National Endowment for the Humanities, September 1992).
5. Quotations of Joshua Steiner and his diary are from the Federal News Service transcript of his testimony at a hearing before the Senate Banking, Housing and Urban Affairs Committee, 2 August 1994.
6. Thomas Bender, " 'Facts' and History," *Radical History Review* (March 1985), 83.
7. Quoted in George Kalogerakis, "Hype & Glory," *Vanity Fair* (October 1993), 184.
8. Stanley Diamond, "Reversing Brawley," *Nation* (31 October 1988), 409.

9. Homi K. Bhabha, "A Good Judge of Character: Men, Metaphors, and the Common Culture," *Race-ing Justice, En-gendering Power: Essays on Anita Hill, Clarence Thomas, and the Construction of Social Reality*, Toni Morrison, ed. (New York: Pantheon, 1992), 249.

10. Mike Causey, "Defense Adds Hiring Rule," *Washington Post* (13 September 1994), B2.

11. See Iver Peterson, "Justice Dept. Switches Sides in Racial Case," *New York Times* (14 August 1994), Sec. 1, p. 37.

12. Stanley Fish quoted in Carol Jouzaitis, "NIU Divided at Debate on Political Correctness," *Chicago Tribune* (24 October 1991), Chicagoland section, 8.

13. Benjamin H. D. Buchloh, "The Whole Earth Show: An Interview with Jean-Hubert Martin by Benjamin H. D. Buchloh," *Art in America* (May 1989), 158.

14. An unnamed university administrator quoted in Alan Charles Kors, "It's Speech, Not Sex, the Dean Bans Now," *Wall Street Journal* (12 October 1989), A16.

15. See Barry R. Gross, "Salem in Minnesota," *Academic Questions* (Spring 1992), 70; Marcia Bedard and Beth Hartung, "Blackboard Jungle Revisited," *Thought & Action* (Spring 1991), 7–20.

16. Quoted in Bill Gifford, "The Unbearable Whiteness of Being," *Washington City Paper* (12 November 1993), 30.

17. U.S. Bureau of the Census, *Statistical Abstract of the United States: 1994*, 114th ed. (Washington, D.C.: U.S. Department of Commerce, September 1994), tables 12, 296.

18. See DeNeen L. Brown and Charles W. Hall, "A Complaint, a Harassment Probe, a Teacher's Suicide," *Washington Post* (3 June 1993), A1; and DeNeen L. Brown and Charles W. Hall, "Girl Blamed, Defended After Teacher's Suicide," *Washington Post* (4 June 1993), D1.

19. William C. Chicca, letter to the editor, *Washington Post* (13 June 1993), C6.

Chapter 1: Politics in the Schoolroom

1. Patricia G. Ramsey, *Teaching and Learning in a Diverse World: Multicultural Education for Young Children* (New York: Teachers College Press, 1987), 73.

2. Marilyn Frankenstein, "A Different Third R: Radical Math," *Politics of Education: Essays from Radical Teacher*, Susan Gushee O'Malley, Robert C. Rosen, and Leonard Vogt, eds. (Albany: State University of New York Press, 1990), 220.

3. Christine I. Bennett, *Comprehensive Multicultural Education: Theory and Practice* (Boston: Allyn and Bacon, 1990), 287; Eugenie C. Scott, "The Social Context of Pseudoscience," *The Natural History of Paradigms*, J. H. Langdon and M. E. McGann, eds. (Indianapolis: University of Indianapolis Press, 1993), 350.

4. Maria Sweeney, "Columbus, A Hero? Rethinking Columbus in an Elementary Classroom," *Radical Teacher* (Fall 1993), 25–29.

5. Quoted in Robert Holland, "Re-education, the Multicultural Way," *Richmond Times-Dispatch* (21 February 1993), F7.

6. "Spelling Test 3" given in October 1992 to a fourth-grade gifted and talented class in the Chapel Hill–Carrboro, North Carolina, school district.

7. Conversation with author, 27 May 1993.

8. Sandra Stotsky, "Multicultural Education in the Brookline Public Schools: The Deconstruction of an Academic Curriculum," *Network News & Views* (October 1991), 30, 32.

9. Charlotte Crabtree and Gary B. Nash, *National Standards for United States History: Exploring the American Experience, Grades 5–12* (Los Angeles: National Center for History in the Schools, University of California at Los Angeles, 1994), 48, 44, 139.

10. Sandra Harding, *The Science Question in Feminism* (Ithaca: Cornell University Press, 1986), 113.

11. Andrew Ross, *Strange Weather: Culture, Science, and Technology in the Age of Limits* (London: Verso, 1991), 11; Paul R. Gross and Norman Levitt, *Higher Superstition: The Academic Left and Its Quarrels with Science* (Baltimore: Johns Hopkins University Press, 1994), 235.

12. Charlotte Crabtree and Gary B. Nash, *National Standards for World History: Exploring Paths to the Present, Grades 5–12* (Los Angeles: National Center for History in the Schools, University of California at Los Angeles, 1994), 274.

13. Ibid., 52, 79.

14. Ibid., 177, 268.

15. Ibid., 270–71; Crabtree and Nash, *National Standards for United States History*, 214–15.
16. Betty Jean Craige, "Multiculturalism and the Vietnam Syndrome," *Chronicle of Higher Education* (12 January 1994), B8.
17. Martha Nussbaum, "Patriotism and Cosmopolitanism," *Boston Review* (October/November 1994), 3.
18. Ibid., 6.
19. "Basic Instructional Program: Related Curriculum Issues," policy 10 (Tavares, Fla.: Lake County Schools, 1994).
20. Professor and education association quoted in Rick Badie, "Teaching Battle Could Be Needless," *Orlando Sentinel* (12 May 1994), 1.
21. Richard Cohen, ". . . To Multiculturalism," *Washington Post* (19 May 1994), A21.
22. *How Schools Shortchange Girls* (Washington, D.C.: American Association of University Women, 1992).
23. Diane Ravitch, "What Gender Bias?" *Washington Post* (21 November 1993), C7.
24. Alexander W. Astin, William S. Korn, and Ellyne R. Riggs, *The American Freshman: National Norms for Fall 1993* (Los Angeles: Higher Education Research Institute, December 1993), 2; Alexander W. Astin et al., *The American Freshman: National Norms for Fall 1994* (Los Angeles: Higher Education Research Institute, December 1994), 48, 32.
25. See Diane Ravitch and Chester E. Finn, Jr., *What Do Our 17-Year-Olds Know?* (New York: Harper & Row, 1987), 263.
26. Robert Lerner, Althea K. Nagai, and Stanley Rothman, "Filler Feminism in High School History," *Academic Questions* (Winter 1991–1992), 31, 36–37.
27. Paul C. Vitz, *Censorship: Evidence of Bias in Our Children's Textbooks* (Ann Arbor, Mich.: Servant Books, 1986), 38. An indignant mother in the Wallingford-Swarthmore school district of Philadelphia pointed out to me the way this theme carried over into exercises sixth-graders were asked to do in the school district in which she lived. A handout given to her son declared "the traditional nuclear family" to be a relic of the past and deservedly so since it "depended on the wife subordinating many of her individual interests to those

of her husband and children." The handout further asked sixth-graders to assess who in their families was responsible for such tasks as grocery shopping, preparing meals, making major expenditures, and disciplining children. On the basis of the answers, each sixth-grader was to decide whether his or her family was "egalitarian or traditional"—and report the results to the school.

28. Jackie DeFazio, letter to the editor, *Washington Post* (25 December 1993), A21.
29. *How Schools Shortchange Girls,* 62.
30. *Hostile Hallways: The AAUW Survey on Sexual Harassment in America's Schools* (Washington, D.C.: American Association of University Women, 1993), 7, 10, 8.
31. Albert Shanker, "Lewd or Rude?" *New Republic* (23–30 August 1993), Advertisement.
32. Cynthia Crossen, *Tainted Truth: The Manipulation of Fact in America* (New York: Simon & Schuster, 1994), 17.
33. Vivien Ng (Washington, D.C.: Presentation to National Women's Studies Association Annual Conference, 20 June 1993).
34. McIntosh quoted in Robert Costrell, "The Mother of All Curriculums," *Brookline Citizen* (15 March 1991), 7.
35. Ibid.
36. Rita Kramer, *Ed School Follies: The Miseducation of America's Teachers* (New York: Free Press, 1991), 28–29.
37. Carol Gilligan, *In a Different Voice: Psychological Theory and Women's Development* (Cambridge: Harvard University Press, 1982); Mary Field Belenky et al., *Women's Ways of Knowing: The Development of Self, Voice, and Mind* (New York: Basic Books, 1986).
38. Randy Moore, "Grades and Self-Esteem," *American Biology Teacher* (October 1993), 388.
39. Astin et al., *The American Freshman* (1994), 13.
40. Suzanne Alexander, "Trophy Transcript Hunters Are Finding Professors Have Become an Easy Mark," *Wall Street Journal* (27 April 1993), B1; Committee on Academic Appraisal and Achievement, "A Study of Grading Practices at Stanford University: Faculty Attitudes, Student Concerns, and Proposed Changes to Grading Policy" (Stanford, Calif.: Stanford University, April 1994), figure 3.

41. William Cole, "By Rewarding Mediocrity We Discourage Excellence," *Chronicle of Higher Education* (6 January 1993), B1.
42. Quoted in John Leo, "A for Effort. Or for Showing Up," *U.S. News & World Report* (18 October 1993), 22.
43. "Making the Grades," *New York Times* (5 June 1994), Sec. 4, p. 16.
44. *How Schools Shortchange Girls,* 66.
45. Melinda Henneberger, "New Gym Class: No More Choosing Up Sides," *New York Times* (16 May 1993), A1.
46. Ann Landers, "Part of Me Will Always Be Missing," *Chicago Tribune* (17 January 1994), Tempo section, 3.
47. Quoted in Patrick F. Bassett, "The Academy of (Lesser) Science," *Education Week* (3 August 1994), 51.
48. Mark A. Mlawer, " 'My Kid Beat Up Your Honor Student,' " *Education Week* (13 July 1994), 39.
49. Nicholas C. Burbules, "Tootle: A Parable of Schooling and Destiny," *Harvard Educational Review* (August 1986), 253, 250.
50. Quoted in Kramer, *Ed School Follies*, 95.
51. "The Ultimate Mother," *New York Times* (12 May 1991), Sec. 4, p. 16.
52. Quoted in Louise Derman-Sparks and the A.B.C. Task Force, *Anti-Bias Curriculum: Tools for Empowering Young Children* (Washington, D.C.: National Association for the Education of Young Children, 1989), 90–91.
53. Emily Culpepper, "The Spiritual, Political Journey of a Feminist Freethinker," *The Tree Book III* (Little Rock: Arkansas Governor's School, 1991), 122, 128, 126.
54. Jack Booth et al., eds., *Impressions* (Toronto: Holt, Rinehart and Winston, 1984–1988), 16 volumes.
55. *Brown v. Woodland Joint Unified School District,* 1992 U.S. Dist. LEXIS 22119, at *38, 56 (E.D. Cal. Apr. 2, 1992), *aff'd,* 27 F. 3d 1373 (9th Cir. 1994).
56. Stephen L. Carter, *Culture of Disbelief* (New York: Basic Books, 1993), 159.
57. Murray Gell-Mann, "First Word," *Omni* (February 1987), 8.
58. Leonard Jeffries, Jr., "Review of the New York State Curricular Materials K-12, Focus: African American Culture," *A Curriculum of*

Inclusion (Albany: New York State Education Department, 1989), 21.

59. "Executive Summary," *A Curriculum of Inclusion* (Albany: New York State Education Department, 1989), iv.

60. Edmund W. Gordon and Francis Roberts, "Reflections on the Work of the NYS Social Studies Syllabus Review Committee," *One Nation, Many Peoples: A Declaration of Cultural Interdependence* (Albany: New York State Education Department, 1991), 69.

61. Ibid., 36, 29, 31, 57.

62. *How Schools Shortchange Girls,* 67.

63. Hunter Havelin Adams III, "African and African-American Contributions to Science and Technology" (Portland, Ore.: Portland Public Schools, 1990), S-41.

64. Ibid., S-v.

65. Bernard Ortiz de Montellano, "Multicultural Pseudoscience: Spreading Scientific Illiteracy Among Minorities—Part I," *Skeptical Inquirer* (Fall 1991), 48–49, 46.

66. Quoted in Erich Martel, "Multiculturalism, Not Afrocentrism, for D.C. Public Schools," *Network News & Views* (February 1991), 48.

67. Quoted in ibid., 48; Frank J. Yurco, "An Evaluation of the Portland Social Studies Baseline Essay," *Network News & Views* (March 1991), 23.

68. Frank M. Snowden, Jr., "Misconceptions About African Blacks in the Ancient Mediterranean World: Implications for Educators" (Washington, D.C.: Presentation to the National Endowment for the Humanities, 23 May 1991).

69. Barnes on *The Education Wars,* Two Cities Film Consortium (23 June 1993), unbroadcast documentary.

70. Sari Horwitz, "From K to 12, Afrocentrism Has Made the Grade in Atlanta; 80% of Teachers Weaving Black History into Lessons," *Washington Post* (17 October 1993), B1.

71. Martin Bernal, a scholar whom Afrocentrists often cite in support of their work, makes this point in his book *Black Athena: The Afroasiatic Roots of Classical Civilization,* Vol. 1 (New Brunswick, N.J.: Rutgers University Press, 1987).

72. Jasper Griffin, "Who Are These Coming to Sacrifice?" *New York*

Review of Books (15 June 1989), 25–27; Mary Lefkowitz, "Not Out of Africa," *New Republic* (10 February 1992), 29–36.

73. George G. M. James, *Stolen Legacy: Greek Philosophy Is Stolen Egyptian Philosophy* (Trenton, N.J.: Africa World Press, 1992), 158.

74. Mary Lefkowitz, "The Myth of a 'Stolen Legacy,' " *Society* (March/April 1994), 28.

75. "Early World History with Multicultural Infusion: Social Studies" (Upper Marlboro, Md.: Prince George's County Public Schools, 1992), 42. See James, *Stolen Legacy*, 42.

76. Mary Lefkowitz, "Afrocentrists Wage War on Ancient Greeks," *Wall Street Journal* (7 April 1993), A14.

77. Nobles and Clarke are quoted in Andrew Sullivan, "Racism 101," *New Republic* (26 November 1990), 20–21. In a 27 June 1989 radio address on WDTR in Detroit, Michigan, Nobles demonstrated the sexism in his repertoire. "White people," he said, "especially European white women . . . when they get to be thirty, forty years, their pineal [gland] calcifies. . . . That's the first example, the first indicator of what they used to call the bonehead."

78. Quotes and details from Sari Horwitz, "A Center of Controversy: Sketchy Plans, Racial Issues Mire Afrocentric Project," *Washington Post* (13 September 1993), B1; and "Abena Walker's Curriculum," *Washington Times* (14 September 1993), A23.

79. Quoted in Sari Horwitz, "Afrocentric Plan Has No Curriculum: D.C. Officials Defend School Experiment," *Washington Post* (10 September 1993), D1.

80. Franklin Smith, "The Project at Webb Will Remain," *Washington Post* (15 September 1993), A19.

81. Quoted in Sari Horwitz, "District to Expand Afrocentric Classes," *Washington Post* (25 July 1994), B4.

82. Quoted in John O'Neil, "On the Portland Plan: A Conversation with Matthew Prophet," *Educational Leadership* (December 1991/January 1992), 25.

83. Alan Keyes, "Heroic Fulfillment Closer to Home," *Washington Times* (3 June 1993), G4.

84. Gerald Early, "The Anatomy of Afrocentrism," *Alternatives to Afro-*

centrism, John J. Miller, ed. (Washington, D.C.: Manhattan Institute, 1994), 14–15.

85. Archie E. Lapointe, Nancy A. Mead, and Gary W. Phillips, *A World of Differences: An International Assessment of Mathematics and Science* (Princeton: Educational Testing Service, January 1989), figure 1.1, table 2.3.

86. U.S. Department of Education, Office of Educational Research and Improvement, *Data Compendium for the NAEP 1992: Mathematics Report Card for the Nation and the States* (Washington, D.C.: National Center for Education Statistics, April 1993), table 4; U.S. Department of Education, Office of Educational Research and Improvement, *Data Compendium for the NAEP 1992: Mathematics Assessment of the Nation and the States* (Washington, D.C.: National Center for Education Statistics, May 1993), table 6.8.

87. Joy Hakim, *A History of US: Book Four, The New Nation* (New York: Oxford University Press, 1993), 148.

88. Joy Hakim, *A History of US: Book Five, Liberty for All?* (New York: Oxford University Press, 1994), 96–100.

89. William Raspberry, "The Afrocentric 'Diet,' " *Washington Post* (24 September 1993), A23.

90. Sophfronia Scott Gregory, "The Hidden Hurdle," *Time* (26 March 1992), 44.

91. Quoted in Ron Suskind, "In Rough City School, Top Students Struggle to Learn—and Escape," *Wall Street Journal* (26 May 1994), A8.

Chapter 2: PC: Alive and Entrenched

1. Quoted in Adam DeVore, "Thought Policed in Poli Sci 111," *Michigan Review* (28 October 1992), 1.

2. Quoted in ibid.

3. "Language Censors," *Wall Street Journal* (5 January 1993), A14.

4. Edie N. Goldenberg, letter to the editor, *Wall Street Journal* (29 January 1993), A15.

5. *Campus Culture Wars: Five Stories About PC,* PBS, WETA, Washington, D.C. (28 December 1993).

6. Asra Q. Nomani, "Was Prof's Lecture Academic Freedom or Sex-

ual Harassment?" *Wall Street Journal* (7 March 1995), A1, A10; professor quoted in Cynthia Hubert, "Sac State Prof Cleared of Sex-Harass Charges," *Sacramento Bee* (19 May 1995), A1.

7. Jerry Adler, "Taking Offense: Is This the New Enlightenment on Campus or the New McCarthyism?" *Newsweek* (24 December 1990), 48.

8. John Taylor, "Are You Politically Correct?" *New York* (21 January 1991), 34.

9. Fred Siegel, "The Cult of Multiculturalism," *New Republic* (18 February 1991), 34.

10. Bettina J. Huber, "Today's Literature Classroom: Findings from the MLA's 1990 Survey of Upper-Division Literature Courses," *ADE Bulletin* (Spring 1992), 40.

11. "MLA Survey Provides New View of Campus Debate" (New York: Modern Language Association, 4 November 1991), Press release.

12. "Footnotes," *Chronicle of Higher Education* (9 December 1992), A6.

13. Michael Abramowitz, "Literature Professors Look Inward and Find Scant Evidence of 'PC': But Right-Wing Misinformation, Media Hype Are Problems, Many Agree," *Washington Post* (3 January 1992), A3.

14. See Gerald Graff and Gregory Jay, "Teachers for a Democratic Culture: Statement of Principles" (Evanston, Ill.: Teachers for a Democratic Culture, 1991); and Scott Heller, "New Group Seeks to Fight a 'Conservative Counterattack,'" *Chronicle of Higher Education* (6 November 1991), A22.

15. Michael Bérubé, "Public Image Limited: Political Correctness and the Media's Big Lie," *Village Voice* (18 June 1991), 36.

16. Cathy N. Davidson, "'PH' Stands for Political Hypocrisy," *Academe* (September/October 1991), 14.

17. Bérubé and Lubiano quoted in Joseph S. Salemi, "Behind the Curtains: TDC and UDI at Hunter College," *Measure* (May 1992), 1ff.

18. Anthony DePalma, "In Campus Debate on New Orthodoxy, A Counteroffensive," *New York Times* (25 September 1991), A1.

19. Michael Kinsley, "P.C. B.S.," *New Republic* (20 May 1991), 8.

20. "Shift in the Wind?" *Democratic Culture* (Fall 1992), 2.

21. Huntly Collins, "PC and the Press," *Change* (January/February 1992), 14.

22. Nancy Welch, "Resisting the Faith: Conversion, Resistance, and the Training of Teachers," *College English* (April 1993), 392.

23. Ibid., 400.

24. John Patrick Diggins, *The Rise and Fall of the American Left* (New York: W. W. Norton, 1992), 291.

25. Bernice R. Sandler, Jean O'Gorman Hughes, and Mary DeMouy, "It's All in What You Ask: Questions for Search Committees to Use," Paper from the Project on the Status and Education of Women (Washington, D.C.: Association of American Colleges, February 1988), 1–2.

26. "Questionnaire for ASA Nominees" (Sociologists for Women in Society, 1990), Photocopy.

27. Barbara R. Bergmann, letter to the editor, *American Economic Association 1991 Committee on the Status of Women in the Economics Profession Newsletter* (October 1991).

28. Quoted in Denise Hamilton, "Two White Professors Accuse College of Racial Discrimination," *Los Angeles Times* (15 July 1992), B3. When a Japanese-American professor, who was less experienced than Waszak, was subsequently hired for this position, Waszak sued Pasadena City College. In August 1994 a Superior Court jury ruled that the college had violated Waszak's civil rights and ordered the college to pay his legal fees. The jury rejected Waszak's contention that race had been a factor in the hiring decision, however, and did not award monetary damages. See Denise Hamilton, "Neither Side Cheers Bias Case Ruling," *Los Angeles Times* (4 August 1994), San Gabriel Valley, Part J, p. 6.

29. Gregory Jay et al., memorandum to Letters and Science Curriculum Committee, University of Wisconsin at Milwaukee (5 December 1994), Photocopy.

30. Lynne Goodstein, "When Is a Women's Studies Course a 'Women's Studies' Course?: Issues of 'Quality Control' of Cross-Listed Courses," an unpublished essay quoted in Daphne Patai and Noretta Koertge, *Professing Feminism: Cautionary Tales from the Strange*

World of Women's Studies (New York: Basic Books, 1994), 178.

31. Anthony DePalma, "Hard-Won Acceptance Spawns New Conflicts Around Ethnic Studies," *New York Times* (2 January 1991), B8.

32. Letter to recipient who wishes to remain anonymous (20 November 1991), Photocopy.

33. Jerry Z. Muller, "Challenging Political Correctness: A 'Paranoid Hysteric' Replies to Joan Scott," *Perspectives* (May/June 1993), 15.

34. Stephen E. Ambrose, "We Hold These Truths to Be Unfashionable," *Wall Street Journal* (13 April 1995), A14.

35. Patricia J. Williams, *The Alchemy of Race and Rights: Diary of a Law Professor* (Cambridge: Harvard University Press, 1991); Eunice Lipton, *Alias Olympia: A Woman's Search for Manet's Notorious Model and Her Own Desire* (New York: Charles Scribner's Sons, 1992); Nancy K. Miller, *Getting Personal: Feminist Occasions and Other Autobiographical Acts* (New York: Routledge, 1991); Frank Lentricchia, *The Edge of Night: A Confession* (New York: Random House, 1994).

36. Conversation with author, 26 April 1993.

37. Stephen Polcari, *Abstract Expressionism and the Modern Experience* (Cambridge: Cambridge University Press, 1991), endnote 1, 374–75.

38. Quoted in Melvin H. Pekarsky, memorandum to Elizabeth Stone and members of Personnel Policy Committee, State University of New York at Stony Brook (26 June 1989), 2, Photocopy.

39. Don Ihde, memorandum to Tilden G. Edelstein, State University of New York at Stony Brook (28 June 1989), Photocopy.

40. John H. Marburger, letter to Stephen Polcari (31 August 1989), Photocopy.

41. Stephen Polcari, letter to author (21 September 1993).

42. Stephen Polcari, letter to Eugene Eisner (n.d.), 9, Photocopy.

43. Review of *Abstract Expressionism and the Modern Experience*, by Stephen Polcari, *Publishers Weekly* (19 July 1991), 41; David Anfam, "Of War, Demons and Negation," *Art History* (September 1993), 483; Gijs Van Hensbergen, review of *Abstract Expressionism and the Modern Experience*, by Stephen Polcari, *Burlington Magazine* (February 1993), 157.

44. Stephen Polcari, letter to author (21 September 1993).
45. Political Organization of Women Radicals in Sociology et al., letter to Department of Sociology Executive Committee, Affirmative Action Office, and President James Duderstadt, University of Michigan (31 March 1993), Photocopy.
46. Derek Green, "The Goldberg Affair," *Ann Arbor Observer* (September 1993), 53.
47. Quoted in ibid., 57.
48. Quoted in ibid., 58.
49. Richard Levin, "Feminist Thematics and Shakespearean Tragedy," *PMLA* (March 1988), 125, 135, 136.
50. Janet Adelman et al., letter to the editor, *PMLA* (January 1989), 78.
51. Richard Levin, letter to the editor, *PMLA* (January 1989), 79.
52. Elizabeth Coleman, letter to the editor, *PMLA* (October 1989), 896.
53. Sandra Lee Bartky, letter to William Whitworth (27 March 1990), Photocopy.
54. Quotes from Scott Jaschik, " 'Squelching' the Opposition: Row Over an Unpublished Article Illustrates the Enmity in the 'Political Correctness' War," *Chronicle of Higher Education* (15 January 1992), A18.
55. Quotes from Matt Sclafani, "Fish Asks Provost to Exclude NAS Members from Committees," *Chronicle* (5 October 1990), 1.
56. Quoted in Thomas Short, "How Politicized Studies Enforce Conformity: Interviews with Julius Lester and Elizabeth Fox-Genovese," *Academic Questions* (Summer 1992), 52.
57. I wrote a fuller account of the Gribben affair in *Telling the Truth: A Report on the State of the Humanities in Higher Education,* 30–34.
58. Letter to author (19 April 1991).
59. Michelle Colitsas, "Education Based on Violated Trust," *Catalyst* (September 1991), 3.
60. "From the Editor: Dubious Dialogue," *Catalyst* (November/December 1991), 11.
61. Marc Shachtman, "Learning and Losing: The Need for a Balance in Political Views," *Oberlin Forum* (October 1990), 3.

62. Quoted in Dale M. Bauer, "The Other 'F' Word: The Feminist in the Classroom," *College English* (April 1990), 385–86.

63. Ibid., 387.

64. Elizabeth A. Fay, "Anger in the Classroom: Women, Voice, and Fear," *Radical Teacher* (Fall 1992), 14–15.

65. James N. Laditka, "Semiology, Ideology, *Praxis*: Responsible Authority in the Composition Classroom," *Journal of Advanced Composition* (Fall 1990), 366.

66. James A. Berlin, "Freirean Pedagogy in the U.S.: A Response," *Journal of Advanced Composition* (Winter 1992), 419.

67. Donald Lazere, "Back to Basics: A Force for Oppression or Liberation?" *College English* (January 1992), 17–18.

68. Maxine Hairston, "Diversity, Ideology, and Teaching Writing," *College Composition and Communication* (May 1992), 180.

69. Paula S. Rothenberg, *Racism and Sexism: An Integrated Study* (New York: St. Martin's, 1988); Gary Colombo, Robert Cullen, and Bonnie Lisle, *Rereading America: Cultural Contexts for Critical Thinking and Writing* (Boston: St. Martin's, 1992).

70. Karen Lehrman, "Off Course," *Mother Jones* (September/October 1993), 48.

71. Kathleen Weiler, *Women Teaching for Change: Gender, Class & Power* (New York: Bergin & Garvey, 1988), 63.

72. Susan Swartzlander, Diana Pace, and Virginia Lee Stamler, "The Ethics of Requiring Students to Write About Their Personal Lives," *Chronicle of Higher Education* (17 February 1993), B1.

73. Quoted in Frances A. Maher and Mary Kay Thompson Tetreault, *The Feminist Classroom: An Inside Look at How Professors and Students Are Transforming Higher Education for a Diverse Society* (New York: Basic Books, 1994), 54.

74. Patai and Koertge, *Professing Feminism*, 13–17.

75. Bradley R. Smith, "The Holocaust Controversy: The Case for Open Debate," *Chronicle* (5 November 1991), 14, Advertisement.

76. See Deborah E. Lipstadt, *Denying the Holocaust: The Growing Assault on Truth and Memory* (New York: Free Press, 1993), 194–95.

77. Ann Heimberger, "First Amendment Protects Controversial Advertisers, Too," *Chronicle* (5 November 1991), 9.

78. "The History Department Responds to Holocaust Ad," *Chronicle* (13 November 1991), 7.

79. Lipstadt, *Denying the Holocaust,* 17.

80. Quoted in Lehrman, "Off Course," 49–50.

81. Conversation with author, 27 April 1993.

82. Susan C. Jarratt, "Rhetorical Power: What Really Happens in Politicized Classrooms," *ADE Bulletin* (Fall 1992), 36.

83. Conversation with author, 27 April 1993.

84. Conversation with author, 1 April 1993.

85. Conversation with author, 27 April 1993.

86. Alan Charles Kors, "The Politicization of the University, In Loco Parentis," *The World & I* (May 1991), 486.

87. Beverly Guy-Sheftall quoted in Candace de Russy, "Whole-Campus Multiculturalization (Brought to You by Ford)," *Measure* (January 1995), 6–7.

88. "Diversity Education Labor Day Program: Facilitator's Guide" (Philadelphia: University of Pennsylvania, 1989), 11.

89. Ibid., 12.

90. Michael Cohen, "What Is Happening and Why?" *Daily Pennsylvanian* (2 October 1989), 6.

91. Conversation with author, 26 April 1993.

92. "Building Pluralism at Bryn Mawr College" (Bryn Mawr, Penn.: Bryn Mawr College, 1988), 44.

93. W. Terrell Jones and Art Costantino, "Agent of Oppression Group Awareness," handout circulated at State University of New York at Binghamton, 1.

94. Quoted in David Rossie, "SUNY-B's First Lesson: Get Correct," *Press & Sun-Bulletin* (4 August 1991), E1.

95. Jennifer George, letter to the editor, *Skidmore Scope* (June 1994), 2.

96. Nicholas A. Damask and Craig T. Cobane, "Our Little Workshop in Thought Control on Campus in Ohio," *Washington Times* (20 October 1993), A23.

97. John H. Bunzel, *Race Relations on Campus: Stanford Students Speak* (Stanford, Calif.: Stanford Alumni Association, 1992), 36, 38.

98. Quoted in Bunzel, *Race Relations,* 65–66.

99. Ibid., 54.

100. Ibid., 74.
101. Ibid., 45.
102. Conversation with author, 27 April 1993.

Chapter 3: From Truth to Transformation

1. See "Report by the Cantonal Judge" and "Death Certificate by the Doctors Who Examined the Bodies," *I, Pierre Rivière, having slaughtered my mother, my sister, and my brother . . .*, Michel Foucault, ed. (Lincoln: University of Nebraska Press, 1975), 3–7.
2. Pierre Rivière, "The Memoir," *I, Pierre Rivière*, 105.
3. Foucault, "Foreword," *I, Pierre Rivière*, x–xi.
4. Jean-Pierre Peter and Jeanne Favret, "The Animal, the Madman, and Death," *I, Pierre Rivière*, 175–77.
5. Foucault, "Foreword," *I, Pierre Rivière*, xiii.
6. Michel Foucault, *Folie et déraison* (Paris: Librairie Plon, 1961), ix.
7. Raymond Aron, *The Elusive Revolution: Anatomy of a Student Revolt* (New York: Praeger, 1969), 110–11, 126.
8. James Miller, *The Passion of Michel Foucault* (New York: Simon & Schuster, 1993), 165–207.
9. Betty Jean Craige, *Reconnection: Dualism to Holism in Literary Study* (Athens: University of Georgia Press, 1988), 9.
10. J. Hillis Miller, "The Critic as Host," in *Deconstruction and Criticism* (New York: Continuum, 1986), 251.
11. Ross, *Strange Weather*, 8.
12. Allan Bloom, *The Closing of the American Mind* (New York: Simon & Schuster, 1987).
13. Thomas S. Kuhn, *The Structure of Scientific Revolutions* (Chicago: University of Chicago Press, 1970).
14. Lawrence Stone, letter to the editor, *New York Review of Books* (31 March 1983), 42.
15. Quoted in Mark Muro, "Derrick Bell—In Protest," *Boston Globe* (25 March 1992), 69.
16. Quoted in "Harvard Law School: Role Models," *Economist* (26 May 1990), 28.
17. Peggy Means McIntosh, "Curricular Re-Vision: The New Knowledge for a New Age," *Educating the Majority: Women Challenge Tradition in*

Higher Education, Carol S. Pearson, Donna L. Shavlik, and Judith G. Touchton, eds. (New York: Macmillan, 1989), 106, 402.

18. Yolanda T. Moses, "The Challenge of Diversity: Anthropological Perspectives on University Culture," *Education and Urban Society* (August 1990), 404.

19. Mark Lilla, "A Taste for Pain: Michel Foucault and the Outer Reaches of Human Experience," *Times Literary Supplement* (26 March 1993), 4.

20. For Foucault's attitude toward mob violence, see Michel Foucault, "On Popular Justice: A Discussion with Maoists," *Power/Knowledge: Selected Interviews & Other Writings, 1972–1977*, ed. Colin Gordon, trans. John Mepham (New York: Pantheon, 1980), 1–36. Discussion first appeared in a special issue of *Les Temps Modernes* 310 *bis* (1972).

21. "The Concern for Truth: An Interview by Francois Ewald," *Politics, Philosophy, Culture: Interviews and Other Writings of Michel Foucault, 1977–1984*, ed. Lawrence D. Kritzman, trans. Alan Sheridan (New York: Routledge, 1988), 265. Interview first appeared in *Magazine littéraire* (May 1984), 18–23.

22. Charles Paine, "Relativism, Radical Pedagogy, and the Ideology of Paralysis," *College English* (October 1989), 563.

23. Richard Ohmann, "Political Correctness and the Obfuscation of Politics," *Radical Teacher* (Fall 1992), 32.

24. Gross and Levitt, *Higher Superstition*, 6–8.

25. Ross, *Strange Weather*, Acknowledgments.

26. Quoted in Maher and Thompson Tetreault, *The Feminist Classroom*, 86.

27. Al Gore, *Earth in the Balance: Ecology and the Human Spirit* (New York: Penguin, 1992), 216–65.

28. Ibid., 256.

29. Ibid., 217.

30. See, for example, Carolyn Merchant, *Radical Ecology: The Search for a Livable World* (New York: Routledge, 1992), 45ff.

31. Will Morrisey, "Ideology and Literary Studies: *PMLA* 1930–1990," *Academic Questions* (Winter 1992–1993), 58–61.

32. Patricia Bizzell, "Beyond Anti-Foundationalism to Rhetorical Au-

thority: Problems Defining 'Cultural Literacy,' " *College English* (October 1990), 672; Bauer, "The Other 'F' Word," 564.

33. Scott Heller, "Magazine Offers a Radical Perspective on Teaching," *Chronicle of Higher Education* (10 July 1991), A3.

34. Gerald Graff, "Academic Writing and the Uses of Bad Publicity," *South Atlantic Quarterly* (Winter 1992), 13.

35. See Linda Bamber, "Class Struggle," *Women's Review of Books* (February 1990), 20–21.

36. Anne Fausto-Sterling, "Race, Gender and Science," *Transformations* (Fall 1992), 5–6.

37. Annette Kolodny (New York: Presentations to Modern Language Association Annual Convention, 27 & 29 December 1992).

38. Paul Heilker, "Academic Freedom, the Thesis/Support Form, and the Essay" (New York: Presentation to Modern Language Association Annual Convention, 29 December 1992).

39. Lisa Jadwin, "Mirroring: Some Strategies for Handling Hate Speech in the Classroom" (New York: Presentation to Modern Language Association Annual Convention, 29 December 1992).

40. Olivia Frey, "It's Enough To Make You Cry: Playing God in the Ivory Tower" (New York: Presentation to Modern Language Association Annual Convention, 28 December 1992).

41. Susan J. Delaney, "How to See Ancient Near Eastern Art in a New Light" (Seattle: Presentation to College Art Association Annual Conference, 6 February 1993); Ann Derbes, " 'The Devil Is in You': The Eroticized Eve in Medieval and Renaissance Art" (Seattle: Presentation to College Art Association Annual Conference, 6 February 1993).

42. Frances Pohl, "Some Thoughts on 'Misbehavin' and the Disciplin-(ing) of Art History" (Seattle: Presentation to College Art Association Annual Conference, 6 February 1993).

43. Elizabeth Minnich (Washington, D.C.: Presentation to National Women's Studies Association Annual Conference, 18 June 1993); Carol Wolfe Konek, "The Movement Against the 'Political Correctness Movement': Resistance to Inclusion of Ethnicity and Gender in Higher Education" (Washington, D.C.: Presentation to National Women's Studies Association Annual Conference, 19 June 1993); Berenice Fisher, "The Politically Committed Profes-

sor: In the Wake of Second Wave Feminism" (Washington, D.C.: Presentation to National Women's Studies Association Annual Conference, 19 June 1993); Sherry Gorelick, "Is It Time for a Paradigm Shift? Students and Faculty Confront the Joys and Dangers of Feminist Methodology" (Washington, D.C.: Presentation to National Women's Studies Association Annual Conference, 19 June 1993).

44. Vivien Ng (Washington, D.C.: Presentation to National Women's Studies Association Annual Conference, 20 June 1993).

45. Richard Rorty, "Two Cheers for the Cultural Left," *The Politics of Liberal Education*, Darryl J. Gless and Barbara Herrnstein Smith, eds. (Durham: Duke University Press, 1992), 233.

46. Bernstein, "Academia's Liberals Defend Their Carnival of Canons," 26.

47. Arthur M. Schlesinger, Jr., *The Disuniting of America: Reflections on a Multicultural Society* (New York: W. W. Norton, 1992).

48. Patti Lather, *Getting Smart: Feminist Research and Pedagogy With/in the Postmodern* (New York: Routledge, 1991), 71, xiv.

49. Gerald Graff and Gregory Jay, "Fact Sheet: Funding of Conservative Academics and Intellectuals by the Olin Foundation" (Evanston, Ill.: Teachers for a Democratic Culture, 1991).

50. Nineteen ninety-three's asset figures were obtained from the Ford and John M. Olin foundations. In the interests of full disclosure: While I have not directly benefited from grants from either of these foundations or from the John D. and Catharine T. MacArthur Foundation, discussed below, two organizations whose boards I chair, the National Alumni Forum and the Committee to Review National Standards, have received Olin grants, as has the Madison Center, on whose board I serve. The Aspen Institute, on the board of which I served in 1993 and 1994, has received funding from both the Ford and MacArthur foundations.

51. Althea K. Nagai, Robert Lerner, and Stanley Rothman, *Giving for Social Change: Foundations, Public Policy, and the American Political Agenda* (Westport, Conn.: Praeger, 1994), 125–30.

52. Ford Foundation, *1990 Annual Report* (New York: Ford Foundation, 1991), 91.

53. "Initiatives for the Race and Gender Enrichment of Tulane Univer-

sity of Louisiana" (New Orleans: Tulane University, 4 June 1990), 1–4.

54. Paul H. Lewis, letter to the editor, *New Orleans Times-Picayune* (22 November 1990), B14.

55. Paul H. Lewis, conversation with author, 23 August 1993.

56. Nagai, Lerner, and Rothman, *Giving for Social Change*, 130.

57. Joshua Muravchik, "MacArthur's Millions," *American Spectator* (January 1992), 34.

58. McIntosh, "Curricular Re-Vision," 406, 403.

59. Robin Bartlett, "Improving Introductory Economics Education by Integrating the Latest Scholarship on Women and Minorities," conference announcement, Wellesley College, 15–20 June 1995, Photocopy.

60. Susan Hill Gross, *Wasted Resources, Diminished Lives: The Impact of Boy Preference on the Lives of Girls and Women* (St. Louis Park, Minn.: Upper Midwest Women's History Center, 1992), 33.

61. Ibid., 81.

62. U.S. Bureau of the Census, *Statistical Abstract of the United States: 1994*, tables 274, 293, 294, 12.

63. J. Diane Cirksena and Valija Rasmussen, *Women on the American Frontier: Deferring Domesticity* (St. Louis Park, Minn.: Upper Midwest Women's History Center, 1991).

64. The New Jersey Project received $784,307.45 from the New Jersey Department of Higher Education from 1986 until the department was abolished in June 1994. The project's life was extended when it was given $100,000 from Governor Christine Todd Whitman's discretionary fund in July 1994.

65. Nancy Ashton, "Involving Faculty in Curricular Transformation," *The New Jersey Project: Integrating the Scholarship on Gender, 1986–1990*, Carol H. Smith and Ferris Olin, eds. (New Brunswick: Institute for Research on Women, Rutgers, State University of New Jersey, Spring 1990), 50.

66. Modern Language Association of America, "Faculty Development Through Curriculum Review," grant application submitted to the Fund for the Improvement of Postsecondary Education (1 March 1990), 1.

67. Ohmann, "Political Correctness," 32; Richard Ohmann, "State University of New York, College at Oswego: First Report on the Department of English" (1992), 6. Special thanks go to American Enterprise Institute interns who used college and university catalogs to piece together information regarding this report. Full documentation of this FIPSE grant was withheld by the Department of Education which, after over a year of delay in response to a Freedom of Information Act request, provided only MLA-censored documents.

68. Program for New Jersey Project national conference, "The Inclusive Curriculum: Setting Our Own Agenda" (Parsippany, N.J.: New Jersey Project, 16–18 April 1993).

69. Marvin Hunt, "Commotion in the Winds! Fright, Changes, Horrors: Radical Scholars Deconstruct the Bard," *Spectator Magazine* (8 December 1988), 5.

70. Ibid.

71. Charlotte Crabtree et al., *Lessons from History: Essential Understandings and Historical Perspectives Students Should Acquire* (Los Angeles: National Center for History in the Schools, University of California, Los Angeles, 1992).

72. Commission on the Humanities, "Report of the Commission on the Humanities" (New York: American Council of Learned Societies, 1964), 4.

73. Ibid., 115.

Chapter 4: Justice Without the Blindfold

1. Quoted in Ruth Milkman, "Women's History and the Sears Case," *Feminist Studies* (Summer 1986), 385–86.

2. Quoted in Carol Sternhell, "Life in the Mainstream: What Happens When Feminists Turn Up on Both Sides of the Courtroom?" *Ms.* (July 1986), 88.

3. Quoted in Milkman, "Women's History," 392.

4. Ann C. Scales, "The Emergence of Feminist Jurisprudence: An Essay," *Yale Law Journal* (June 1986), 1383, 1387.

5. Mary E. Becker, "Contracts and Feminism" (New Orleans: Presen-

tation to Women and Legal Education Section of the American Association of Law Schools, 6 January 1989), 2.

6. Lani Guinier, Michelle Fine, and Jane Balin, "Becoming Gentlemen: Women's Experiences at One Ivy League Law School," *University of Pennsylvania Law Review* (November 1994), 84.

7. Catharine A. MacKinnon, "Feminism, Marxism, Method, and the State: Toward Feminist Jurisprudence," *Signs* (Summer 1983), 638.

8. Catharine A. MacKinnon, "Difference and Dominance: On Sex Discrimination," *Feminism Unmodified: Discourses on Life and Law* (Cambridge: Harvard University Press, 1987), 44–45. Speech originally delivered in October 1984.

9. MacKinnon, "Afterword," *Feminism Unmodified*, 217–18.

10. See "Not by Law Alone: From a Debate with Phyllis Schlafly," *Feminism Unmodified*, 30. Remarks first delivered at Stanford Law School, 26 January 1982.

11. Catharine A. MacKinnon, *Only Words* (Cambridge: Harvard University Press, 1993), 3.

12. Andrea Dworkin (Chicago: Presentation to Center on Speech, Equality, and Harm conference, 6 March 1993).

13. Diana E. H. Russell, *Sexual Exploitation: Rape, Child Sexual Abuse, and Workplace Harassment* (Beverly Hills: Sage Publications, 1984), 34–37.

14. MacKinnon, *Only Words*, 7.

15. MacKinnon, *Feminism Unmodified*, endnote 18, 232–33.

16. MacKinnon, "Francis Biddle's Sister: Pornography, Civil Rights, and Speech," *Feminism Unmodified*, 171. Speech first delivered at Harvard Law School, 5 April 1984.

17. Clinton statement on Violence Against Women Act, Federal News Service (21 March 1995); Ann Devroy, "Analysts Dispute Clinton on Crime Against Women," *Washington Post* (22 March 1995), A8; Devroy quoted in Cathy Young, "Exaggerating the Dangers Women Face," *Detroit News* (28 March 1995), 9A; John Schwartz, "In Debate Over Crimes Against Women, Statistics Get Roughed Up," *Washington Post* (27 March 1995), A4.

18. Smeal and Dworkin quoted in Ruth Shalit, "Caught in the Act," *New Republic* (12 July 1993), 14–15.

19. MacKinnon, "Not a Moral Issue," *Feminism Unmodified*, 148. Speech first delivered at the University of Minnesota, 23 February 1983.

20. *Donald Victor Butler v. Her Majesty the Queen, Canada Supreme Court Reports* (1992), Part 3, Vol. 1, p. 497.

21. MacKinnon, *Only Words*, 102.

22. MacKinnon, "Not a Moral Issue," 152–53.

23. Kathleen Currie and Art Levine, "Whip Me, Beat Me and While You're at It Cancel My N.O.W. Membership," *Washington Monthly* (June 1987), 17; James R. Petersen, "Catharine MacKinnon," *Playboy* (August 1992), 37.

24. Andrea Dworkin (Chicago: Presentation to Center on Speech, Equality, and Harm conference, 6 March 1993).

25. Strossen in John Leo, "Censors on the Left," *U.S. News & World Report* (4 October 1993), 30.

26. Andrew J. Kleinfeld, "Politicization: From the Law Schools to the Courts," *Academic Questions* (Winter 1993–1994), 17.

27. *Meritor Savings Bank, FSB v. Mechelle Vinson et al.*, 477 US 57, 66, 67 (1986).

28. *Robinson v. Jacksonville Shipyards, Inc.*, 760 F. Supp. 1486, 1495, 1501, 1524 (M.D. Fla. 1991).

29. *Tunis v. Corning Glass Works*, 747 F. Supp. 951, 954–955 (S.D. N.Y. 1990), *aff'd*, 930 F.2d 910 (2d Cir. 1991).

30. Kingsley R. Browne, "Title VII as Censorship: Hostile-Environment Harassment and the First Amendment," *Ohio State Law Journal* (April/May 1991), 493, 495, 508–9. While the court declared the specific gender-based language cited by plaintiff not to be a Title VII violation, it based its conclusion on the language's having been used before there was widespread awareness of its discriminatory nature and on the fact that the company was in the vanguard of establishing policies to eliminate it. 747 F. Supp. 951, 959.

31. Browne, "Title VII as Censorship," 505.

32. "Shattering the Glass Ceiling," *Myers Reports*, Vol. 10, No. 1.

33. Quoted in Gifford, "Unbearable Whiteness," 28.

34. Quoted in Andrew Ferguson, "Chasing Rainbows," *Washingtonian* (April 1994), 38.

35. Quoted in Michele Galen, "White, Male, and Worried," *Business Week* (31 January 1994), 53–54.
36. Frederick R. Lynch, "Workforce Diversity: PC's Final Frontier?" *National Review* (21 February 1994), 34.
37. Robert Bolt, *A Man for All Seasons* (London: Samuel French, Inc., 1960, 1962), Act 1, Scene 6, p. 56.
38. See MacKinnon, *Only Words*, 7.
39. Jerry Frug, "Henry James, Lee Marvin and the Law," *New York Times* (16 February 1986), Sec. 7, p. 1.
40. Foucault, *Folie et déraison,* ix.
41. Mark G. Kelman, "Trashing," *Stanford Law Review* (January 1984), 293–348.
42. Lani Guinier, "The Triumph of Tokenism: The Voting Rights Act and the Theory of Black Electoral Success," *Michigan Law Review* (March 1991), 1102–1104.
43. Lani Guinier, "Keeping the Faith: Black Voters in the Post-Reagan Era," *Harvard Civil Rights–Civil Liberties Law Review* (Spring 1989), footnote 171, 431.
44. Derrick A. Bell, Jr., "A Question of Credentials," *Harvard Law Record* (17 September 1982), 14.
45. Mari J. Matsuda, "Looking to the Bottom: Critical Legal Studies and Reparations," *Harvard Civil Rights–Civil Liberties Law Review* (Spring 1987), 324.
46. Mari J. Matsuda et al., *Words That Wound: Critical Race Theory, Assaultive Speech, and the First Amendment* (Boulder, Colo.: Westview Press, 1993), 5.
47. Richard Delgado, "When a Story Is Just a Story: Does Voice Really Matter?" *Virginia Law Review* (February 1990), 105–6.
48. Randall L. Kennedy, "Racial Critiques of Legal Academia," *Harvard Law Review* (June 1989), 1779, 1786–87.
49. Randall L. Kennedy, "Lani Guinier's Constitution," *American Prospect* (Fall 1993), 46.
50. Mari J. Matsuda, "Public Response to Racist Speech: Considering the Victim's Story," *Michigan Law Review* (August 1989), 2358.
51. Arati R. Korwar, *War of Words: Speech Codes at Public Colleges and*

Universities (Nashville: Freedom Forum First Amendment Center, Vanderbilt University, 1994), 25.

52. *Federal Register* (10 March 1994), 11449–50.

53. A mid-March 1995 check of NEXIS shows that since January 1, 1990, there have been 2,857 articles about free speech on campus, 718 about free speech in the workplace.

54. Browne, "Title VII as Censorship," 482.

55. Shelby Coffey III, "Guidelines on Ethnic, Racial, Sexual and Other Identification" (Los Angeles: Los Angeles Times, 10 November 1993), 7, 10, Photocopy.

56. See "Fighting Words," *New Yorker* (3 May 1993), 34; and Daniel Seligman, "PC Comes to the Newsroom," *National Review* (21 June 1993), 30.

57. See Richard Harwood, " 'Diversity' Comes Home," *Washington Post* (27 November 1993), A27; and Alicia C. Shepard, "High Anxiety," *American Journalism Review* (November 1993), 19–24.

58. Alfred J. Tuchfarber, "Summary Report: Cincinnati Federation of Teachers Survey" (Cincinnati: University of Cincinnati Institute for Policy Research, 23 October 1991), 1; Peter D. Hart Research Associates, memorandum to Cincinnati Federation of Teachers and American Federation of Teachers (31 May 1994), 5, Photo-copy.

59. Albert Shanker, "Discipline by the Numbers," *Washington Post* (17 January 1994), Advertisement. See also Ann Bradley, "The Discipline Dilemma," *Education Week* (19 January 1994), 20–24.

60. A fine account of how legislation that prohibited race and gender discrimination was transformed into legal requirements for race and gender preferences is Herman Belz, *Equality Transformed: A Quarter-Century of Affirmative Action* (New Brunswick, N.J.: Trans-action, 1991).

61. *Health Security Act*, 103d Congress, 504–6; U.S. Department of Commerce, Economics and Statistics Administration, Bureau of the Census, *1990 Census of Population, Supplementary Reports: Detailed Occupation and Other Characteristics from the EEO File for the United States*, 2.

231

62. See Al Kamen's column, "In the Loop," *Washington Post* (23 February 1994), A15.
63. Scott Jaschik, "Education Department Upholds Most Minority Scholarships," *Chronicle of Higher Education* (23 February 1994), A24.
64. Shepard, "High Anxiety," 19.
65. Matsuda et al., *Words That Wound*, 14.
66. Quoted in Arlynn Leiber Presser, "The Politically Correct Law School: Where It's Right to Be Left," *ABA Journal* (September 1991), 53.
67. Thadd A. Prisco, conversation with author, 17 November 1993; Thadd A. Prisco, letter to author (20 November 1993), 2.
68. ABA General Practice Section, Law Student Opinion Survey (Spring 1991), 1.
69. Steven C. Bahls, "Political Correctness and the American Law School," *Washington University Law Quarterly* (Fall 1991), 1057.
70. Karl Johnson and Ann Scales, "An Absolutely, Positively True Story: Seven Reasons Why We Sing," *New Mexico Law Review* (Fall 1986), 445.
71. Richard F. Devlin, "Legal Education as Political Consciousness-Raising or Paving the Road to Hell," *Journal of Legal Education* (June 1989), 216, 219–20, 226–27.
72. Morrison Torrey, Jackie Casey, and Karin Olson, "Teaching Law in a Feminist Manner," *Harvard Women's Law Journal* (Spring 1990), footnote 59, 111–12.
73. Patricia J. Williams, *The Alchemy of Race and Rights* (Cambridge: Harvard University Press, 1991), 28, 32, 95, 97.
74. Quoted in Sam Roberts, "An Integrationist to This Day, Believing All Else Has Failed," *Washington Post* (7 May 1995), E7.

Chapter 5: Museums, Moving Images, and False Memories

1. Quoted in Celia McGee, "High Priestess of Trendiness," *New York Times* (17 January 1993), Sec. 2, p. 31.
2. Fred Ho, "Artists & Social Issues," panel discussion in conjunction with the exhibition Etiquette of the Undercaste (Washington, D.C.: Smithsonian Institution, 7 April 1992).

3. Pamela Sommers, "The Couple in the Cage," *Washington Post* (20 October 1992), E3.

4. "Do You Have Questions About Mining the Museum?" handout accompanying Mining the Museum exhibit (Baltimore: Maryland Historical Society, 1992).

5. Quoted in Angamela Rollins, *Morning Edition,* National Public Radio, Bob Edwards, host (21 September 1992).

6. Robert Sullivan, "Trouble in Paradigms," *Museum News* (January/February 1992), 41.

7. Lisa Phillips, "No Man's Land: At the Threshold of a Millennium," *1993 Biennial Exhibition* (New York: Whitney Museum of American Art, 1993), 53.

8. Mary Abbe, "Bloody Performance Draws Criticism," *Minneapolis Star Tribune* (24 March 1994), 1A.

9. Thelma Golden, "What's White . . . ?" *1993 Biennial Exhibition,* 35.

10. Conversation with author, 6 May 1993.

11. Benjamin H. D. Buchloh, "The Whole Earth Show: An Interview with Jean-Hubert Martin by Benjamin H. D. Buchloh," *Art in America* (May 1989), 158.

12. Simon Taylor, "The Phobic Object: Abjection in Contemporary Art," *Abject Art: Repulsion and Desire in American Art* (New York: Whitney Museum of American Art, 1993), 76.

13. See Bill Briggs, "Black and White Art," *Denver Post Magazine* (28 March 1993), 11–13.

14. This phrase is used in the exhibition catalogue to describe the exhibition's intent. Elizabeth Broun, Foreword, *The West as America: Reinterpreting Images of the Frontier,* William H. Truettner, ed. (Washington, D.C.: Smithsonian Institution Press, 1991), vii.

15. Dominick A. Pisano, "Constructing the Memory of Aerial Combat in World War I," *Legend, Memory, and the Great War in the Air,* Dominick A. Pisano et al., eds. (Washington, D.C.: National Air and Space Museum, 1992), 11–17.

16. See Ken Ringle, "A-Bomb Exhibit Plan Revamped: Smithsonian Acts to Defuse Criticism," *Washington Post* (30 August 1994), C1; Eugene L. Meyer and Jacqueline Trescott, "Smithsonian Scuttles

Exhibit; Enola Gay Plan Had 'Fundamental Flaw,' " *Washington Post* (31 January 1995), A1.

17. Robert D. Sullivan, letter to Frank H. Talbot (29 June 1990), Photocopy.

18. Sullivan, "Trouble in Paradigms," 41.

19. Booklet accompanying Science in American Life exhibit (Washington, D.C.: National Museum of American History, 1995).

20. Helen Frankenthaler, "Did We Spawn an Arts Monster?" *New York Times* (17 July 1989), A17.

21. Larry Clark, *Teenage Lust* (New York: 1987, Larry Clark). The Supreme Court ruled in 1982 in *New York v. Ferber* that although portrayals of explicit sex between adults cannot be prohibited if they have "serious literary, artistic, political, or scientific value," visual depictions of sex involving children can be banned no matter what the circumstance because of the state's "compelling interest in prosecuting those who promote the sexual exploitation of children."

22. Alvin Kernan, *The Death of Literature* (New Haven: Yale University Press, 1990), 126–51.

23. Neil Postman, *Amusing Ourselves to Death: Public Discourse in the Age of Show Business* (New York: Penguin, 1986).

24. Barry S. Sapolsky and Joseph Tabarlet, "Sex in Primetime Television: 1979 Versus 1989," *Journal of Broadcasting & Electronic Media* (Fall 1991), 509.

25. S. Robert Lichter, Linda S. Lichter, and Stanley Rothman, *Prime Time: How TV Portrays American Culture* (Washington, D.C.: Regnery, 1994), 403.

26. Jean Bethke Elshtain, *Democracy on Trial* (New York: Basic Books, 1995), 51–52.

27. *TV Guide* (1 April 1995), 88, 106, 124, 141.

28. Douglas L. Wilson, "Thomas Jefferson and the Character Issue," *Atlantic* (November 1992), 58.

29. Ron Kovic, *Born on the Fourth of July: A True Story of Innocence Lost and Courage Found* (New York: Pocket Books, 1976); eyewitness and police officer quoted in Nick Ravo, " 'Fourth of July' Unfair to Syracuse Police, Some Residents Say," *New York Times* (15 January 1990), B3.

30. Jay Sharbutt, "New Film Brings the Old War Home," *Los Angeles Times* (22 January 1989), Calendar section, p. 24; Kovic, *Born on the Fourth of July*, 152–57, 176–84.

31. As Jim Garrison himself tells it in his book, *On the Trail of the Assassins* (New York: Warner, 1988), Ferrie died without acknowledging he ever knew Oswald.

32. Stone quoted in Jan Herman, "UCI Panel to Take Close-Up Look at War Psychology," *Los Angeles Times* (6 February 1990), F1.

33. "A Backgrounder Unit for the Film 'JFK'" (New York: Learning Enrichment, 1991).

34. Oliver Stone (New York, NY: Presentation to Nation Institute panel on "Hollywood and History: The Debate Over *JFK*," 3 March 1992).

35. Ellen Somekawa and Elizabeth A. Smith, "Theorizing the Writing of History or, 'I Can't Think Why It Should Be So Dull, for a Great Deal of It Must Be Invention,' " *Journal of Social History* (Fall 1988), 154.

36. Stone, Nation Institute presentation.

37. Bloodworth-Thomason and English quoted in Richard Zoglin, "Sitcom Politics," *Time* (21 September 1992), 47.

38. Quoted in Robert O'Harrow, Jr., "Conspiracy Theory Wins Converts," *Washington Post* (2 January 1992), B1, B5.

39. Quoted in Haynes Johnson, *Divided We Fall: Gambling with History in the Nineties* (New York: W. W. Norton, 1994), 48.

40. Close-Up Foundation interviews, C-SPAN (27 March 1995).

41. *Crossfire,* CNN (24 April 1995).

42. Richard Leiby, "Black Out: What a New Movie About the Black Panthers Remembers—and What It Forgets," *Washington Post* (30 April 1995), G7.

43. *Liberators: Fighting on Two Fronts in World War II,* PBS, WETA, Washington, D.C. (11 November 1992).

44. Quoted in Jeffrey Goldberg, "The Exaggerators," *New Republic* (8 February 1993), 13.

45. Quoted in ibid., 14.

46. Quoted in Stephen J. Dubner, "Massaging History," *New York* (8 March 1993), 50.

47. Kenneth S. Stern, "Liberators: A Background Report" (New York: American Jewish Committee, 1993).

48. Quoted in Goldberg, "The Exaggerators," 13–14.

49. Quoted in John Carmody, "WWII Documentary on Black GIs Pulled," *Washington Post* (13 February 1993), G1.

50. Edward Jay Epstein, *The Assassination Chronicles: Inquest, Counterplot, and Legend* (New York: Carroll & Graf, 1992), 575.

51. Quoted in Michael D. Yapko, *Suggestions of Abuse: True and False Memories of Childhood Sexual Trauma* (New York: Simon & Schuster, 1994), 25.

52. Yapko, *Suggestions of Abuse*, 28.

53. Quoted in Daniel Goleman, "Childhood Trauma: Memory or Invention?" *New York Times* (21 July 1992), C1.

54. Ethan Watters, "Doors of Memory," *Mother Jones* (January 1993), 29.

55. Renee Fredrickson, *Repressed Memories: A Journey to Recovery from Sexual Abuse* (New York: Simon & Schuster, 1992), 171.

56. Ibid., 204.

57. Ellen Bass and Laura Davis, *The Courage to Heal: A Guide for Women Survivors of Child Sexual Abuse* (New York: HarperCollins, 1992), 22.

58. Quoted in Mark Pendergrast, *Victims of Memory: Incest Accusations and Shattered Lives* (Hinesburg, Vt.: Upper Access, 1995), 208.

59. Quoted in Kathryn Robinson, "Memories of Abuse," *Seattle Weekly* (11 August 1993), 27.

60. Elizabeth F. Loftus, "Therapeutic Recollection of Childhood Abuse: When a Memory May Not Be a Memory," *Champion* (March 1994), 6.

61. See ibid., 7.

62. Richard Ofshe and Ethan Watters, "Making Monsters," *Society* (March/April 1993), 5, 8–9.

63. These and all other details of the Ingram story are from Lawrence Wright, *Remembering Satan: A Case of Recovered Memory and the Shattering of an American Family* (New York: Alfred A. Knopf, 1994).

64. Elizabeth Loftus and Katherine Ketcham, *The Myth of Repressed*

Memory: False Memories and Allegations of Sexual Abuse (New York: St. Martin's, 1994), 59.

65. Richard Ofshe and Ethan Watters, *Making Monsters: False Memories, Psychotherapy, and Sexual Hysteria* (New York: Charles Scribner's Sons, 1994), 272.

66. See Fox Butterfield, "Silent Decades Ended, Dozens Accuse a Priest," *New York Times* (9 June 1992), A18.

67. Quoted in Michael Hirsley and Jan Crawford, "Bernardin Accuser Recants," *Chicago Tribune* (1 March 1994), 1.

68. Jane Gross, "Bitter Closing Arguments in 'Recovered Memory' Abuse Case," *New York Times* (12 May 1994), B13.

69. Bass and Davis, *The Courage to Heal*, 347.

70. Frederick Crews, "The Unknown Freud," *New York Review of Books* (18 November 1993), 61.

71. Quoted in Elizabeth F. Loftus, "The Reality of Repressed Memories," *American Psychologist* (May 1993), 528.

72. *Primetime Live*, ABC (2 April 1992).

73. See "True Tales of False Memories: Childhood Sexual Abuse?" *Psychology Today* (July 1993), 11; and Leon Jaroff, "Lies of the Mind," *Time* (29 November 1993), 52.

74. Crews, "The Unknown Freud," 66.

75. Ofshe and Watters, "Making Monsters," *Society*, 15–16.

76. Judith Lewis Herman, *Trauma and Recovery* (New York: Basic Books, 1992), 9.

77. Linda R. Silver, "Oberlin College: Self-Empowerment and Difference," *The Courage to Question: Women's Studies and Student Learning*, Caryn McTighe Musil, ed. (Washington, D.C.: Association of American Colleges, 1992), 172. A Freedom of Information Act request submitted to the Department of Education on 23 February 1995 for access to the research (paid for by a FIPSE grant) on which *The Courage to Question* was based had not been fulfilled by the time that *Telling the Truth* was ready for publication—apparently because of objections posed by the grantees, the Association of American Colleges and the National Women's Studies Association.

78. Quoted in Katie Roiphe, *The Morning After: Sex, Fear, and Feminism on Campus* (Boston: Little, Brown, 1993), 40, 42.

79. Quoted in Nancy Gibbs, "When Is It Rape?" *Time* (3 June 1991).
80. Morris Freedman, letter to the editor, *Washington Post* (20 June 1993), C7.
81. Pendergrast, *Victims of Memory*, 452.
82. Ralph Vance (pseudonym), "After the Fall: Cast Out of His Family After Accusations of Sex Abuse, a Father Searches for the Truth," *Chicago Tribune* (27 February 1994), Sunday magazine, 14.

Chapter 6: The Press and the Postmodern Presidency

1. Price memorandum published in Joe McGinniss, *The Selling of the President 1968* (New York: Trident, 1969), 193–94.
2. Peggy Noonan, *What I Saw at the Revolution: A Political Life in the Reagan Era* (New York: Random House, 1990), 143.
3. Quoted in *Covering the Presidential Primaries* (New York: Freedom Forum Media Studies Center, Columbia University, June 1992), 27.
4. David S. Broder, "Five Ways to Put Some Sanity Back in Elections," *Washington Post* (14 January 1990), B1.
5. Kiku Adatto, *Sound Bite Democracy: Network Evening News Presidential Campaign Coverage, 1968 and 1988* (Cambridge: Joan Shorenstein Barone Center, Harvard University, 1990), 23.
6. S. Robert Lichter and Linda S. Lichter, eds. "Clinton's the One: TV News Coverage of the 1992 General Election," *Media Monitor* (November 1992), 2.
7. Thomas E. Patterson, *Out of Order* (New York: Vintage Books, 1994), 75.
8. Ibid., 168.
9. Lichter and Lichter, "Clinton's the One," 2.
10. Quoted in Renee Loth, "Studies Find Tilt in TV Coverage of Campaign," *Boston Globe* (2 September 1992), 1.
11. Edwin Diamond, "Getting It Right," *New York* (2 November 1992), 18.
12. Smith, Cohen, and King quoted in *The Finish Line: Covering the Campaign's Final Days* (New York: Freedom Forum Media Studies Center, Columbia University, January 1993), 111, 118, 127.
13. *Inside Washington,* WUSA (15 August 1992).

14. Howard Kurtz, "Republicans and Some Journalists Say Media Tend to Boost Clinton, Bash Bush," *Washington Post* (1 September 1992), A7.
15. Tom Rosenstiel, *Strange Bedfellows: How Television and the Presidential Candidates Changed American Politics, 1992* (New York: Hyperion, 1994), 333.
16. S. Robert Lichter, Stanley Rothman, and Linda S. Lichter, *The Media Elite: America's New Powerbrokers* (Bethesda, Md.: Adler & Adler, 1986), 21, 28–30; David Weaver, Roy W. Howard, and G. Cleveland Wilhoit, *The American Journalist in the 1990s* (Arlington, Va.: Freedom Forum, 17 November 1992), 7.
17. Craige, *Reconnection*, 10.
18. Joann Byrd, "73 Days of Tilt," *Washington Post* (8 November 1992), C6.
19. Joann Byrd, "Son of Objectivity," *Washington Post* (15 November 1992), C6.
20. Howard Kurtz, *Media Circus: The Trouble with America's Newspapers* (New York: Times Books, 1993), 48, 41.
21. Max Frankel, "Journalism 101," *New York Times Magazine* (22 January 1995), 18.
22. Richard Harwood, "How Objective Can the Media Really Be?" *Washington Post* (16 August 1992), C7.
23. Michael Lewis, "Lights! Camera! News!" *New Republic* (28 February 1994), 12.
24. Jon Katz, "Rock, Rap and Movies Bring You the News," *Rolling Stone* (5 March 1992), 33, 40.
25. Fred Barnes, "O.K., You Win," *New Republic* (30 November 1992), 43.
26. Paraphrased and quoted in Bob Woodward, *The Agenda: Inside the Clinton White House* (New York: Simon & Schuster, 1994), 110.
27. Ibid., 175.
28. Ibid., 115, 255.
29. Quoted in Paula Dwyer, "Clinton Bashes Business—But Does He Mean It?" *Business Week* (10 February 1992), 97.
30. Bill Clinton, *Putting People First: A National Economic Strategy for America* (Little Rock: Clinton for President Committee, 21 June 1992), 4, 1.

31. Elizabeth Drew, *On the Edge: The Clinton Presidency* (New York: Simon & Schuster, 1994), 58.

32. Robert Pear, "Health-Care Costs May Be Increased $100 Billion a Year," *New York Times* (3 May 1993), A1.

33. Isabel V. Sawhill and Mark Condon ["Is U.S. Income Inequality Really Growing?" *Policy Bites* (June 1992), 3] write that in both the decade from 1967 to 1976 and from 1977 to 1986, on average, the poor "grew much richer by 72–77 percent" and the rich "grew a little richer, by 5–6 percent." They arrived at these figures by taking income mobility—the fact that in the U.S. people do not tend to stay in the same income category—into consideration. Sawhill and Condon write: "These figures will not surprise the experts. Any significant mobility should lead to the same pattern. People who start at the bottom have nowhere to move but up, and are likely to do so as they become older, gain work seniority, and earn higher incomes. People who start at the top, some of whom may be there because of temporary sources of income like capital gains, have nowhere to go but down. This pattern, however, may be surprising to the general public, which has been led to believe that the poor were literally getting poorer over the last decade or two, and that the incomes of the rich were skyrocketing." Christopher Jencks of Northwestern University concludes from research that focuses on consumption rather than income that during the past two decades "Rich families with children do seem to have grown richer. But poor families with children did not necessarily grow poorer." Jencks quoted in David Whitman, "The Poor Aren't Poorer: Liberal Researchers Rebut a Popular Lament and Applause Line of the '90s," *U.S. News & World Report* (25 July 1994), 33.

34. Moore on *Journalists' Roundtable,* C-SPAN (1 May 1992); Marc Levinson, "The Fat and Happy '80s," *Newsweek* (4 May 1992), 63; John Greenwald, "How I Won the War," *Time* (25 May 1992), 67. Excerpts appear in Brent H. Baker and Tim Graham, eds., *Notable Quotables* (11, 25 May 1992).

35. Patterson, *Out of Order,* 113. Statistics are derived from S. Robert Lichter and Linda S. Lichter, eds., "The Boom in Gloom: TV News Coverage of the American Economy, 1990–1992," *Media Monitor* (October 1992), 3.

36. Quoted in McGinniss, *The Selling of the President*, 192.

37. Quoted in Steven Mufson, "Economy's Growth Rate Strengthens," *Washington Post* (28 October 1992), A1.

38. Brokaw on *NBC Nightly News,* NBC (27 October 1992); Jennings and Jamieson on *World News Tonight with Peter Jennings,* ABC (27 October 1992).

39. Rather and Spencer on *CBS Evening News with Dan Rather,* CBS (27 October 1992); Engberg on *CBS Evening News with Dan Rather* (28 October 1992).

40. Quoted in Kathleen Hall Jamieson, *Dirty Politics: Deception, Distraction, and Democracy* (New York: Oxford University Press, 1992), 204.

41. *Good Morning America,* ABC (23 June 1992).

42. Press conference in Little Rock, Arkansas (14 January 1993).

43. One who did notice was Dan Balz who wrote perceptively of the shift in "End Attained, Clinton Mutes Talk of Middle-Class Tax Cut, a Campaign Exercise in Rewriting History," *Washington Post* (23 June 1992), A1.

44. "Clintonspeak, Clinton Doublespeak, Clinton Doublespokesperson," *American Spectator* (November 1993), 28.

45. See "Statement by Gov. Clinton on Haitian Refugees," U.S. Newswire (27 May 1992).

46. Press conference in Little Rock, Arkansas (14 January 1993).

47. Quoted in Steven Greenhouse, "Aristide Condemns Clinton's Haiti Policy as Racist," *New York Times* (22 April 1994), A1.

48. Bob Herbert, "The Truth Sculptor," *New York Times* (12 January 1994), A21.

49. Remarks at White House Briefing with President of Namibia Sam Nujoma, Federal News Service (16 June 1993); "Somalia Message to Congress from President Clinton," U.S. Newswire (13 October 1993).

50. S. Robert Lichter and Linda S. Lichter, eds. "They're No Friends of Bill: TV News Coverage of the Clinton Administration," *Media Monitor* (July/August 1994), 2. Percentage of positive network coverage of Bush provided by Richard Noyes, Center for Media and Public Affairs.

51. Joe Klein, "The Politics of Promiscuity," *Newsweek* (9 May 1994), 19, 18.

52. Michael Kelly, "Bill Clinton's Climb," *New York Times Magazine* (31 July 1994), 45.

53. Ibid., 25.

54. Richard A. Lanham, *The Motives of Eloquence: Literary Rhetoric in the Renaissance* (New Haven: Yale University Press, 1976), 4.

55. Ibid., 1.

56. Michel Foucault, *The Order of Things: An Archaeology of the Human Sciences* (New York: Vintage, 1994), 387. Originally published as *Les Mots et les choses* (Paris: Editions Gallimard, 1966).

57. Richard Rorty, "The Fate of Philosophy: What Will a Post-Philosophical Culture Look Like?" *New Republic* (18 October 1982), 33.

58. Speech at University of Texas, Austin (6 April 1993).

59. Kelly, "Bill Clinton's Climb," 40.

60. Ifill on *Frontline: What Happened to Bill Clinton?* PBS (13 January 1995).

Chapter 7: Living in Truth

1. Andrew Kohut et al., *More Clinton Leadership Wanted: Now the GOP Faces Cynical, Dissatisfied Public* (Washington, D.C.: Times Mirror Center for the People and the Press, 13 April 1995), 25.

2. Stephan Budiansky, "A Museum in Crisis," *U.S. News & World Report* (13 February 1995), 73.

3. David Remnick, *Lenin's Tomb: The Last Days of the Soviet Empire* (New York: Random House, 1993), 36–51.

4. Václav Havel, "The Power of the Powerless," *Living in Truth*, Jan Vladislav, ed. (London: Faber & Faber, 1986), 56.

5. Richard Bernstein, *Dictatorship of Virtue: Multiculturalism and the Battle for America's Future* (New York: Alfred A. Knopf, 1994), 241.

6. Kathryn Robinson, "Memories of Abuse," *Seattle Weekly* (11 August 1993), 18–28.

7. John R. Searle, *The Construction of Social Reality* (New York: Free Press, 1995), 158.

8. Frank M. Snowden, Jr., *Before Color Prejudice: The Ancient View of Blacks* (Cambridge.: Harvard University Press, 1983), 64.

9. Martin Bernal, *Black Athena: The Afroasiatic Roots of Classical Civi-*

lization, Vol. 1 (New Brunswick, N.J.: Rutgers University Press, 1987), 52; Frank M. Snowden, Jr., "Bernal's 'Blacks,' Herodotus, and Other Classical Evidence," *Arethusa* (Fall 1989), 83–93.

10. Bernal, *Black Athena*, Vol. 1, 434–36.

11. Frank M. Snowden, Jr., commencement address at University of Maryland at College Park (20 May 1993), 6.

12. I am indebted for much information in this profile to "Professor Elizabeth Fox-Genovese Interviewed by Carol Iannone," *Academic Questions* (Summer 1992), 56–65.

13. Ibid., 61, 64–65.

14. Quoted in Courtney Leatherman, "Colleague Sues Ex-Director of Women's Studies at Emory U. for Sexual Harassment and Bias," *Chronicle of Higher Education* (3 March 1993), A18.

15. Elizabeth Fox-Genovese, "Save the Males?" *National Review* (1 August 1994), 52.

16. Elizabeth Fox-Genovese, conversation with author, 13 July 1994.

17. Alan Charles Kors, conversation with author, 26 April 1993.

18. Ibid.

19. Kors, "The Politicization of the University," 485.

20. Ibid., 495.

21. Stephen Burd, "President Bush Names 8 Scholars to Sit on Humanities Board," *Chronicle of Higher Education* (8 April 1992), A30.

22. Alan Charles Kors, letter to the editor, *Chronicle of Higher Education* (6 May 1992), B3–B4.

23. Alan Charles Kors, conversation with author.

24. Quoted in Dinah Wisenberg Brin, "Ice Cream Truck Driver Killed in Robbery, 16-Year-Old Arrested," Associated Press report (17 June 1994).

25. Bob Greene, "Society's Crumbling, and We're Watching," *Chicago Tribune* (27 June 1994), Sec. 5, p. 1.

26. Josiah Royce, *The Religious Aspect of Philosophy: A Critique of the Bases of Conduct and of Faith* (Boston: Houghton, Mifflin, 1885), 157–58.

ಕಾ Index

Index

Index

❧ About the Author

LYNNE V. CHENEY is the W.H. Brady, Jr., Distinguished Fellow at the American Enterprise Institute and was Chairman of the National Endowment for the Humanities from 1986 through 1992. She has a Ph.D. in English, has taught at several colleges and universities, and was a senior editor at *Washingtonian* magazine. She is the author of two previous books and co-author of two others, including *Kings of the Hill,* which she wrote with her husband, Richard Cheney, former Secretary of Defense.